IONA NATIONAL AIRWAYS

IRELAND'S FIRST COMMERCIAL AIRLINE

By MICHAEL TRAYNOR

To my wife, Anne and our children,
Ross, Dáire, Aisling, Cian and Odhrán

ISBN 0-9549194-0-8

Cover Design and editorial layout by Direct Print Limited.

This book is typeset in Palatino 10 pt.

Printed by Direct Print Limited.
Published November 2004 by Michael Traynor.

Copyright © 2004 Michael Traynor, 36 Anne Devlin Avenue, Rathfarnham,
Dublin 14. Tel 00-353-1-4941280. E-mail-traynorm66@hotmail.com

For additional copies please send payment to Michael Traynor at above
address. Please add 79 to cover postage and packing in Ireland.

ACKNOWLEDGEMENTS

To undertake the compilation of the story of Ireland's first commercial aviation company proved to be quite an extensive task. An undertaking I was unaware would involve so much assistance from so many people. As always, it is almost an impossible task to mention those that have given generously to this story. However, there are some that bear a special word of thanks, particularly for their unselfish efforts at offering information and data essential to the history of the airline.

In May 2000, I approached Pearse Cahill, son of the founder of Iona National Airways. Pearse opened his house and files for unlimited perusal. He gave most openly of his time whenever requested. Hopefully his efforts will bear fruit in the publication of this book. I then contacted Paul Cunniffe, editor of *Irish Air Letter*, who provided a vast amount of information from the files of this monthly publication, spanning almost 30 years, and covering the most active years at Iona. Paul also gave considerable assistance with editing and proof reading towards the end of the work. Further gratitude to Eamon Power, Karl Hayes, and Eleanor Flegg for editorial assistance. I am also grateful to Paul Duffy for the time he afforded me throughout my research and for providing editorial assistance with the final text.

The National Library, Kildare Street and National Archives, Bishop Street, provided further historical data along with several visits to the Military Archives, Cathal Brugha Barracks during summer 2000, where I received tremendous assistance from Commandant Victor Laing and his staff. Bob Montgomery at the Royal Irish Automobile Club Archive provided further information of Pearse's motoring achievements. Leo Murray, Meath Aero Museum, provided archive material. Flan Garry at Irish Aviation Authority permitted access to IAA aircraft register files to verify details.

Contemporary historical aviation data was extracted from the many publications covering the various aspects of this important period. A list of these publications is included in the bibliography and referred to throughout the text where appropriate.

When the data had been collated and in draft form the work of accumulating photographs commenced. The initial batch of several hundred photographs was borrowed from Pearse Cahill's vast personal collection. Many readers will be familiar with prints that adorned the walls of the Iona clubhouse for many years. Other sources were from individuals that had personally spent many, many years photographing aircraft and whose efforts will be valued and appreciated by generations to come. Thankfully those individuals have been forthcoming and generous in making available their personal collections to me. They include Paul Duffy, (including his unique collection of air to air photographs of Iona aircraft taken from aircraft chartered by him for this purpose), Liam Byrne, (whose collection is now in the caring possession of Ronny Vogt), Paul Cunniffe, George Flood, Chris Bruton, Leo Murray, Hugo Wilhare, Patrick J. Cummins, Simon Nolan and many, many others. Without the persistent efforts of these individuals to obtain photographs of Irish aircraft this publication would be lacking much pictorial content. I sincerely thank you all. Photographs of incidents, in which Iona aircraft were chartered to take exclusive media photographs, were provided from The *Irish Times* archives with the kind assistance of Peter Thursfield. The *Examiner* was also forthcoming from its archives.

When all the above was collated, the task commenced to put it all into book form. For that I am grateful to the staff at Direct Print for their advice, guidance, and particularly patience during the design, layout and printing work. For their professionalism I am grateful.

Last, but by no means least, I wish to say a very special 'thank you' to my wife, Anne and our children, Ross, Dáire, Aisling, Cian and Odhrán for their unbelievable tolerance and patience with me - sometimes through difficult periods - while this work was progressing! For hundreds of hours that might otherwise have belonged to them - thank you. Their encouragement throughout ensured I was motivated to complete this work.

The author gratefully acknowledges the financial support of the following. Without such support this publication would not have been possible. (Individuals listed in alpabetical order.)

Desmond Cahill

Pearse Cahill

Peter Cahill

Martin Clancy

Brendan Davis

Paul Flanagan

Peter Flanagan

Catherine Greene

Brian Higgins

Enda Hopkins

Eric Hopkins

Desmond McEvaddy

Kieran A. O' Connor

Dr. Tony Walsh

Fingal County Council

SUPPORTED BY THE HERITAGE COUNCIL

LE CUIDIÚ AN CHOMHAIRLE OIDHREACHTA

Oifig an Taoisigh
Office of the Taoiseach

FOREWORD

It is a pleasure for me to have the honour to place a foreword in a publication of this nature. Down through the years Iona National Airways were there to witness the whole history of flight being unfolded and the early adventures and indeed difficulties of those early Irish Aviators who looked to the air and the aircraft for a career.

Throughout this book you see the panorama of achievement revealed. For many who took to the air they realised that aircraft had revolutionised their conception of distance. They paved the way and made air transport the accomplished fact it is today.

In the early 30's, in the worldwide arena, almost every month, new records were set, whether for speed, long distance or endurance in the air. The company which Hugh Cahill founded, in Kildonan, also played its part in fostering a love of aviation in the youth of its time.

In those days a 15 minute introductory flight at Kildonan cost the pupil 10 shillings and a solo flight in the ever popular Gipsy Moth could cost you 7 shillings and 6 pence.

The most famous Irish airwoman of the time, Lady Mary Heath, flew at Kildonan and eventually took over the operation of the airfield. She obtained her Pilots Certificate and there followed many offers from aircraft manufacturers for her to demonstrate the quality of their products. She made several attempts on the height record and flew from Cape Town to London - a remarkable feat at that time.

Hugh embued a love of flying in his son Pearse, and at an early age would airlift the family to Sligo to have a picnic on the beach and be home by teatime. Most of Pearse's classmates would be satisfied with a bus trip out to nearby Dollymount Strand. However, everyone growing up in the north city area would be acutely aware of the engineering works at Cross Guns Bridge which was a landmark at the time.

Prior to the security conscious era, passengers at Dublin Airport could sip coffee and look across the runway at the Iona aircraft and hangars and for some the first inquisitive steps would be taken on a road that would lead to a rewarding career in aviation.

You could be met at Cloghran by the roar of a Gipsy Major engine at full power on a test bench. As well as training pilots, Iona also offered training to young technical apprentices interested in a career in aeronautical engineering.

Pearse Cahill's interest in all things aeronautical is infectious and he has a detailed knowledge of the operation and function of every pump and generator on all his aircraft - and could quote their part numbers as well!

In 1972 Pearse supplied eight Cessna 172 Aircraft to the State. Six of these aircraft are still flying with the Irish Air Corps and this fine service reflects well on the after sales product support given by Iona.

The tradition of the Cahills in Irish aviation is continued to this day with both Pearse's son and granddaughter flying as commercial pilots - how Hugh would be pleased.

Bertie Ahern T.D.
Taoiseach

PREFACE

Very few people involved in aviation in Ireland over the past seventy years would not have encountered, either directly or indirectly, the name 'Iona' in their aeronautical experiences. I was one of those that encountered that organisation indirectly. As a member of Dublin Airport Flying Club since 1988 we were 'guests' of the Iona organisation at the Iona ramp for many years.

In May 2000 Ronan Lee contacted me, through Liam Byrne, about another aviation matter, totally unrelated to Iona; however, after a few drinks we began discussing the Pearse Cahill story. We formed the opinion there was a story to be told, either by way of television documentary or in published format, or both. Contact was made with Pearse and he proved a most willing and co-operative subject. We were granted unlimited access to his files, photographic collection and memorabilia. We filmed him at various 'Iona' locations around Dublin and he gave us many hours of his time. For that we are grateful. Without that level of assistance, the story of Ireland's first commercial aviation operator would have proven more difficult to relate.

I had only seen Iona operate from the outside, nonetheless, I could not have realised the vast work that lay ahead in accumulating and collating all the data necessary to produce this publication. In excess of two thousand hours were spent over a three-year period to arrive at the final product. Some might argue, the full story is not even told yet!

Undoubtedly, there are stories and anecdotes that are omitted. Some may not even be printable! For any omissions I apologise. I made several requests through various bodies and organisations for contributions to this story. Some replied and many were of tremendous assistance.

I wish to 'steal' the opening paragraph from the 'Iona Aeroplane' chapter in *History of Aviation in Ireland* by Liam Byrne:

> 'The story of Iona National Airways is more than just the story of Ireland's first airline. It embraces the golden era of aviation in Ireland when aircraft and flying first became within reach of the ordinary people of the country. When Iona was founded only three private aircraft carried Irish registration marks, no commercial airline existed and a sighting of one of the few aircraft operated by the Irish Army Air Corps was a rare event. Hugh Cahill, the founder of Iona, was a true pioneer not only as a result of his zeal and dedication but also in his exceptional business ability. He brought aviation to the people and consequently the people to aviation.'

I could not have introduced the Iona story any better.

Michael Traynor
November 2004.

IONA NATIONAL AIRWAYS

CONTENTS

Chapter

1

GETTING OFF THE GROUND

*The acquisition of Ireland's first commercial aircraft
and attempts at establishing an aviation business,
sometimes thwarted by lack of Government support*

Chapter One

GETTING OFF THE GROUND

In the early 1920s the motor industry in Ireland was in its infancy. Although only a few motor vehicles existed in Dublin, car owners were a growing minority. The horse was still the main form of transport for most rural families and only the occasional prosperous member of society possessed a motorcar. Air travel was even more exotic, and the sight or sound of an aeroplane in the Irish skies was cause for great excitement.

Hugh Cahill was a man of vision. He saw the potential of motorised transport and became involved in the motor industry in 1923. The new Irish Free State was only a year old, the country had been broken by the harsh years of the civil war, and few people had cars. Despite this, Hugh realised that cars were the vehicles of the future and, more importantly, that they would need to be serviced and maintained. Seeing a business opportunity of tremendous possibility he set up shop, selling and hiring new and second-hand cars, servicing vehicles, and teaching people how to drive.

Born in 1883, Hugh had grown up on the north side of Dublin(*i). Throughout his twenties he witnessed the strife and poverty of the workers' strikes, followed by World War One, the years when emigration was a regular necessity for many families, and the nation was embroiled in the struggles for Irish freedom. It was during Ireland's fight for Independence that Hugh met Caroline O'Connor. Caroline was born 31 December 1894 to James O'Connor and Rose Byrne. Hugh and

Caroline were married on 22 September 1915 in the Church of the Sacred Heart, Donnybrook, and settled in Prospect Villa, Glasnevin to rear their family. The house was to become the family home for the Cahill family for almost 60 years. Their first son was born on 26 January 1917, nine months after the Easter Rising, and was christened Matthew Pearse in memory of Padraig Pearse. Six other children were born to Caroline and Hugh and were reared beside the banks of the canal.

Hugh Cahill and Caroline O'Connor photographed in the gardens of 27 Chelmsford Road, Ranelagh, Dublin. The occasion was their wedding in September 1915.

Photograph courtesy Pearse Cahill collection

FOOTNOTE (*i)
Hugh was the eldest of three sons born from the marriage of Matthew Cahill, 24 Summerhill Place, on Dublin's north side, and Martha Marshall (nee Shaw) no. 1 Marshall Terrace. Matthew was originally from County Cavan and operated a public house in the Broadstone area of Dublin. Martha's maiden name was Shaw and she had one daughter, Ruth, from her first marriage. Martha and Matthew moved to 36 Lower Ruthland Street and had three sons. Their first child, Hugh, was born on 23 June 1883. The next son, Philip, was to become involved in the engineering business. He was regarded as a designer and, while employed with the Great Southern Railways, was responsible for designing some of their carriages. The youngest was Harry. Sadly, he met an untimely death in 1961. Matthew died at the early age of 55 years on 23 October 1899 when his eldest son was only 16 years of age. Martha, on the other hand, lived until her 81st year when she died on 21 December 1935.

Promotional brochure advertising services of Iona Motor Engineering Works, 1923

Brochure courtesy Pearse Cahill collection

Iona Engineering Works, Cross Guns Bridge, 1930

Photograph courtesy Pearse Cahill collection

'Shaft Making, Gear Cutting, Slotting, Case Hardening, Metal Turning, Bearings, Spring Making and Valve Grinding. Craftsmen do their work with good tools. In the metal turning section alone there is £2,000 worth of the very latest machines. These embody every gadget, device hitherto thought of. We know that this combination of craftsmen and machinery is quite unrivalled. If the job is a tough one let us handle it.'

Hugh was a man of slight stature. As a consequence of him being slightly deaf; he had a habit of saying 'which' and 'what' during the course of conversations with people. He had a good sense of humour and was noted for pranks and tricks that many fell victim to.

The Cahill's became involved in engineering and Hugh constructed an engineering works adjoining the family home. These premises were on a site currently located at the rear of Hedigan's *Brian Boru* public house at Cross Guns Bridge. The streets in the vicinity of Prospect Villa were named in commemoration of Saint Columba; names such as Iona Road, Iona Park, Iona Drive, Iona Crescent, and Iona Villas. From this Hugh got the inspiration for his new company, Iona Engineering Works, which opened its doors for business in 1923. He quickly developed the business to the extent that he was running machines worth several thousands of pounds – a vast amount by early 1920s standards. Most of the machines were of a specialist type and Hugh employed skilled men to operate them. Promotional literature for Iona Motor Engineering Works of the period listed the available skills and services:

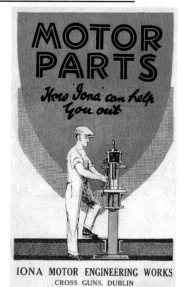

Promotional brochure advertising services of Iona Motor Engineering Works, 1923

Brochure courtesy Pearse Cahill

The combination of engineering works and motor repairs gave Iona the capability to have parts specially made for particular needs. At peak periods, the premises functioned twenty-four hours a day, providing necessary maintenance for many of the private bus companies throughout the city. It was to continue to operate for a half a century.

As well as selling and servicing new and used vehicles, Iona hired out cars, including Rolls Royce, promoting the business as 'The Pioneering Hiring Firm for Taximeters'; the meters

Pearse, aged 9 years, in model Citroen car, obtained
by Hugh Cahill from Citroen motor company, *Iona
Garage* is inscribed on the door.

Photograph courtesy Pearse Cahill collection

converted Vickers Vimy bomber. Sixteen hours and twenty-eight minutes later, and having covered 1,700 miles, they crash-landed at Clifden, County Galway. They were later Knighted for their achievement. Some further unsuccessful attempts were made, and the world was to wait almost eight years before a twenty-five year old Detroit born pilot, with Limerick connections, was to make a successful solo crossing. Charles A. Lindbergh left Roosevelt Field, New York, at 07.54am on 20 May 1927. Flying the *Spirit of St Louis*, he crossed the Kerry coastline twenty-eight hours later. After flying a total of 3,400 miles he landed at Le Bourget airport, near Paris, thirty-three and a half hours after leaving New York. This flight received

displaying fares for passengers in the taxicabs. The offices of the Irish Taximeter Hire Company were given as 5 D'Olier Street, Dublin, although it later moved to 33/34 North Brunswick Street, Dublin, with Desmond and Caroline Cahill quoted as its directors. Eventually, Hugh decided it was time to separate the engineering works from the motor business. He purchased a site at the junction of Prospect Road and Whitworth Road. The rear of the premises adjoined the old Glasnevin rail station. In front were petrol pumps. The premises opened on 8 June 1931.

The 1920s and early 1930s were the romantic and glamour days of aviation in Ireland. It was the period of air displays and air circuses, and the days when thousands of curious sightseers and well wishers flocked to Baldonnel and Portmarnock to witness the aerial attempts to cross the Atlantic from east to west. Two Royal Air Force veterans of World War One, John Alcock and his companion Arthur Whitten-Brown, successfully crossed the Atlantic on 14 June 1919, taking off from St John's, Newfoundland, in a

Pearse, aged 9 years, in model Citroen car, on
O'Connell Street, Dublin in 1926 under the watchful eye
of a 7 foot tall Garda, affectionately known as 'Tiny'.

Newspaper photograph courtesy Pearse Cahill

worldwide acclaim for the aviator and also focused attention on the crossing of the Atlantic in the opposite direction, east to west.

Four months later, on 16 September 1927, Captain Robert 'All-Weather' McIntosh, of Imperial Airways, and his co-pilot Commandant James C. Fitzmaurice, Officer Commanding the Irish Air Corps, departed Baldonnel in a Fokker *Princess Xenia*. Due to deteriorating weather they were forced back and crash-landed at Beale strand, near Ballybunion, County Kerry. Commandant Fitzmaurice did not have long to wait for another opportunity at the Atlantic crossing. In the company of two Germans, Captain Hermann Koehl and Baron Guenther Von Huenefeld, he made another attempt in the Junkers built *Bremen*. On Thursday morning, 12 April 1928, the aircraft roared down the runway at Baldonnel, much to the

all over the world. This event was probably the catalyst for the rejuvenation of the Irish Aero Club, which was formally re-inaugurated with Fitzmaurice as chairman, on 15 August 1928. (This club was originally formed in 1909, but had become somewhat defunct). Seven weeks later the fledgling club took delivery of its first aeroplane, a brand new Avro 594B Avian. On 5 October 1928, it was to become the first civil aircraft to be registered in the six-year-old Irish Free State, as EI-AAA. Colonel Fitzmaurice was, despite his world fame, to become the forgotten hero of Irish aviation. He died on 26 September 1965 and was buried in Glasnevin Cemetery with full military honours, receiving due recognition only in death.

Among the people at Baldonnel who witnessed the take-off of the *Bremen* on that famous occasion were Hugh Cahill and his friend James (Jim) C. Malone.

Hugh Cahill was among the many thousands of onlookers and well-wishers that gathered at dawn on 12 April 1928 to witness the take-off of the *Bremen* on the occasion of the first successful crossing of the Atlantic from east to west. It was this event that spurred Hugh Cahill towards commercial aviation in Ireland

Photograph courtesy Irish Air Corps

delight of the several thousand sightseers gathered in the early dawn to witness this historic event. Thirty-six and a half hours after leaving Baldonnel they landed on the ice at Greenly Island, Newfoundland, having flown 2,215 miles. Fitzmaurice was immediately promoted to Major (later Colonel) and received many accolades from

Jim, then Transport Manager with the Irish-American Oil Company, had been closely involved in the preparation and fuelling of the *Bremen*, and shared Hugh's interest in aeroplanes and flying. No flight training was available in Ireland in the early twenties so Jim had to go to an air school at Lympne in Kent; there he earned his Class 'A' flying certificate. Following his return to Dublin he went on to become one of the founders of the Irish Aero Club. Some sources state he was probably one of the first Irishmen to qualify as an air pilot but did not pursue a career in commercial aviation. Hugh Cahill also went to England to train as a pilot, where he received instruction at Stag Lane Aerodrome, outside London. Though Hugh logged approximately twenty hours instructional flying, he never completed his flying training; in fact he never got as far as flying solo. Hugh did not become a member of the Irish Aero Club, but his interest in aviation evolved from discussions he held with Jim Malone about the commercial possibilities of aviation. Not alone did Hugh Cahill anticipate the growth in the motor industry, but also he anticipated a similar growth in the aviation industry. Conscious that the principal function of the Irish Aero Club was to provide instruction to pilots, Hugh realised there was a gap in the market. Commercial aviation had not yet been explored in Ireland. Throughout 1930 he put together a plan to develop an enterprise that would meet the demands of the business community, yet would not clash with the operations of his comrades in the Irish Aero Club.

The *Dublin Evening Mail* newspaper reported on 31 May 1930 that Air Taxis were coming to Dublin with the headline: *"Service of Aeroplane Taxis to link up Irish towns with Dublin – Great project to be launched by local firm in September."* The article made reference to the acquisition of premises at Cross Guns Bridge by a Glasnevin based engineering company. It further added: *"the company intended to extend the air-service to London, Berlin, Paris and other big Continental cities using a Desoutter aircraft."* The following week, 4 June 1930, the *Southern Cross* arrived at Baldonnel. The country was again riding on the crest of a euphoric wave at yet another attempt on the Atlantic, over two years after the *Bremen* departed from Baldonnel. On the morning of the latest attempt, 24 June 1930, thousands of spectators gathered on Portmarnock Strand to bid *bon voyage* to the Australian Charles Kingsford-Smith and his crew of John Stannage, Evert van Dyk and Skerries, County Dublin born navigator Paddy Saul, in their Fokker aircraft *Southern Cross*.

In July 1930 Hugh Cahill formed Iona National Air Taxis and Flying School. A few weeks later he purchased his first aircraft, a Gipsy Moth, that was granted its Certificate of Airworthiness number 2599 on 26 July 1930 as G-ABBV (see Table 1). This aircraft was intended for pilot training. It was over a month later when the aircraft was ferried from Stag Lane Aerodrome, London, to Baldonnel by Jim Malone.

The aircraft Hugh Cahill intended for use as an air taxi was a Desoutter. In England in 1929, Marcel Desoutter formed the Desoutter aircraft company to manufacture the Dutch-designed Koolhoven F.K.41 high wing light aircraft under licence. Desoutters' chief engineer, C. H. Handasyde, later modified the design. Handasyde and Mr. Martin were the co-designers of the Martinsyde, the *Big Fella*, which was the first aircraft purchased by the newly formed Irish Air Corps. The first Desoutter intended for operation by Iona was a Mark I registered G-AATX, with constructors' number D18. On 1 April 1930 it completed its Certificate of Airworthiness and was registered ten days later to National Flying Services Limited, Hanworth. It was purchased by Hugh Cahill and its intended delivery routing was Croydon to Dublin, via Blackpool and Stranraer. This was to allow the shortest sea crossing to Ireland. G-AATX began its ferry flight on 29 July 1930. On board, along with the pilot from National Flying Services, were Hugh Cahill and a reporter from the *Dublin Evening Mail*. North of Liverpool, en route to Blackpool, some smoke was observed emanating from the engine compartment. It was later discovered that the Zenith type carburettor had two thumbscrews holding the cover on which were not wire locked, and the vibration caused them to come loose. As a consequence fuel began to leak from the carburettor and poured onto hot engine components causing a lot of smoke. They made a precautionery landing at Barfield Farm, near Bootle. The aircraft ran through a hedge at the end of the field and nosed over. Nobody on board was injured and the damaged aircraft was taken by rail to the Desoutter plant at Croydon for repair. This flight was the last entry in Hugh Cahill's logbook. He returned to Ireland by boat from Liverpool. The Desoutter was repaired and registered on 25 April

1931 to P. H. Meadway, West Malling. Its next owner was J. L. Burgess, Maidstone Aerodrome to whom it was registered in September 1931. Its final transfer of ownership was on 25 July 1932 to Maidstone Airport Limited in Kent. Unfortunately, it crashed at Edenbridge, Kent on 1 October 1932 and was removed from the UK civil aircraft register in December 1932.

Throughout 1930, Handasyde made improvements to the previous model: a dH Gipsy III engine in place of the earlier version's Cirrus Hermes; redesigned ailerons and tail surfaces; and provision for wheel brakes. The prototype of the modified design first flew in June 1930 and was known as the Desoutter, Mark II. It rolled off the production line with a price tag of £875; with a deluxe finish £15 extra. It weighed 1,100 pounds empty and 1,800 pounds loaded. It was not

Hugh Cahill (left) and Jim Malone pictured in the Desoutter factory at Croydon in 1930, beside the Desoutter aircraft which was to be bought by Iona National Airways. However the above aircraft was found to have "wing fluttering" problems so c/n D.30, later EI-AAD, was taken instead

Photograph courtesy Ronny Vogt collection

The Desoutter Mark I, G-AATX, left Croydon on its ferry flight to Dublin, on delivery to Iona National Airways. Owing to smoke emanating from the engine compartment they were forced to make a landing at Barfield Farm, Bootle near Liverpool on 29 July 1930 en route Stanley Park, Blackpool to Baldonnel with Hugh Cahill on board. Hugh is on the left in above photograph along with a reporter from the *Evening Mail*

Photograph courtesy Pearse Cahill collection

equipped with any radio, had a cruising speed of 96 to 100 miles per hour and a range of 400 miles. Hugh Cahill visited the Desoutter factory on a number of occasions throughout the summer 1930, usually in the company of Jim Malone, and subsequently purchased a Desoutter Mark II, bearing the constructors' serial number 30.

On 30 August 1930 the Desoutter performed a 30-minute test flight. It was granted an Export Certificate of Airworthiness, number 2647, by P. W. Everson on 1 September 1930. The registration marks EI-AAD were allocated and it was the fourth aircraft on the Saorstat civil aircraft register. It was the first commercial aircraft registered in Ireland.

The welcoming party at Baldonnel on 5 September 1930 to greet the first two aircraft to form Hugh Cahill's new aviation company, Desoutter EI-AAD and Gipsy Moth G-ABBV. Left to right: Pearse (age 13 years), 3 reporters, L. S. Tyndall (ferry pilot EI-AAD), Jim Malone (ferry pilot G-ABBV) and John Cummins

Photograph courtesy Pearse Cahill collection

The Certificate of Airworthiness later bore the endorsement:

> 'The aircraft to which this certificate relates being registered in Saorstat Eireann, this certificate has been validated by the Minister for Industry and Commerce, and has hereby conferred upon it the same validity as if it had been issued by the Minister, Director, Transport and Marine branch, 20 October 1930.'

On 1 September 1930, the Desoutter undertook three local flights at Croydon, south of London. On 2 September the blue and silver aircraft flew from Croydon to Grimsby, at the mouth of the river Humber on the east coast of England, returning to Croydon the following day. Its ferry flight to Ireland commenced on Thursday, 4 September 1930 at 1.30pm with a one-hour flight from the Desoutter factory at Croydon, Surrey, to Bicester, Oxfordshire. Accompanying the Desoutter was the Gipsy Moth, G-ABBV, purchased a number of weeks earlier by Hugh Cahill. At Bicester a heavy fog covered the aerodrome and the crews waited for more favourable weather. From Bicester they continued, the same day, and, following a flight of one hour 15 minutes EI-AAD reached Sealand, located in north east Wales and five miles west of Chester on the border of England and Wales.

G-ABBV was forced to divert to a Royal Air Force base where Jim Malone was arrested for making an unauthorised landing at a military establishment. Both Jim and the aircraft were detained and, following some legal argument, released to continue the journey to Baldonnel where it landed that Thursday evening, 4 September 1930. This was the first aircraft to be owned by Iona Engineering Works and was operated from Baldonnel. It was to remain on the British register for its first year of operation.

EI-AAD overnighted at Sealand. The following morning, Friday, 5 September, according to the log book for EI-AAD, a ten-minute 'weather test' flight was conducted. On determination that the weather would be satisfactory for the flight, the Desoutter, piloted by Mr. L. S. Tyndall, who, the previous month was appointed Chief Pilot with Iona, departed Sealand and routed to Baldonnel in a flight that took one hour 45 minutes. One of the people to meet the aircraft was the young 13-year-old Pearse Cahill. The *Dublin Evening Mail* of 6 September 1930 carried a photograph of Gipsy Moth, G-ABBV and Desoutter, EI-AAD at Baldonnel, referring to the establishment of '*an air taxi business.*' The Desoutter was not entered on the Irish register to Hugh Cahill until 20 October 1930. Along its fuselage was painted the logo '*Iona*

Ireland's first commercial aircraft, under military guard at Baldonnel, with *'Iona National Air Taxis & Flying School'* on the fuselage

Photograph via Pearse Cahill collection

National Air Taxis and Flying School'. Both the Desoutter and the Gipsy Moth went to work immediately, providing instruction and undertaking air taxi assignments.

The arrival of the new Iona aircraft attracted widespread media attention. All Dublin and National newspapers captured the event in photographic and dialogue format. Typical was the article produced by the *Irish Independent*, Saturday, 6 September 1930:

> 'The De Soutter three-seater monoplane ordered by Mr. H. Cahill of the Iona Taxi and Engineering Works, Dublin, who is inaugurating an aerial taxi service between Dublin and England arrived at Baldonnel yesterday. The plane was piloted from Sealand aerodrome, Chester by Mr. L. S. Tyndall and the journey was completed in one hour 45 minutes.
>
> The machine which bears the markings EI-AAD is the fourth plane to carry a Saorstat registration. It is the second of two machines to be used on the service, the other being a de Havilland Gypsy Moth.
>
> When the machine arrived it was received by Mr. J. Malone, Branch Manager, Irish-American Oil Company, who is assisting Mr. Cahill in the establishment of the air taxi service.'

At the time Hugh Cahill was promoting his aviation business, the media were keen to promote aviation events as they unfolded throughout the world. A sample of such reportings around the time Iona took delivery of their aircraft related to: Costes and Bellonte completing their crossing from Paris to New York; The R100 airship flight from England to America; Flying boats arriving at Queenstown (Cobh); Master of Semphill's flight from London to Sweden; Irish Aero Club Moth on display in Clery's window, Dublin; Amy Johnson's flight from England to Australia and many others. All these events helped to portray aviation in a positive light and thus make the Irish public more air-minded.

Twenty-first century pilots may wish to draw comparisons with the aircraft they fly, compared with what pilots had to contend with in 1930's. Aircraft then were small, unheated and noisy. They were 'tail-draggers' with a tail wheel or tailskid – which would regularly dig into the grass. Many aircraft lacked brakes, retractable undercarriage and had no flaps - to lose height it was necessary to sideslip. Hand starting by swinging the propeller was normal. Most aircraft were non-radio and there were few navigation aids on the ground. Instruments were basic – compass, altimeter, airspeed indicator, turn and bank, rev counter, oil pressure and a type of petrol gauge. Still, with this basic equipment, many pilots did manage to get to their destination. Weather forecasting for aircraft was in its infancy and the Irish Meteorological Service was not formed until 1936. The complexities and security of air traffic control and

Instrument panel of Desoutter EI-AAD. Top, left to right: Altimeter, Turn & Bank indicator, Airspeed indicator. Bottom, left to right: Magneto switches, Oil pressure gauges, engine RPM

Photograph courtesy Pearse Cahill collection

avionics were in the future and there was a great sense of adventure and freedom in the skies. Most aeroplanes had an open cockpit with leather helmet, goggles and a heavy sheepskin coat being necessary parts of the pilot's attire. The aircraft were small but sturdy and capable of aerobatics as a general rule. Frequently they were poor performers in a crosswind situation and forced landings were a much more common occurrence than today, regularly attracting the attentions of the media.

Hugh Cahill looked continuously to the future. Events in his aviation life were stepping up a gear, and his vision of a commercial aviation enterprise was looming more prominently in his mind. He realised more than ever that the military airfield at Baldonnel was not a suitable base for his operations. Within days of its arrival, Hugh Cahill was most anxious to have some airfields approved

for operation by the Desoutter. Some flying had taken place at Derham's field, a 12-acre site in Skerries, north County Dublin. Hugh examined the prospect of developing that field and Captain W. P. Delamere, of the Air Corps, examined it as a potential landing airfield. In his report dated 10 September 1930, he commented:

> 'The field in my opinion is suitable for aircraft of the Gipsy Moth type only, and can be regarded merely as an emergency landing ground for other aircraft types.'

The Desoutter underwent weekly maintenance inspections. Its first 25-hour scheduled inspection occurred on 12 October 1930. Maintenance was performed by Iona's first engineer, Mr. T. Murray. He was appointed to the position of Chief Engineer following the arrival of the Desoutter. He remained at Iona in this capacity for two years until replaced by John R. Currie in September 1932. During this period, Iona also availed of the services of two Air Corps licensed engineers - Rudi Bracken and Johnny Maher.

During October 1930, Hugh had arranged pleasure flights in the Desoutter from a field at the Curragh, County Kildare. This field was located on the southern side of the Newbridge-Kildare road to the west of the military camp buildings. Despite the rejection by the authorities of the field at Skerries, he applied to the Department of Industry and Commerce for a licence to operate at the Curragh. An internal memorandum from the Department seems to indicate that there was some support for this Cahill plan:

> 'I am to add that the Minister is anxious to encourage such national enterprise as that of Mr. Cahill, who has been the first to enter the sphere of aviation on a commercial basis in the Saorstat, and whose flying school and air taxi service may well be the nucleus of an air transport undertaking of some magnitude. At the moment, it is understood that if facilities are made available, a number of officers at the Curragh are anxious to undergo training for their pilots' licences.'

L. S. Tyndall, Hugh Cahill and Gerry Malone beside Gipsy Moth, G-ABBV, in Derham's field, Skerries, County Dublin

Photograph courtesy Pearse Cahill collection

Iona pilot, L. S. Tyndall, and his bride receiving best wishes as they prepare to depart Kildonan for their honeymoon in France using the Desoutter, EI-AAD. To wish them *bon voyage* is, left to right, Pearse and Hugh Cahill along with Cummins junior. On the right are Mr. and Mrs. Cummins

Photograph courtesy Pearse Cahill collection

On 26 October the Desoutter was flown to Drogheda, County Louth where over three hours of 'joy-rides' were given. In those days it was necessary to obtain a licence to do 'joy-rides' from a field and, on 3 November 1930, Hugh wrote again to the Department of Industry and Commerce seeking application for a licence to operate from a field at Mornington, County Meath. This field, the property of a Mr. Lynch and located directly behind the Roman Catholic Chapel, was exceptionally large and level. The British Government confirmed it was on their list of selected fields before they decided on Gormanstown for an aerodrome. Yet again, the military and civil authorities thwarted his attempts to develop commercial aviation and declined his request. Other potential airfields were also examined, including a site on the main Dublin to Belfast road at Santry, currently occupied by the Airport Industrial Estate. Hugh Cahill was not to be put off by his unsuccessful attempts at locating a suitable site for his aerodrome.

The Desoutter undertook some local flights at Baldonnel on 1 and 3 November 1930. By this time the logbook recorded a flight time totalling 35 hours 50 minutes. No further flights were recorded until almost six months later when it flew to Stag Lane aerodrome, London, where Hugh had received some previous flight instruction. The Desoutter's next mission was a romantic one; Iona pilot L. S. Tyndall got married, and Hugh Cahill graciously offered the newly married couple the aircraft for a flight to France for their honeymoon. On 21 April 1931 Hugh and Pearse Cahill saw them off from Kildonan. This was to be the last Irish flight of Ireland's first commercial aircraft. Hugh Cahill realised the aircraft was too large for most of the airfields he had hoped to operate from. He was also becoming somewhat frustrated with his attempts at obtaining official sanction for his commercial aviation operations with the Desoutter. After a few days in London, the Desoutter departed Stag Lane on 28 April 1931 bound for Paris. It returned to London after an overnight in Paris. The following day, 30 April, it again flew to France. This time the destination was Lyons and the flight time was five hours 5 minutes. Next day, following a flight lasting three hours 50 minutes, it arrived at Nice on the Mediterranean Sea, near the border with Italy. On 2 May it commenced its return leg with a flight of five hours 15 minutes to Paris. A two-day stop over and it was London bound, taking two hours 30 minutes to reach Heston aerodrome, London. Its log book entry after this flight on 4 May 1931 stated: '*Aircraft taxied into lock-up at Stag Lane Aerodrome.*'

In May 1931 EI-AAD was to earn the distinction of becoming the first aircraft to be removed from the Irish civil aircraft register.

Desoutter EI-AAD continued to lead an active life after leaving Iona National Airways. On 29 July 1931 the new British registration marks G-ABOM were painted on the fuselage, a 15 minute test flight was conducted at Hanworth, five miles south of Heston and near Staines. It was later submitted to Messrs Lloyds Surveyor for renewal of the Certificate of Airworthiness. On 6 August 1931 it appeared on the British register as G-ABOM, to Robert Lewis Baker, Draycot, Mildred Avenue, Boreham Wood, Herts. On 11 November 1931, it was registered to two Melbourne airmen resident in London, J. H. Jeffrey and E. H. Jenkins. It was their intention to acquire an aircraft that they could utilise to get them back home to Australia at a somewhat leisurely pace departing after Christmas. They left London on 28 December 1931 and arrived in Darwin, North Australia, on 10 February 1932.

Lawrence McK. Johnson of Launceston, Tasmania purchased the Desoutter from the Melbourne based Hart Aircraft Service in 1932. He used it to commence a bi-weekly mail service between Launceston and Flinders Island, a distance of approximately 120 miles, mostly over water. The aircraft, now registered as VH-UEE, was named *Miss Flinders*. In September 1932, the Holyman brothers began a service to the island with the deHavilland 83 Fox Moth VH-UQM *Miss Currie*. Johnson amalgamated with the Holyman Company, and the joint company was named Tasmanian Aerial Services Pty. Ltd. (later Holyman's Airways Pty. Ltd.). Both companies used the Desoutter on the Launceston – Flinders Island service and later on the Hobart – Launceston service. With gradual expansion of services and acquisition of other airlines, the company evolved into Australian National Airways. Ironically, Australian National Airways was co-founded by Sir Charles Kingsford-Smith; a member of the crew that departed Portmarnock Strand on 24 June 1930 in the *Southern Cross* to complete the second non-stop transatlantic crossing from east to west; only six weeks before the Desoutter EI-AAD arrived at Baldonnel. The other co-founder of Australian National Airways, Charles Ulm, had also been to Ireland. On 27 July 1933, he attempted another Atlantic crossing from Portmarnock until his

aircraft, *Faith in Australia,* sank in the sand overloaded by the fuel.

With the growth in traffic a larger aircraft was required and in mid 1935 the Desoutter was traded with deHavilland Aircraft Pty Ltd, Mascot, New South Wales in part payment for another aircraft. Over the years the aircraft changed hands many times until the 1950s when it was used as a crop sprayer, operating from Bourke N.S.W. In 1958 the Certificate of Airworthiness was allowed to lapse and the aircraft was stored in a hangar. On 5 September 1961 it was struck off the register and withdrawn from use. In 1962, when a new passenger terminal building for Launceston Airport, Tasmania, was being planned, it was suggested that the Desoutter VH-UEE, which had important links with the early history of domestic air services operating from Launceston, should be restored and displayed in the building. Rainair Taxis Pty Ltd donated the aircraft, and the owner of the hangar was prepared to release the aircraft on payment of a debt of £200 for rental over eight years. The Air Force Association of Launceston purchased the aircraft at this price. It was transported to Melbourne and on 26 March 1966, the week after Hugh Cahill died, the dismantled aircraft was air freighted, free of charge, to Launceston airport. Members of the local aero club carried out the restoration on a voluntary basis.

Desoutter VH-BQE (formerly EI-AAD) at Bourke, New South Wales, 13 June 1961, following termination of service with Rainair Taxis Ltd and withdrawal from use. It was struck off the Australian register 5 September 1961

Photograph via Pearse Cahill collection

Desoutter VH-BQE, (formerly EI-AAD) at Essendon, Victoria, 26 March 1966, the wings and tail section were removed and many parts cannibalized. Owners donated the remains to Launcestown airport for restoration

Photograph via Pearse Cahill collection

A public appeal in Launceston raised the money to pay for the partitions and display lighting and, on 29 October 1966, the new passenger terminal building was opened and the aircraft placed on public display.

The historically important aircraft, once so central to Hugh Cahill's business plans, was now many thousands of miles away from Ireland. On 2 July 1969, Pearse Cahill wrote to the Commonwealth of Australia, Department of Civil Aviation, Melbourne, and requested information on its fate. The reply dated 26 August 1969 and signed by S. J. Gilbertson for Director General of Civil Aviation, describes the Desoutter's long and chequered career. (His response is summarised in Table 2).

Thankful that such a piece of Irish aviation history was preserved, albeit at the other side of the globe, Pearse Cahill went to visit *Miss Flinders* in October 1988 and found her well preserved:

'She hadn't changed a bit; I'd have recognised her anywhere. Even the colour scheme was pretty much close to the original. My father arranged to have us taken up for about 15 minutes when I was only a 13 year old boy.'

During 1997, when Launceston airport was undergoing a major refurbishment, the Desoutter was moved, after over 30 years, from its pride of place in the terminal building and was temporarily retained in storage at Inveresk Rail Yard. A new museum has now been constructed in Launceston, Tasmania, and the Desoutter again is one of the prominent display items and cherished by the staff there. The original logbooks form part of the display.

In February 1990 a newspaper article carried a report concerning the head of an Aboriginal Prince that was in the Royal College of Surgeons, St Stephen's Green, Dublin. The Aboriginals were seeking the return of the head from the Irish Government. On 21 February 1990, Pearse wrote to the Taoiseach of the time, Charles Haughey, suggesting the Government should engage in a trade with the Australians with the head returning to Australia and *Miss Flinders* returning to Ireland. An Taoiseach acknowledged his suggestion, but nothing came of the proposal.

On 11 February 1931, Iona National Airways Limited was registered as a limited liability company. It was allocated Certificate of Incorporation number 8085. The directors of the new company were given as Hugh Cahill, Prospect Villa, Glasnevin, Dublin and Caroline Cahill of the same address. Paul Callan of Cremin McCarthy and Company, Auditors and Accountants, 12–14 College Green, Dublin, acted as accountant on behalf of the company. Hugh Cahill was now formally in business and ready to let his mark be felt on the Irish aviation industry. It was now time to press ahead with his plans for civil aviation in Ireland.

Desoutter VH-UEE (formerly EI-AAD), on display at Launcestown airport terminal building showing the name *'Miss Flinders'* on nose section

Photograph via Pearse Cahill collection

Desoutter VH-UEE (formerly EI-AAD), on display at Launcestown airport terminal building

Photograph via Pearse Cahill collection

Table 1

Registration	G-ABBV (EI-AAK)
Aircraft Type	de Havilland dH60X Moth, 2-seater bi-plane
Constructors Serial Number	1276
Place & Year of Manufacture	Stag Lane, London, 1930
Previous Registrations	New aircraft
Registered to	Hugh Cahill, July 1930
Delivery date	4 September 1930
Remarks	On 9 July 1931, G-ABBV, was taking off from a field at Collooney, Co. Sligo when it crashed into a haystack and overturned. Following repair it was transferred to the Irish register as EI-AAK to Iona National Airways Limited on 22 August 1931. EI-AAK and Fox Moth, EI-AAP were transferred to Caithleen Nelson on 2 December 1933 for operation by Everson Flying Services. On 22 March 1935 it transferred to another owner at Kildonan - Dublin Air Ferries Ltd. On 7 April 1936, EI-AAK was ferried to Hanworth for overhaul and sale. It was cancelled from the Irish register 2 June 1936. Following its return to England, it reverted to its original registration of G-ABBV. It had a few owners in the UK until it crashed at Churchdown, Glostershire on 15 July 1939, after nine years of service. UK registration cancelled 24 August 1939.

Table 2: THE FATE OF EI-AAD WHILE IN AUSTRALIA.

11 March 1932	Lawrence McK. Johnson, Western Junction, Tasmania as *Miss Flinders*
18 October 1932	Tasmanian Aerial Services Ltd, Launceston, Tasmania. (later Holyman Airways Ltd,)
18 July 1935	Struck off register;
23 July 1935	deHavilland Aircraft Pty. Ltd. Mascot,
26 March 1936	J. J. Larkin, Sydney, N.S.W.
18 August 1936	G. P. Hoskins, c/o Airlines of Australia, Townsville, Queensland. On 24 January 1937 it was struck by Eagle, VH-USI during take off and port wing torn off.
15 November 1938	J. Pater, Warragul, Victoria.
24 April 1939	C. D. Pratt, Melbourne, Victoria. Stored during World War Two.
28 September 1946	Wollonggong & South Coast Aviation Services, N.S.W.
7 December 1949	South Coast Airways Pty. Ltd, Wollongong
6 August 1951	Struck off register and withdrawn from service.
30 August 1951	NEW REGISTRATION MARKS VH-BQE ALLOCATED (Change in registration was a consequence of an amendment to international regulations concerning the use of successive 'Es' in aircraft registrations)
25 January 1952	South Coast Airways Ltd, Wollongong, N.S.W.
5 January 1953	W. E. James, Wollongong, N.S.W.
14 July 1953	Airmech, Bankstown Airport, N.S.W.
14 May 1954	R. C. Burt, Baradine, N.S.W.
25 May 1956	Australian Aircraft Sales, Sydney, N.S.W.
17 January 1957	Rainair Taxis Ltd., Sydney, N.S.W.
5 September 1961	Struck off register and withdrawn from use.

Chapter

2

PASTURES NEW

*Development of Ireland's first commercial aerodrome
and promotion of aviation activities to instill an
awareness of aviation among the public*

Chapter Two

PASTURES NEW

Baldonnel was essentially a military airfield and was never intended for ongoing civil aviation purposes. There were to be certain curtailments for the embryo airline, and Hugh Cahill also feared that his interests would be seen to conflict with those of his comrades at the Irish Aero Club. Hugh was not in any way deflected from his efforts to find his, and subsequently Ireland's, first civil aerodrome. Many possibilities were examined in the early months of 1931. Eventually Hugh approached friends of his with whom he worked, the Fitzpatrick family who owned Kildonan House, on the Ashbourne road, about a mile and a half north of Finglas, in north county Dublin. They agreed to lease some land. Two fields comprising approximately 50 acres adjoining the house were selected for use as an airfield (*ii). Many modern aviators when driving northbound on the M50 motorway will pass the Finglas intersection in relatively good sunshine, yet a mere four miles ahead, Dublin airport and its environs will be fog-bound. This contrasting weather difference is due in principle to the proximity of the coastline. One can reflect on the decision of Major Sholto Douglas in 1917 to select Collinstown as his choice of an ideal location for an aerodrome while fourteen years later Hugh Cahill opted for the site four miles further inland at Kildonan.

A certain amount of work was done at Kildonan by way of joining the two fields and levelling them. Three runways were created; two ran in an east-west direction, either side of the avenue leading to Kildonan House, and another crossed the avenue, running northeast to southwest. A hangar capable of holding approximately eight aircraft was constructed on the east side of the airfield at the entrance to the farm. In addition a clubhouse was also built. The contractors were P. & W. MacLellan, Structural Engineers, of Glasgow. Fuel facilities were incorporated. In front of the clubhouse was a small paddock area in which a small sun-house was built; this could rotate 360 degrees, a favourite place for people to congregate while waiting for their flight.

In her talk to the Old Dublin Society, dated 18 January 1984, Sr. Katherine Butler, RSC, described the aerodrome:

'In the early 1930s Finglas, in the north county Dublin was a small village consisting mainly of one hilly street with some little houses and shops, a church and a school. A left turn at the top of the street led to a muddy or dusty road, depending on the weather, little better than a country lane that brought one to Cappagh Hospital. Continuing on the main road one passed Flood's public house, Parke's garage, a few clusters of cottages with vegetable gardens, then along by the road flanked by fields and hedges until about a mile out on the left a house named 'Kildonan' came into view, the property of people named Fitzpatrick. A path by the side of this led to a field with a hangar, some aircraft, a clubhouse, a petrol pump, a windsock – Kildonan aerodrome.'

'On the roof of the hangar was painted the name 'KILDONAN' in large letters. This was frequently the only means of identifying the airfield to visiting aircraft. Literature promoting the new enterprise referred to the company as 'Iona National Aerial Taxi Service and Flying School'. The company headed notepaper at the time was showing the title 'Iona National Flying School and Motor Engineering Works'. Either way it captured the idea that Iona would be offering all aviation services.'

Early promotional leaflet material described the facilities:

'Our Aerodrome situated as it is within four miles of the city can be reached within 15 minutes – a ring on the phone and the machine is ready awaiting your arrival at any hour of the day, or we can arrange to call for you with one of our motor taxis if you so desire. There is no waiting list, no schedule of time to which you must adhere, the instructional experience available is unique and will enable the highest standard to be reached by all pupils.'

FOOTNOTE (*ii)
The Byrne family are the current owners of this land. An Electricity Supply Board sub-station now occupies the eastern end of the field, and is clearly visible from the northbound carriageway of the M50 Motorway.

Aerial view of the aerodrome at Kildonan early 1930's, indicating the lengths of runway available both sides of the avenue leading to Kildonan House - partially obscured by wing brace in top photograph. In the centre of the photograph is the Iona hangar.

Photograph via Pearse Cahill collection

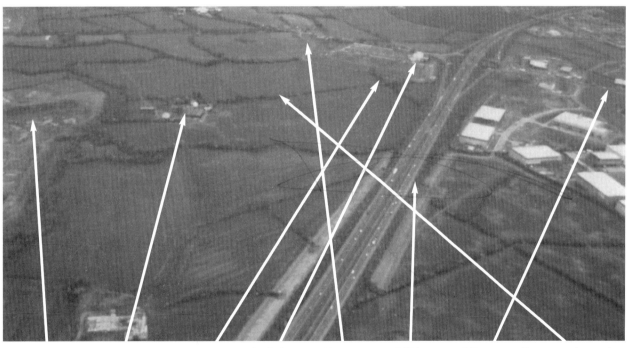

| Roadstone Huntstown Quarry | Kildonan House | Site of former Kildonan Hangar | ESB Sub Station | N2 to Ashbourne | M50 Motorway | N2 to Finglas | Runways formerly located both sides of avenue to Kildonan House |

Aerial view of lands at Kildonan taken from a similar postion in May 2004

Photograph courtesy Brian Higgins

Promotional poster advertising services offered by Iona National Aerial Taxi Service and Flying School

Poster courtesy Pearse Cahill collection

Iona had just commenced operations at their newly acquired aerodrome, when they received a request for assistance for a novel flight. Crabtree's were motorcycle specialists and engineers, located at Warrington, Cheshire, east of Liverpool. On 15 May 1931 they wrote to the Royal Irish Automobile Club: *'a very difficult position has arisen through the I.O.M., T.T. practice on 6th June.'* Mr. S. A. Crabtree was due to race in the club's Grand Prix in the Phoenix Park on Thursday 4 and Friday 5 June. Yet, Mr. Crabtree was employed by Excelsior Motor

Company to partake in the practice on the Saturday morning in the Isle of Man. Neither *'the Free State Air Force nor the local flying club'* could assist Mr. Crabtree. The Royal Irish Automobile Club contacted Hugh Cahill who offered to assist in any way possible, subject to insurance. The rate was one shilling per mile. Mr. Crabtree was collected by car from the Phoenix Park immediately following his last race and driven to Kildonan. From there he was flown to the Isle of Man arriving on the Friday evening in good time for his practice on Saturday morning.

The Desoutter, EI-AAD was found to be too large and therefore unsuitable for many of the small airfields for which it was planned to operate and was sold in England in May 1931. This temporarily reduced the Iona fleet to one aircraft. The Gipsy Moth, G-ABBV, proved a success; consequently Hugh Cahill elected to purchase two further similar aircraft. G-ABAH was a Gipsy Moth, identical to G-ABBV, and was registered to Iona National Airways Limited on 3 June 1931 as EI-AAF (see Table 3). G-EBYV a Cirrus Moth was registered to the new company on 2 June 1931 as EI-AAG (see Table 4). One of the pilots who ferried the aircraft from the UK was Sir Geoffrey de Havilland, owner of the company who manufactured these aircraft; having produced his first light aircraft in 1923. Hugh purchased a fur flying coat for Pearse and Geoffrey de Havilland brought it to Ireland in the aircraft. Pearse had travelled in the Iona taxi from Whitworth Road along with the Customs man to meet the arriving aircraft. When Geoffrey saw the Customs man he called Pearse over and told him to hide the coat quickly before the Customs man saw it.

Iona, now with three aircraft, decided to highlight and promote its activities. The first such event took place on Monday, 8 June 1931 when the official opening of the airfield at Kildonan took place. The ceremony was performed by Mr. Seamus Dolan, TD, Parliamentary Secretary to the Minister for Industry and Commerce. This launched the first civil commercial airport in Ireland, preceding Dublin airport by almost nine years. From this field operated Irelands' first commercial civil aviation company, preceding Aer Lingus by over five years. The ceremony was high profile and included senior officers of the Air Corps, the Governor General MacNeill and other Government officials. (In 1928, James MacNeill was the second person appointed Governor General of the Free State.) Pleasure flying in the three Moths was available to many members of the public who attended. The new operation received widespread coverage in the national newspapers. *The Irish Times*, Tuesday, 9 June 1931 in an article headed *'Air Taxi Service Inaugurated'* included the comments:

'Mr. Cahill must be congratulated on his efforts to establish civil aviation in this country. For many years the Irish Free State has lagged behind other countries of the world in this respect. Until Mr. Cahill established Iona National Airways there was no air taxi service

The garage premises at the junction of Whitworth Road and Prospect Road, Cross Guns Bridge opened 8 June 1931

Photograph courtesy Pearse Cahill collection

here, although the Irish Aero Club were always prepared to use their machines as air taxis.

'Mr. Cahill has selected a fine field which, with some alterations he proposes to make, will make an excellent aerodrome in which big machines will be able to land and take off. He has constructed a hangar that can hold twenty aeroplanes, in addition to a large clubhouse, where ground instruction will be given to members of the flying school.'

The Head Office of the company was at the garage Hugh Cahill had erected at the junction of Prospect Road and Whitworth Road at Cross Guns Bridge, Phibsborough, Dublin. This garage was constructed around the time the field at Kildonan was being developed and was located across the road from the family engineering works, then in operation for about eight years.

Official opening day at Kildonan 8 June 1931, depicting the Iona fleet of, left to right, Gipsy Moths EI-AAF,G-ABBV and EI-AAG

Photograph courtesy Pearse Cahill collection

The first time the garage opened for business was the same day the airfield at Kildonan was officially opened – Monday, 8 June 1931. A taxi business was also located on the new premises, from where many patrons hired a taxi to take them the five miles out in the countryside to the aerodrome at Kildonan. The windows on the side of the garage facing the canal were adorned with stained glass and emblazoned with the company's business: 'IONA NATIONAL AIRWAYS LIMITED, ACCESSORIES, TAXIS DAY AND NIGHT.' The front of the building had a canopy similarly portraying the company operation. A few weeks after the official opening of the field at Kildonan, Hugh Cahill arranged the transportation by road of the Gipsy Moth, G-ABBV, to the premises at the top of Whitworth Road. There the aircraft was placed on display in the window to the public as a means of promoting the activities at Kildonan.

Iona National Airways also had offices at 26 Westmoreland Street, Dublin. They were located in rooms overhead Watson's fish shop, opposite the present location of Bewley's Café. (In 2004 these premises were occupied by Black Tie Ltd and John J. Walker & Co., Solicitor). A good social atmosphere evolved around the airfield, which had

Hugh Cahill (centre) with Lord Mayor, Alfie Byrne. In the background is Governor General MacNeill. The occasion was the Air Display, Baldonnel, 15 August 1931

Photograph courtesy Pearse Cahill collection

its own club attendant offering tea and sandwiches to patrons and visitors. Short air races were organised from the airfield to Dunsoghly Castle turning toward the church in Finglas and back to the aerodrome, all the time being in view of spectators at the aerodrome.

Promotional poster advertising services offered by Iona National Airways Ltd

Poster courtesy Pearse Cahill collection

The main activities at Kildonan were air-taxi work and pleasure flights ('joy-rides' as they were termed in that wonderful romantic era in reasonably care-free Ireland). 'Joy-rides' then cost 7 shillings. Instruction also took place at Kildonan. The flying bug got to Hugh's 14-year-old son, Pearse, whose first instructional flight is recorded as 27 June 1931. This flight took place in the Gipsy Moth EI-AAF, with J. C. Coogan as his instructor. Prior to this Hugh had told another instructor, Captain Tyndall, 'to take Pearse up and scare the living daylights out of him,' so that he would have no further interest in flying. Despite the aerial manoeuvres, Pearse said he had the best aerobatics of his life – there was no shaking the flying bug from the young Cahill. After 13 hours logged instruction, Pearse was authorised by John R. Currie to undertake his 'First Solo' on 30 April 1933, a mere 12 weeks after his 16th birthday, in Gipsy Moth EI-AAK. There were no recorded flights in Pearse's logbook between 8 June 1933 and 23 May 1952.

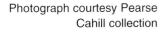

16-year-old Pearse Cahill in the cockpit of Gipsy Moth, EI-AAK, following his 'First Solo' on 30 April 1933

Photograph courtesy Pearse Cahill collection

The staff at Kildonan showed certain intent on the company developing as a business offering full aeronautical services. The airport manager was ex-Air Corps officer Captain Tom Young. Pilots included Captain Tyndall, J. C. Coogan, J. M. St-John Kearney and Eric Stewart. The ground engineer was John R. Currie. Captain Young was charged with running a ground school in aeronautical matters in addition to performing his role as having responsibility for aerodrome operations. The Chief Flying Instructor was J. C. Coogan. The assistant ground engineer at Kildonan was Mick Brady. Born in 1913, Mick lived at 44 Lower Dodder Road, Rathfarnham, Dublin.

Iona's Ground Engineer, John R. Currie and Assistant Ground Engineer, Mick Brady (left) in the workshop at Kildonan. The photo tells who's doing the work and who's posing for the camera!!

Photograph courtesy Chris Bruton collection

John R. Currie joined Iona in September 1932 as Instructor and Chief Engineer. He later achieved fame as the designer of the Currie Wot aircraft

Photograph courtesy Chris Bruton collection

Coogan was an officer with the Free State Army Air Corps. When aviation ceased to operate at Kildonan, Tom Young returned to the Defence Forces, serving throughout the war years as an Administrative Officer in the Air Corps. Later he was personnel officer with Aer Lingus. He finished his career in the Department of Defence.

John Robert Currie was a young Southampton born engineer of Irish extraction. He was regarded as a superb all round engineer and an excellent carpenter, as well as an engine fitter. His aeronautical training was with the Royal Air Force towards the end of World War One. He held early (British) Ground Engineers licences in categories A, B, C and D. In addition he held a lapsed pilot's licence, which he renewed at Kildonan, as an Irish pilot's 'A' (private) licence. He joined Iona in September 1932 and did some additional flying in order to gain his 'B' (commercial) licence. His 'B' Irish pilot's licence was number 13. At his request the Irish authorities changed it to number 14. He remained on at Kildonan with Everson Flying Services. He later returned to England, and took up a position as lecturer at the College of Aeronautical Engineering, Chelsea. It was before World War Two that the brilliant engineer gained prominence as the designer and builder of the *Currie Wot*. The *Wot* was a wood and fabric aerobatic single seat bi-plane, with plywood fuselage. Two examples, G-AFCG and G-AFDS, built by Cinque Ports Aviation Ltd at Lympne, near Folkestone, Kent in 1937, shared a single 40 hp Aeronca JAP. J-99 two-cylinder engine (salvaged from a wrecked Aeronca C-3, G-ADZZ) but differed in detail and were known as Wot 1 and Wot 2 respectively. Both were destroyed in a German air raid on Lympne in May 1940. After the war J. R. Currie, then chief engineer at the Hampshire Aeroplane Club, Eastleigh, north of Southampton, was persuaded to produce original drawings from which two more *Wots*, financed by V. H. Bellamy, were built at the club by J. O. Isaacs. These two aircraft, G-APNT and G-APWT, were first flown 11 September 1958 and 20 October 1959, respectively. In addition to the four aircraft referred to above and the six in the following paragraph, Currie placed a further six Currie Wots on the UK civil aircraft register up to 1972.

The most sensational *Wots* were six, G-AVOT to G-AVOY, built by Slingsby Sailplanes Ltd. at Kirkbymoorside, Yorkshire in 1967 with changes in external profile to resemble 0.83 scale S.E.5A replicas under the designation Slingsby Type 56. They were powered by 115hp Lycoming engines with $2 1/2$ inch plastic rainwater pipes as dummy exhausts. Derek Piggott flew the first machine, G-AVOT, from Welburn airfield alongside Slingsby's factory on 20 June 1967. This and G-AVOU and G-AVOV were ferried to Casement Aerodrome, Dublin via Squires Gate in a flying time of four hours by Lorne Welch, John Oxborough and Henryck Doktor on 27 June; and the remaining three by John Oxborough, Henryck Doktor and Derek Goddard on 30 June. On 21 June 1967 they were registered to Shillelagh Productions Inc. as EI-ARH to EI-ARM and equipped with dummy guns initially for the film *Darlin' Lili*, These replicas were flown again in August 1969 during the filming of *I shot down Richthofen*, after which EI-ARI and EI-ARJ were crated for sea and

The original 1937 Currie Wot 1, G-AFCG, with Cinque Ports Flying Club Crest, at Lympne, December 1937. The diagonal centre section struts were reversed on all later Wots

Photograph courtesy *'Aeroplane'* collection

Slingsby Type 56 Wot / S.E.5A replica EI-ARM at Kirkbymoorside, north Yorkshire, in June 1967 prior to delivery to Baldonnel as G-AVOY for film work.

Photograph courtesy Norman Ellison

Six Currie Wots ferried to Ireland for film work, and
photographed at Baldonnel Aerodrome

Photograph courtesy Paul Duffy

Currie Wot, EI-ARM, repainted for film work at
Baldonnel Aerodrome

Photograph courtesy Paul Duffy

road transport to Aksaray, 300 miles south east of
Ankara, Turkey where they were flown for 1914 –
1918 war sequences for the film *Dubious Patriot*.
The aircraft were then shipped back to Ireland.

In 1931 a new company, the Irish Aviation
Company, based at the old disused Royal Air Force
base at Collinstown, commenced operations using
a Desoutter Mark I, G-AAPY. They were operating
mail and small parcel services initially to Sligo. On
behalf of the *Daily Mail* they collected the
newspapers in Manchester and had them delivered
to Sligo before Dublin printed newspapers reached
the town in the morning. This service commenced
on 10 July 1931. Their Chief Pilot was a New

Zealander, Eric Stewart. He had served with the
Royal Air Force and Imperial Airways. He also had
a fine record flying the Indian Air Mail route Basra-
Baghdad-Cairo. During World War One he flew
Sopwith Camels. When operations at Irish Aviation
Company ceased in November 1931, Stewart joined
Iona National Airways at the nearby aerodrome,
Kildonan. He later transferred to Waterford where
he went into business with Arthur Westcott-Pitt
and J. M. St. Kearney to establish Irish Air Lines.
Stewart died when an aircraft he was piloting
crashed in the Irish Sea.

The Iona aircraft toured the country promoting
aviation and giving pleasure flights to many
members of the public who were now gradually
becoming accustomed to aeroplanes yet, who
found a certain fascination and attraction to them
when they visited their area. On 9 July 1931, one
month after the official opening, one of the Moths,
G-ABBV, was taking-off from a field at Collooney,
County Sligo when it crashed into a haystack and
overturned. The pilot, the sole occupant, received
slight injuries. The aircraft was not too badly
damaged and was removed to Kildonan for repair.
Following repair it was transferred to the Irish
register as EI-AAK to Iona National Airways
Limited on 22 August 1931.

Gipsy Moth, G-ABBV, upturned at Collooney, Co. Sligo
following impact with a haystack 9 July 1931

Photograph courtesy Pearse Cahill collection

Unfortunately, the company suffered an accident to
the second of their three aircraft within weeks. On
31 July 1931, EI-AAF was coming in to land at
Bundoran, County Donegal. In an effort to avoid

some of the on-lookers who had gathered in the field the pilot, Mr. Coogan, elected to go around; he was unable to gain sufficient altitude and collided with the thatched roof of a house, belonging to a Miss McCoughrey, which adjoined the field. Both pilot and passenger received injuries and were removed to hospital in Ballyshannon. The passenger, John O'Doherty, was a visitor from Belfast. According to a report in the *Donegal Democrat*:

> 'The engine of the plane was severed from the body by the impact and flew into the upstairs room of the house; fortunately, Miss McCoughrey was downstairs at the time.'

The aircraft never flew again and was subsequently removed from the register on 31 July 1932. Part of the airframe was used as a link-trainer at Kildonan to provide instruction to student pilots. The engine was placed in the Cirrus Moth, EI-AAG, thus converting this aircraft to a Gipsy Moth.

This accident had a court sequel that was a first of its type in legal aviation history in Ireland. The summons, issued by the Dublin District Court to Iona National Airways Limited as Defendant and naming The Attorney General as plaintiff, was dated 7 November 1931. It stated:

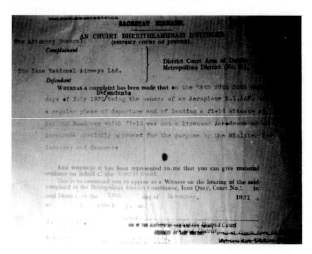

A copy of the Summons served on Iona following the accident involving EI-AAF at Bundoran, Co. Donegal, 31 July 1931

Copy summons courtesy Pearse Cahill collection

'That on 28th, 29th, 30th and 31st July 1931, Defendants being the owner of an aeroplane EI-AAF, used as a regular place of departure and of landing a field situate at Westend, Bundoran which field was not a licensed Aerodrome or an Aerodrome specially approved for the purpose by the Minister for Industry and Commerce.'

The company received a fine as a consequence.

During January and February 1932 further work was carried out on the Kildonan aerodrome. The airfield was enlarged to 75 acres, giving a run of 600 metres in all directions. The work involved a considerable amount of levelling of the field and removal of trees and hedges.

On 20 May 1932 a Lockheed Vega took off from Harbour Grace, Newfoundland. Its pilot was the thirty-one year old wife of a wealthy American publisher – Mrs. G. P. Putnam, otherwise known as Amelia Earhart. Fifteen hours later she arrived over Ireland, and landed in a field near Culmore, County Derry, five years to the day after Charles

Amelia Earhart (left of centre of photograph and still wearing her leather flying helmet) is surrounded by well-wishers at Culmore, Derry, following her solo transatlantic flight 20 May 1932. This flight gave Hugh Cahill a further boost in his efforts to promote aviation in Ireland

Photograph via Pearse Cahill collection

Lindbergh's historic flight from New York to Paris. She became the first female to successfully complete a solo crossing of the Atlantic. Her arrival aroused great excitement in Ireland at such a feat. Her crossing beat the record, by two hours, set by Alcock and Brown on 14 June 1919.

In June 1932, Iona National Airways were successful in having their request to upgrade the status of the airfield to fully licensed, with Customs facilities. This required a Customs and Excise official to attend the airfield and meet the arriving aircraft and its passengers. Hugh Cahill had the contract to bring the Customs and Excise official by Iona taxi from the city centre to Kildonan and Baldonnel. The advantage of this was the greater utilisation of the airfield by visitors from the United Kingdom. No records survive of aircraft movements at Kildonan in those early days. From then on, aircraft arriving at Dublin requiring Customs clearance could elect to land at either Baldonnel or Kildonan. The first foreign visiting aircraft to land at Kildonan after being licensed was a Junkers F13, G-ABDC, of Personal Flying Services, flown by Captain W. Ledie and a Hendy 302, G-AAVT, which both arrived from Heston. The four seater Junkers was later leased in by Iona to give 'joy-rides' and pleasure flights.

In June 1932, Iona received authorization to permit aircraft coming from abroad to land at Kildonan, instead of having to clear Customs at Baldonnel. The first aircraft to avail of this facility was Junkers, F-13, G-ABDC. This Junkers was leased in by Iona during the Eucharistic Congress in June 1932

Photograph courtesy Pearse Cahill collection

Certainly 1932 saw an increase in aviation activity. For Ireland to host the Eucharistic Congress between 22 and 26 June of that year was a significant Ecumenical coup, proving a major event in the Irish calendar. On 21 June, ocean liners carrying many thousands of pilgrims from the United States, Lapland and Holland arrived in Irish ports for the Eucharistic Congress. An occasion that comes infrequently to a nation and 1932 was the only occasion to date that Ireland has hosted such an event. In this instance it was to commemorate the 1,500th anniversary of the coming of Saint Patrick to Ireland. Those days and the period leading to the occasion were very active for Iona. They had on lease the Junkers G-ABDC that was utilised to great effect to fly many reporters and photographers to and from United Kingdom in order that their stories and photographs could appear in the next edition of the British newspapers. At the end of the Congress, Iona flew the Lord Mayor of New York from Dublin to Portsmouth to catch the liner departing Southamouth for USA.

In July 1932 it was decided to further extend the fleet and a larger aircraft was acquired. This was a new deHavilland dH83 Fox Moth, registered EI-AAP to Iona National Airways on 20 July 1932 (see Table 5). It was delivered by William Gairdner, employed by Brian Lewis and Company, agents for deHavilland, arriving at Kildonan at 6.30pm on Saturday, 23 July 1932. It was a single engine bi-plane where the pilot sat in an open cockpit. In front of him was an enclosed cabin that could accommodate up to four passengers. The range of the Fox Moth was 360 miles, an incredible distance for that period. It was immediately put to use doing air taxi work, charged at one shilling per mile. 'Joy-rides' cost five shillings. Wherever the aircraft went to provide such displays to the public, it was necessary for a truck or tender-car to go to the location bringing fuel, fire extinguishers, a pole and windsock. Some of the more regular venues were: a field adjacent to the military camp on the Curragh, County Kildare; at Mornington, County Meath and Bettystown Strand, County Louth. Air tours were also arranged. One such example was an aerial tour advertised as follows: -

'Flying from Kildonan aerodrome, the first landing will be at Limerick for lunch, passengers being taken by car to Ardnacrusha to view the Shannon power works. The flight over the Lakes of Killarney and other parts of Kerry will occupy most of the afternoon, returning to Limerick for tea before flying back to Dublin.'

In July 1932 it was decided to further extend the fleet and a larger aircraft was acquired. This was a new de Havilland dH83 Fox Moth, registered EI-AAP to Iona National Airways on 20 July 1932.

Photograph courtesy Pearse Cahill collection

In July 1932, two world famous pioneering aviators, Jim Mollison and Amy Johnson, were married. Two weeks later, on 9 August, they were at Baldonnel preparing for Jim's solo attempt on the Atlantic. The euphoria surrounding the successful achievement of Amelia Earhart had barely subsided when the public were filled with excitement at the prospect of another attempt on the Atlantic. While in Dublin the trio of renowned aviators met up. They attended many venues in each other's company. One such occasion saw them visit the new airfield at Kildonan. Yet again, Paddy Saul was involved in an attempt to navigate the Atlantic. He plotted the course for the Scot. On Thursday, 11 August 1932, Paddy flew with W. R. Elliott (Chief Flying Instructor, Irish Aero Club) on a flight to the west of Ireland, accompanying them in Amy's plane. Jim Mollison examined possible alternative take-off points. In the end, Jim elected to depart from Portmarnock strand. On 18 August 1932, the *Heart's Content* roared down the beach to the cheers of the thousands of well-wishers gathered to see him embark on the first successful

Three famous flyers together in St. Stephen's Green, Dublin in August 1932. During their stay in the capital they visited Kildonan. Left to right: Amy Johnson, Amelia Earhart and Jim Mollison

Photograph via Pearse Cahill collection

solo non-stop westbound crossing of the Atlantic. Thirty hours 15 minutes later he landed successfully at New Brunswick. There was still a large sense of romance attached to aviation in Ireland, and Hugh Cahill was determined to harness this feeling and convert it into a reality.

A report in the *Cork Examiner* covered a visit to Ballincollig, County Cork of Gipsy Moth, EI-AAK. On Friday, 26 August 1932, an American priest missed the train to Cork. He was endeavouring to catch the US liner, *Manhattan*, at Cobh. He telephoned Iona at Kildonan and Oliver Armstrong agreed to fly the priest. They departed Kildonan at 10.50am and arrived at Ballincollig at 12.20pm, where a taxi took the passenger to Cobh in time to connect with the liner. At Ballincollig the Moth was refuelled by arrangement with Jim Malone's Irish American Oil Company, who sent a tanker out to the airfield. According to the newspaper report, this was not Oliver Armstrong's first visit to Ballincollig as had flown there several times already and knew his way about the ruins of the old Ballincollig barracks quite well. His landing attracted a handful of people to the field and while the plane was at rest the keenest interest was taken in its appearance. The fuselage was a dark blue colour and the wings were painted silver.

In August 1932, as a consequence of the licensing of Kildonan, the Department of Industry and Commerce issued Civil Aviation Notice, No. 3 of 1932, titled *'Revised arrangements for reporting the passage of aircraft crossing the Irish Sea.'* It outlined the arrangements for reporting an aircraft's passage across the Irish Sea from Baldonnel or Kildonan to Holyhead. These included the pilot notifying, by telegram or telephone, to the Officer Commanding Army Air Corps, Baldonnel or Aerodrome Manager, Kildonan, details of the pilot and passengers, the aircraft and relevant times. Baldonnel or Kildonan were to relay this information to the Holyhead Meteorological Station. The time of departure was also to be advised when the aircraft was airborne. Baldonnel or Kildonan were to observe the true course made good by the aircraft as long as possible. Clause (iv) stated:

> 'Aircraft to circle over the Meteorological Station, Holyhead, after crossing the Irish Sea, at such a height as will, having regard to the condition of visibility, enable the nationality and registration marks to be readily identified.'

When the personnel of the Meteorological Station observed him, they would flash a white light at the pilot. The pilot could not continue his flight until he had received this light signal. Baldonnel or Kildonan would then be advised of the aircraft's passage over Holyhead. On arrival at its destination aerodrome in Great Britain on the outward journey or on landing at Baldonnel or Kildonan on their return, an arrival signal was immediately dispatched to Holyhead.

In the event that the aircraft was not observed over Holyhead after one hour since from departure,

Baldonnel or Kildonan were to be notified, who in turn would notify the Department of Industry and Commerce. In addition, Holyhead would contact Seaforth W/T station, which would broadcast shipping, giving all details available. For aircraft returning to the Irish Free State a similar procedure operated in reverse direction. An amendment was later issued, whereby the pilot would include in his initial notification the proposed height and cruising air speed. The amendment included the clause:

> 'The controlling authority at Met. Office, Holyhead will estimate trip time. In the event of non arrival of any such aircraft when the estimated trip time has been exceeded by 25% from the time of departure from Baldonnel or Kildonan or at the discretion of the Controlling Authority, the various bodies would be notified.'

From this it was evident a number of false alarms had been unnecessarily activated.

The acquisition of the Fox Moth, EI-AAP, proved so successful that Iona decided to dispose of one of the two remaining Gipsy Moths. EI-AAG was cancelled from the Irish register 17 August 1932 as sold in England and returned to its former registration G-EBYV on 16 September 1932. Newcastle upon Tyne Light Aeroplane Club, Cramlington, operated it. On 30 June 1936 it crashed at Medomsley, Durham and was cancelled from the UK register in October 1936. For the winter of 1932 Iona operated EI-AAP and the other Gipsy Moth EI-AAK. Activities now offered by the company included banner-towing and aerial photography.

Another event to capture the public imagination was the dropping of a ball to start a Gaelic Athletic Association football match. The match was the 1932 game in Croke Park, Kerry versus Dublin for the McKee-Clancy Memorial fund held on 16 October 1932. The aircraft was the Gipsy Moth EI-AAK owned by Iona National Airways Limited. The pilot on the occasion was Oliver Armstrong. The 'observer' and ball-dropper was the airfield Manager, Tom Young. A special 'basket' was prepared at Iona's engineering works at Cross

Guns Bridge. It was affixed to the underside of the aircraft with wires. The ball was placed in the basket and some practice flights took place at Kildonan, with Tom Young pulling a cord from his seat in the cockpit when he felt he was positioned over the target. Following a few practice runs, the duo set off for Croke Park. The ball hopped almost to the roof of the old Hogan Stand and landed in the 'square' of the railway end!

Iona's chief pilot, Oliver Eric (Paddy) Armstrong was born in Terenure, Dublin on 19 March 1903. He enlisted in the Royal Air Force in 1919, having been inspired by the Alcock and Brown flight. It proved a difficult route and he did not earn his 'wings' until 1927, aged 24 years. His service with the Royal Air Force ended in 1931. He joined Iona in early 1932 and was appointed Chief Pilot in July 1932. The majority of his flying for Iona was in the Fox Moth, EI-AAP, mostly charter, air-taxi work and 'joy-riding'. In October 1932 he left Kildonan.

In August 1934 'Ollie' Armstrong joined London based Olley Air Services, owners of Blackpool and West Coast Air Services. They provided the aircraft and pilot to launch Aer Lingus. The pilot of EI-ABI, *Iolar*, on Aer Lingus' inaugural flight from Baldonnel to Bristol, 27 May 1936 was Oliver E. Armstrong. In January 1938 he moved from Olley to Aer Lingus to become their Chief Pilot and later Operations Manager. In his book *Pioneers in Flight*, Niall G. Weldon describes his career thereafter:

'He tried to again enlist with the Royal Air Force, but at 42, was considered too old. He did, however, join the Air Transport Auxiliary, stationed at Belfast, he ferried aircraft in all kinds of weather to bases all over Britain. During his flying career he flew nearly 100 different types of aircraft – an experience he might never have had as a military pilot. After the war, he returned to civil aviation and flew aircraft for Morton Air Services and Cambrian Airways. Later, he went to Birmingham to fly for Don Everall Aviation,

The first twin-engine aircraft on the Irish register was the Kildonan based Monospar, EI-AAQ, registered to Oliver Armstrong

Photograph via Pearse Cahill collection

In February 1933 he was involved in the formation of Western Air Transport Limited, with the intention of operating a London to Galway air service. This service never materialised. He did not sever his links with Kildonan for on 20 February 1933 a Monospar, G-ABVS, was placed in his name on the Irish register as EI-AAQ and based at Kildonan. On 2 November 1933 it was sold back in England and reverted to its original registration marks.

piloting charter and scheduled flights. He was appointed Commercial Manager of that company. In 1957, to mark the 21st birthday of Aer Lingus he was invited to cut the cake at a public engagement. It was in a Birmingham hospital in 1959, aged 56 years, that Oliver Eric Armstrong passed away. The *Birmingham Post* 28 December 1959 described him as a major contributor to the development of aviation in Britain, having completed 15,000 flying hours.'

The *Who's Who in British Aviation*, 1933 recorded the following entries: -

'**Armstrong, Oliver Eric.** Chief pilot, Iona National Airways, Dublin. Born Dublin 19 March 1903. Educ. Diocesan Intermediate School, Dublin. Sergt Pilot RAF 1919. Served in Egypt, Iraq and India. Discharged 1931. Address 55 Brighton Road, Rathgar, Dublin. I.F.S. Tel Terenure 207.'

'**Cahill, Hugh.** Managing Director, Iona National Airways Ltd. Born Dublin. Address Prospect Lodge, Glasnevin, Dublin. Tel Dublin 22586.'

The Fox Moth further allowed Hugh Cahill to develop some plans he had been nurturing, one of which was a regular air service linking Dublin to the Continent. Liners regularly sailed the Atlantic docking at Galway. In 1929 Galway was the venue for the first airmail service linking Ireland and the UK. Obtaining the loan of Vickers Vixen, G-EBEC from the Vickers aircraft company, Brooklands, Flying Officer J. 'Mutt' Summers, along with Colonel Charles Russell, left Croydon and flew via Newbridge-on-Wye, Sealand, Baldonnel and arrived in Oranmore Aerodrome, County Galway at 4.05pm on 25 August 1929. The German liner, *Karlsruhe* docked at Galway from America at 6.15 am on the morning of 26 August 1929. At 7.30am that morning the duo took-off from Oranmore in the Vixen with seven bags of US mail from the liner. An hour later they were airborne from Baldonnel, they then continued, routing via Sealand (near Chester), until touching down at Croydon, south of London at 11.37am. The cargo of mail was unloaded and they departed Croydon at 2.10pm, returning the same route, and arriving back at Oranmore at 7.10pm, completing the first return air mail service between Ireland and UK. The event was celebrated at a banquet held in the Hotel Royal, Galway that night. Post Officials estimated the flight had reduced the delivery time by twenty-four hours.

In addition to UK mails, the liners carried mails for the Continent. Hugh was to embark on one of his most ambitious plans to date and go further than Colonel Russell. He saw the potential for an air service flying mails between Ireland and the Continent. He developed a relationship with KLM, the Royal Dutch Airline. It was eventually agreed a trial flight would take place. A German liner, the *Bremen* captured the *'Blue Riband'* of the Atlantic on her maiden voyage in July 1932 in a crossing time of 4 days 17 hours and 42 minutes. The publicity surrounding this achievement sparked another idea in Hugh Cahill's head. Newspapers in July 1932 gave further coverage to the prospect of the

GALWAY-LONDON AIR SERVICE

PROSPECT FOR LINK WITH OCEAN LINERS

WOULD HELP COUNTRY

It was announced at a special meeting of Galway Harbour Board that the Iona National Airways, Ltd., would soon establish an air service in Galway, whereby passengers arriving by big liners in Galway could immediately fly from Galway to London.

The arrangement is the inspiration of the Dutch Air Lines, Ltd.

A suitable landing place for the 'planes near Galway, probably the Oranmore Flying Field, is spoken of as a start off and landing place.

Mr. Coleman, on behalf of the company, told the Commissioners that if a suitable landing ground were provided his company would immediately institute an air service to carry passengers, luggage, and mails, if they got them. They were convinced that such a service would help Galway and the Free State.

Mr. Armstrong, Iona Airways pilot, said the landing field at Oranmore was too small, and rather far from the town.

The Chairman, Mr. Young, said that the Harbour Commissioners would give the proposal immediate and sympathetic consideration.

Newspaper article in July 1932 reporting on the efforts of Iona to establish an air link between Galway and London

Newspaper article courtesy Pearse Cahill collection

The KLM Fokker under military guard following arrival from Berlin on 21 October 1932

Photograph via Pearse Cahill collection

The Fokker crew arrives at the hangar at Baldonnel at dawn on 22 October 1932 to prepare for the flight to Berlin

Photograph via Pearse Cahill collection

The Fokker, PH-AID, is taxied from the hangar at Baldonnel to await the arrival of the Iona aircraft from Oranmore, Co. Galway

Photograph via Pearse Cahill collection

proposed air service. On Tuesday, 26 July 1932 a special meeting of Galway Harbour Board was convened. Hugh Cahill, Ollie Armstrong, pilot, and Mr. Coleman, represented Iona National Airways. The proposal was to fly passengers, luggage and mails from the liners docking at Galway and transport them by air to London and beyond. It was suggested the field at Oranmore would be too small for large aircraft and it was a bit far from the town. A deputation had already gone to the Government to extend and improve facilities at Oranmore, but nothing had developed. Mr. Coleman stated KLM would be prepared to send two or three machines to Galway. Mr. Armstrong said it was up to the municipal authorities to provide a landing field, as was the case in England and other countries. The chairman assured the Iona deputation *that the harbour commissioners would give the proposal immediate and sympathetic consideration.'*

The *Bremen* was due to arrive again at Galway port on 21 October 1932. That day a Fokker F.X11, registration PH-AID, landed at Baldonnel and overnighted. The following morning, Saturday, 22 October, a large crowd, estimated to number several thousand, assembled at Baldonnel anticipating, but not really expecting, the arrival of a mail feeder service from Oranmore, County Galway. The reason the crowd were cautiously apprehensive about the arrival of the aircraft from the west was the layer of heavy fog that shrouded the entire country that autumn morning.

Oliver Armstrong arrived at Oranmore early in the morning. He could not see the far end of the runway due to the heavy fog. Nonetheless, he loaded the mailbags from the *Bremen*, along with mail from Galway and surrounding areas bound for Germany. He brought the aircraft to life, and off he went. He had arranged for a man with an acetylene cycle lamp to stand twenty yards from the hedge at the take-off end of the field. His flight across Ireland was 'blind'; only using the few navigational instruments available in those days. Meanwhile, at Baldonnel, two aircraft had taken off but were forced to return immediately due to the lack of visibility. The chances of the feeder service making the journey across the country in such poor

Following his arrival from Oranmore, Co. Galway, Oliver Armstrong (right) hands over mail bags to a Post Office official at Baldonnel, prior to transfer to the Berlin bound Fokker

Photograph via Pearse Cahill collection

conditions appeared slight; in fact, a proposal was being contemplated that the Junkers should depart for Berlin. At 7.30am the sound of a small plane was heard coming from the west. Right on schedule, the small aircraft touched down, taxied

and parked adjacent to the huge Fokker. It was Iona National Airways' Fox Moth, EI-AAP. Ollie Armstrong climbed out, to an incredulous burst of applause, and greeted the pilot of the Fokker, Captain J. B. Scholte. Mr. J. J. Den Outer was wireless operator and Mr. P. Dunk was engineer.

Thirteen passengers climbed aboard. Colonel Charles Russell, a former Commanding Officer of the Air Corps, and promoter of this inaugural Air Mail flight to Berlin, performed the role of co-pilot on the sector from Dublin to Croydon. The mailbags from Galway were added to the thousands of letters sent by van from the General Post Office at 6am that morning and were then loaded on board the Fokker. The three massive engines roared into life and soon the aircraft was on its way following what could be termed a successful feeder service from Galway. The aircraft crossed the coastline at Dun Laoghaire, heading towards Wales and onwards to Croydon, then one of the principle aerodromes near London. Here an hour-long scheduled stop occurred. The next stop was at Rotterdam, with the final leg of the journey terminating in Berlin at 4.30pm. The total journey

A section of the curious and enthusiastic large crowd that gathered at Baldonnel at dawn on 22 October 1932, to witness the first air-mail service between Ireland and mainland Europe. In the background, under the Fokker's starboard (right) engine, is the Iona Fox Moth, EI-AAP

Photograph via Pearse Cahill collection

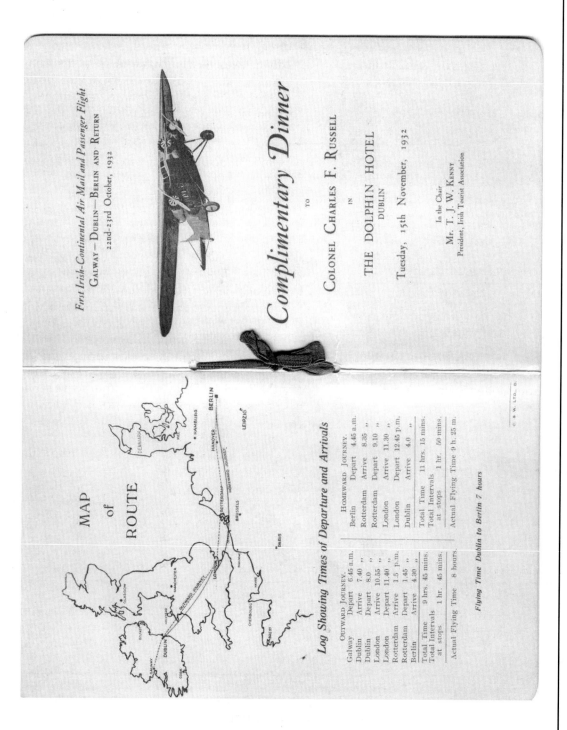

First Irish-Continental Air Mail and Passenger Flight
GALWAY—DUBLIN—BERLIN AND RETURN
22nd-23rd October, 1932

Complimentary Dinner

TO

COLONEL CHARLES F. RUSSELL

IN

THE DOLPHIN HOTEL
DUBLIN

Tuesday, 15th November, 1932

In the Chair
Mr. T. J. W. KENNY
President, Irish Tourist Association

MAP of ROUTE

Log Showing Times of Departure and Arrivals

OUTWARD JOURNEY.

Galway	Depart	6.45 a.m.
Dublin	Arrive	7.40 ,,
Dublin	Depart	8.0 ,,
London	Arrive	10.55 ,,
London	Depart	11.40 ,,
Rotterdam	Arrive	1.5 p.m.
Rotterdam	Depart	1.45 ,,
Berlin	Arrive	4.30 ,,

Total Time	9 hrs. 45 mins.
Total Intervals at stops	1 hr. 45 mins.
Actual Flying Time	8 hours.

HOMEWARD JOURNEY.

Berlin	Depart	4.45 a.m.
Rotterdam	Arrive	8.35 ,,
Rotterdam	Depart	9.10 ,,
London	Arrive	11.30 ,,
London	Depart	12.45 p.m.
Dublin	Arrive	4.0 ,,

Total Time	11 hrs. 15 mins.
Total Intervals at stops	1 hr. 50 mins.
Actual Flying Time	9 h. 25 m.

Flying Time Dublin to Berlin 7 hours

A Complimentary Dinner was held on 15 November 1932 to commemorate the first Irish - Continental Air Mail and Passenger Flight, Galway-Dublin-Berlin and Return

Courtesy Ronny Vogt collection

was 825 miles. The following day PH-AID returned to Baldonnel where it overnighted. Thus the first airmail round trip between Ireland and a Continental city was completed.

In honour of Colonel Charles F. Russell and to commemorate the first Irish – continental airmail and passenger flight, a complimentary dinner was held in the Dolphin Hotel, Dublin on Tuesday, 15 November 1932. The Lord Mayor, Alfie Byrne, Erskine Childers and Paddy Saul were among the many dignitaries in attendance. Hugh Cahill and Oliver Armstrong were among the invited guests(*iii).

Mails were been flown between Ireland and the United Kingdom since 1923. The first such flight was similar to the above. It was to link Plymouth in the south of England with Belfast, with the inaugural flight taking place on 15 September 1923. The pilot on this flight was Alan Cobham. In 1926 he was Knighted in recognition of his services to aviation. Daily flights continued and the British Air Ministry announced that the service would run from Plymouth co-incident with the arrival of the mail steamship from United States of America.

Hugh Cahill was not so fortunate. Though the proving flight from Galway was a success, and despite his offer to establish a feeder service between Cork and Dublin also, his efforts were totally in vain. The Government of the new Free State gave no support for his plans to establish an air-mail service between Ireland and Continental cities. Not deterred by this bitter blow, Hugh Cahill continued his strenuous efforts at promoting aviation in Ireland. The general public, that had encountered Cahill's efforts, were convinced of the place in the new progressive Free State for aviation, unfortunately, the authorities were slower to accept these advances.

Baldonnel was very much the centre of aviation in the country at that time. It was there that medical examinations were conducted. A bone of contention with Iona was the fact they were obliged to pay landing charges to attend such examinations. They appealed these charges in November 1932, but were advised the charges were Statutory and could not be waived.

Thursday afternoon, 19 January 1933, Kildonan was honoured to welcome one of the more prominent promoters of civil aviation in these islands. The Institute of the Irish Motor Trade invited The Hon. William Francis Forbes as guest to Dublin. He was better known as the Master of Sempill and arrived from the UK in his Puss Moth, G-ABJU. William Francis Forbes (*iv) was born in Devonport, near Plymouth, Devonshire in 1893. During World War One he saw service with the Royal Naval Air Service, the Royal Flying Corps and the Royal Air Force, retiring from active service in 1919. In 1921 he was head of a 30-man mission to Japan to organise, equip and train the Japanese Naval Air Service. His success at that venture saw him travel to Greece at the request of the Greek Government to assist with the re-organisation of the Greek Naval Air Service. By the mid-1920s his main focus turned to developments in general and sporting aviation. From 1926 to 1928 he was Chairman of the Royal Aeronautical Society and its President from 1928 to 1930. Along with Sir Alan Cobham they did much to develop, foster and

FOOTNOTE (*iii)
The 13 passengers on the flight formed the dinner committee, they were: Mr. Charles E. McConnell, A.I.P.A., Capt. Hugh St. George Harpur, Mr. T. Hayden, Lieut. Arthur Russell, Mr. Denis Johnston, B.L., Mr. Kevin Smith, Mr. Frank Gallagher, Major Sam Dunckley, Mr. Norman O'Connell Redmond, Major General Hugo MacNeill, Mr. George J. Bonass, Dr. George E. Pepper and Mr. C. H. Manders.

FOOTNOTE (*iv)
William Frances Forbes' accolades and associations include the Air Force Cross; Fellow of the Royal Aeronautical Society; Deputy Chairman of London Chamber of Commerce; Director of National Flying Services; Vice-President International Commission for study of Motorless Flight; member of the Advisory Committee of the Science Museum; Member of the Advisory Committee for Aeronautics, Hull University.

promote civil aviation in Britain and Ireland during the late 1920s and early 1930s. Kildonan was honoured to welcome both these distinguished gentlemen within a few months of each other.

A number of incidents occurred which helped to portray the activities at the aerodrome in a positive light. One of these was a flight to Meath and north County Dublin to drop food supplies to people that were cut-off by road as a result of a very severe snowfall. When the death toll had reached nine people throughout Ireland, the Lord Mayor of Dublin, Alderman Alfie Byrne, TD, issued an appeal to the Department of Local Government and Public Health. On 28 February 1933, Iona National Airways volunteered to give the use of an aeroplane free of charge. Messrs. Alex Findlater and Company, the well-known Dublin provision merchant, immediately undertook to supply all the necessary provisions, consisting 200 loaves, 20 pounds of tea, and a large supply of sugar along with other essential supplies. John R. Currie was pilot, with Pearse Cahill also on board. Due to the density of snow on the ground it was difficult to determine the usual landmarks. To find their way back to Kildonan, they flew south until they crossed the river Liffey. They turned east, passing Leixlip until they reached O'Connell Street. They then turned up O'Connell Street and followed the road to Doyle's corner, where they turned right, again following the road which led them to Finglas. It was nearing nightfall and the countryside around Finglas provided poor reference points for the aviators, until Cappagh Hospital was in sight, which they circled until they were able to identify the airfield at Kildonan. Their approach was assisted by the airfield Manager, Captain Tom Young waving a lantern to guide the weary mercy-flight pilots to a safe landing.

The first fatal air crash in Ireland involving an Irish registered aircraft occurred on 24 May 1933. A Gipsy Moth, EI-AAH, belonging to the Irish Aero Club, on a pleasure flight from its base at Baldonnel crashed into the sea at Dalkey, County Dublin, killing the pilot, Major Sam Dunckley and his passenger and employer, Chris Clayson. This unfortunate and tragic incident did not deter Hugh Cahill continuing with efforts to promote activities at Kildonan. His planned air pageant went ahead on Whit Monday, 5 June 1933. The spectators, undeterred by the tragic event of two weeks previous, turned out in their thousands at Kildonan. Newspaper reports at the time estimated the attendance at fifteen thousand people.

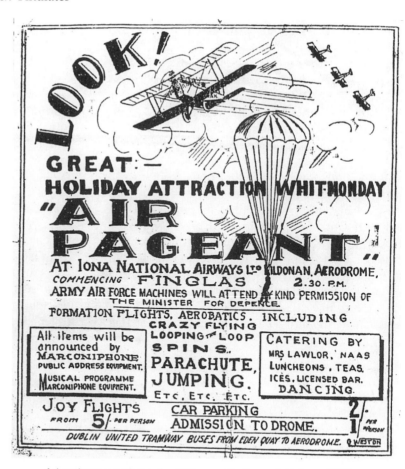

Advertisement poster for Kildonan Air Pagent, 5 June 1933

Poster courtesy Pearse Cahill collection

The spectators were in for a treat as they witnessed Joe Gilmore parachute from EI-AAP. On 17 April earlier that year, Joe, a native of Ardglass, County Down, had the distinction of becoming the first Irishman to parachute from an aeroplane and land on Irish soil. This achievement took place at Baldonnel jumping from Gipsy Moth G-ABXZ. At the Kildonan Air Pageant, the sixteen-year-old Pearse Cahill accompanied Joe on the flight. EI-AAP climbed to 2,500 feet and Pearse held the door open while Joe vacated with parachute packs attached to his back and front. Joe jumped to make a spectacular landing after side-slipping past a grove of trees on the eastern side of the field to land 200 feet from the wood. Joe was to hold another

distinction when he became the owner of the first Civilian Coupe manufactured. Bearing constructor's serial number 1, it was registered on 11 May 1935 to Joseph Gilmore as EI-AAV. Joe bought the aircraft in England in 1933 and apparently it crashed on the flight to Ireland resulting in the aircraft remaining in England for some time. This unique side-by-side high wing monoplane of the time later crashed in Ireland and was written-off on that occasion. Joe moved to England after the start of World War Two, reportedly joining British Imperial Airways and the 44-year-old pilot was killed in a crash on Prince Edward Island, Newfoundland in 1946. The crash of BOAC Liberator G-AGEM on landing in icing conditions at Charlottotown, Prince Edward Island on 21 February 1946 is presumably the accident concerned. EI-AAV was cancelled from the Irish register on 24 January 1949 with the entry *'Cancelled – owner deceased.'*

Joe Gilmore prepares to board EI-AAP at Kildonan in advance of his parachute jump at the Kildonan Air Pagent, 5 June 1933

Photograph via Pearse Cahill collection

Joe Gilmore descending from EI-AAP towards Kildonan during the Air Pagent, 5 June 1933

Photograph via Chris Bruton collection

Also at the Kildonan Air Pagent, Air Corps pilots Lts. Russell, Keane and Twohig gave a thrilling display of aerobatics in their newly delivered Avro 631 Cadets. Part of their act involved the three aircraft having bunting tied between them. They would then perform a loop without breaking the bunting. This was the first occasion the Air Corps performed at a civil event. W. R. Elliott, Chief Flying Instructor of the Irish Aero Club, gave a demonstration of crazy flying. Elliott also won the obstacle race the start of which was novel. The pilots stood twenty-five yards apart, put on their flying clothing, carried a glass of water to the aeroplane and finally started their engines. The following month, on 7 July, Elliott was killed in a mid-air crash in Limerick involving one of Cobham's Air Circus aircraft. Less than a year previous, on 11 August 1932, Elliott and Paddy Saul flew Amy Johnson and her husband Jim Mollison from Baldonnel to the west of Ireland to survey possible sites for Mollisons' attempt on the Atlantic in his *Hearts Content*.

Alan Cobham (left) and Hugh Cahill (right) at Kildonan, 1 July 1933, on the occasion of Cobham's first visit to Ireland with his aerial circus

Photograph courtesy Pearse Cahill collection

A section of the thousands of spectators that attended the Kildonan Air Pagent, 5 June 1933, that included a display by Iona Moths, along with Air Corps Cadets and other local aircraft

Photograph via Pearse Cahill collection

Hugh Cahill was very much intent on bringing aviation to the ordinary people of Ireland. A like-minded person in England at that time was Sir Alan Cobham. Born in London 6 May 1894, he served with the Royal Flying Corps during World War One. Following the war he developed his involvement with civil aviation and did 'joy-rides' and commercial aerial photography, and in 1921 he joined the de Havilland Aircraft Company. The King's Cup was his Trophy in 1924. On 20 November 1924, the 30-year-old aviator set out on what was to become his first epic trail-blazing flight. He departed London in a dH50 biplane with Air-Vice Marshall Sir Sefton Brancker as passenger and landed at Rangoon, Burma, then flew

Cobham's aerial circus lines up in formation over Kildonan prior to a fly-past over Dublin city, 1 July 1933

Photograph via Pearse Cahill collection

back to London, landing there on 17 March 1925, covering a total of 17,000 miles in 220 hours flying time. During 1925 and 1926, he did some very useful work in making flights to various parts of the British Empire. These included Capetown in 1925, Cairo in 1926 and Australia in the same year, with a view to emphasizing the importance of air services, thus laying the foundations for many air routes. In 1926, he was knighted, becoming Sir Alan Cobham. In 1927 he piloted flying boats, mainly in Singapore. From 1927 onwards, he devoted much of his time to establishing landing bases throughout the world and promoting aviation.

In 1931, Alan Cobham formed an air circus, that brought excitement, thrills and the pleasure of seeing the best pilots in the world. They performed outstanding feats in the best aircraft in the world, and 'joy-rides' at a very moderate price, enabling tens of thousands of ordinary folk who could not otherwise afford it to sample the experience of flying.

Sir Alan had sites surveyed throughout Ireland as possible locations for his displays. One of these sites was Baldonnel. However, as the venture was of a commercial nature the military base at Baldonnel had to be excluded. Hugh Cahill invited Sir Alan to perform at Kildonan. The Cobham Circus first visited Ireland during 1933. On Friday, 30 June, seven aircraft of the circus landed at Kildonan, flying in from Stranraer, the remainder arriving the following morning. The first aircraft to arrive was Tiger Moth G-ABUL, flown by Sir Alan. Other aircraft of the Circus visiting Kildonan over the weekend were: Handley Page HP33 Clive G-ABYX, Handley Page W10 G-EBMR, Airspeed Ferries G-ABSI, and G-ABSJ, Fox Moths G-ACEX, G-ACEY, and G-ABWF, Avro 504 G-ABVH, Moth G-ABUB, and Cierva autogyro G-ABGB. There was also a Mongoose-engined Avro 504 and a Blackburn Lincock. Most of these types of aircraft were new to the spectators attending the displays. Aeronautical Rules in the 1930s were not as stringent as present day rules, which permitted

A selection of Cobham's aircraft at Kildonan on 1 July 1933. Kildonan clubhouse is in foreground. Runways are on left and right of avenue leading to Kildonan House, seen at top of photograph and surrounded by trees.

Photograph via Pearse Cahill collection

found themselves being 'flour bombed' by a rogue aircraft above. On at least one occasion, however, the pilot of the diving aircraft slightly misjudged his target, so that sections of the crowd were bombarded instead.

Highlight of the display was always the daring wing-walker, Martin Hearn, who caused many hearts to almost stop as he stood, legs apart, on the upper wing of an Avro 504, as it roared across the airfield. Later he sat astride the machine as it looped the loop – without a safety harness! Strangely, one section of Martin Hearn's act was later omitted from his Irish displays, whether it was thought that Irish audiences were more sensitive than their English counterparts or for

Cobham's Circus to fly low and in tight formation over Dublin city. Some display activity took place on Saturday, 1 July; however, the main display day was reserved for Sunday, 2 July 1933. The Lord Mayor of Dublin, Alderman Alfie Byrne, formally opened the air show. Sir Alan himself gave the commentary as each aircraft went through its paces.

The performance would begin with a fly-past of all participating aircraft. Each machine had its type painted on the fuselage so as to make identification easier for the spectators. After the fly- past, 'joy-rides' would be given. It was not uncommon for hundreds to sample the delights of flying with perhaps several hundred more anxiously awaiting their turn. The start of the performance forced a cessation of this activity. Then the Cobham daredevils would give a hair-raising example of aerobatics that included inverted flying and an air race. Just in case the dangerous stunts proved too exciting, brief periods of humour were included, much to the relief and amusement of their spectators. One such item was when the occupants of a car driving along the airfield unexpectedly

some other reason is not known. But in performances in England, a loudspeaker appeal was made to the crowd inviting any brave member who felt that he could emulate Hearn's performance to come forward and try his luck. Needless to say, there was always one, and dressed in yokel attire, he would run from the crowd and climb awkwardly into the aircraft. Nervously he waved to the spectators and as the aircraft took off, attempted to clumsily pull his way up along the fuselage. Then as the aeroplane flew high above the earth a body would drop from the cockpit and plummet to the ground. First Aid men then worked feverishly trying to revive the numerous prostate bodies of those who had fainted, while representatives of Cobham's Circus attempted to convince people of the real truth.... that the body was in fact only a dummy thrown from the aircraft by the volunteer, who was in reality Martin Hearn in disguise. Perhaps the reason the act was dropped is based on a report that an expectant mother had had her baby on the spot brought on by the sight of Martin Hearn's 'fall' from the aircraft. The world's first autogyro was also demonstrated.

Cobham's Handley Page at Kildonan 1 July 1933. The three men standing beneath the wing give perspective of the size of one of the largest aircraft to visit Ireland in the early 1930s

Photograph via Pearse Cahill collection

Fox Moth, EI-AAP, refueling at Bristol, during an air ambulance flight between Eastbourne and Ballincollig, Co. Cork on 1 July 1933. The insignia on the tail is of INFS (Iona National Flying Services)

Photograph via Pearse Cahill collection

It was the two-seater designed by the Spaniard Don Juan de la Cierva in 1923. The technique for take off was to increase rotor speed to 1200rpm, then release one brake to allow the autogyro tilt into wind. Releasing the other brake and holding the control stick well back allowed the machine to commence its take off run and rise into the air.

Flight Lieutenant Turner Hughes will be remembered for his inverted flying in the Tiger Moth. Flying the yellow coloured aircraft, he thrilled the crowds by flying inverted fifty feet over their heads. His finale was to fly normally, climb suddenly and roll over to inverted flight and dive at the crowd down to one hundred feet above them. During the weekend, it was estimated over 15,000 people attended Kildonan to see the display and many partook of 'joy-rides'. A detailed account of the weekend activities is recounted in Madeline O'Rourke's book *Air Spectaculars – Air Displays in Ireland.*

On the morning of the above referred to air pageant, Saturday, 1 July 1933, Iona's Fox Moth, EI-AAP, departed Kildonan at 6.30am and flew to Liverpool and onward to Croydon with a passenger. It then positioned to Eastbourne where it took on board a passenger who was recuperating from an illness and who wished to be transferred to Cork. The aircraft refuelled at Bristol and thence directly to Ballincollig, County Cork where it left its passenger, returning to Kildonan where it landed at

10.00pm In the course of the day EI-AAP covered 1,000 miles and clocked up ten hours flying time. The pilot was Captain Armstrong, who had returned to Iona again. Ironically, he was to land at Bristol on 27 May 1936 to inaugurate Aer Lingus' first commercial flight.

Another 'first' for Oliver Armstrong was a flight undertaken in the Monospar, EI-AAQ. This was the first twin-engine aircraft to grace the Irish civil aircraft register. The aircraft was chartered to fly to the 1933 Grand National at Aintree, near Liverpool. The purpose was to collect photographs of the days racing and bring them to Dublin. On the return journey he encountered very heavy fog; nonetheless, he successfully navigated his way back to land at Kildonan that evening. The photographs appeared the next morning in the national newspapers. This was the first occasion where the Irish newspapers were able to feature photographs of the English Grand National on the morning after the race.

Another pilot at Kildonan was Ivan Hammond. He did his training for his pilot's licence at Kildonan. He too joined Aer Lingus, becoming their second pilot. He became the first Aer Lingus pilot who was employed with only civil aviation experience.

Further aviation interest and intrigue was caused on the same weekend as the above display when Derry was host to General Balbo - Benito

Mussolini's flamboyant Minister of Air - and his Italian air armada. They landed safely on Lough Foyle on 2 July 1933, with 24 flying boats, having travelled from west Italy via Holland to Lough Foyle. The Irish Air Corps assisted them in County Donegal before their departure for Iceland and thence to Montreal and Lake Michigan at Chicago.

Cobham's display continued to tour the rest of Ireland. Sadly during the display at Limerick the following Friday a mid-air collision occurred involving Gipsy Moth, EI-AAI, belonging to the Irish Aero Club and a Fox Moth G-ABWF belonging to the Air Circus. The pilot of the Gipsy Moth, Mr. W. R. Elliott, Chief Flying Instructor of the Irish Aero Club and his passenger Mr. William Ower, from Newcastle West, County Limerick, were both killed. The circus returned to Kildonan the following day and performed at several other venues until it returned to England on 17 July. The circus returned in September, but this time the Dublin performance took place at Portmarnock.

Ten days later, on 27 July 1933, the population was again filled with enthusiasm at the arrival in Baldonnel of an Australian, Charles Ulm. In 1928, Ulm accompanied Charles Kingsford-Smith on the first trans-Pacific flight. This time Ulm was attempting to continue a round-the-world trip. Unfortunately, the aircraft, an Avro X, VH-UXX, *Faith in Australia*, sank in the sand at Portmarnock's Velvet Strand due to the weight of the fuel. Following completion of repairs in October 1933, weather continued to deteriorate and the transatlantic season ended. Ulm returned to Australia. Undoubtedly, the international interest and local involvement of these pioneering flights did no harm to Hugh Cahill's attempts at raising the awareness of aviation in Ireland.

Midland and Scottish Air Ferries Limited was a company formed by Scottish transport entrepreneur John Sword. It commenced flying operations in Scotland on 14 March 1933. Scheduled services to Aldergrove, Belfast were inaugurated on 30 May 1933. It was only a matter of time before Sword was to extend his operations to Dublin. They were to become the first company to operate scheduled air services between Ireland and England. To promote the service they teamed up with the Irish Aero Club to organise an air pageant for both Dublin and Cork. The Dublin event was scheduled for Saturday, 5 August 1933 at the fifteen acres in the Phoenix Park. At rehearsal on the Thursday evening Lt. Jim Twohig was killed at Clondalkin, when two Air Corps machines collided. John Sword sent all of the available Midland and Scottish Air Ferries aircraft to Baldonnel, arriving on the Friday evening. On the day of the display, a mock dogfight resulted in a further tragedy that marred the weekend, when an Air Corps Vickers Vespa entered a spin at low level. The pilot, Captain Oscar Heron and his observer, Private Richard Tobin were killed. On Sunday the formation departed for Ballincollig, County Cork.

Midland and Scottish Air Ferries Irish operations commenced on Monday, 14 August 1933 with a flight from Hooton Park aerodrome, on the Cheshire side of the river Mersey, near Ellesmere Port to Baldonnel via Speke aerodrome, Liverpool on the opposite side of the river Mersey. This was to clear Customs. This was the first scheduled service between Liverpool and Dublin. The aircraft mainly used were Airspeed Ferry's G-ACBT and G-ACFB and an Avro X, G-ACGF. The Hooton-Speke-Baldonnel service was operated 20 times during September 1933, Sundays excepted, and a total of 62 passengers (and 30 packets newspapers) were carried in all on the 40 sectors – an average of 1 1/2 passengers per flight! Flying between Liverpool and Dublin had not, so far, appealed to the large numbers of businessmen who were catching the sea ferries every day between these two great sea ports and gateways to their industrial hinterlands! The service ceased on 30 September, in the main due to poor loads.

The final display of Cobham's tour was at Colpe Farm, Drogheda, County Louth, on 1 October 1933. A Spartan, owned by Aerofilms, though not part of the circus, was giving pleasure flights. The plane stalled after take off, killing the pilot Captain K. Rose and seriously injuring his passengers Mr. and Mrs. Hoe. Press reports of the time created a most unfortunate impression of aviation, with fatal accidents occurring on an almost monthly basis throughout the summer of 1933.

The summer of 1933 undoubtedly gave the citizens of Dublin more than the normal taste of aviation with four organised events:

• 5 June 1933   Air Pageant, Kildonan

• 1 / 2 July 1933 Cobham's Air Circus, Kildonan

• 5 August 1933 Midland & Scottish Air Pageant, Phoenix Park

• 17 September 1933 Cobham's Air Circus, Portmarnock

August 1933 at Kildonan, left to right: Fox Moth, EI-AAP, Monospar EI-AAQ, Gipsy Moths EI-AAK and G-ACBU

Photograph via Pearse Cahill collection

Between 1932 and 1935 Sir Alan was to give more than 1,200 air displays that were seen by more than four million spectators. He carried more than one million passengers on pleasure flights. Sir Alan Cobham died peacefully at his home in Bournemouth, Hampshire, on 21 October 1973, aged seventy-nine years.

During the course of his aviation operations at Kildonan, Hugh conducted both commercial flying and pilot training functions. By means of segregating these roles he formed two separate entities. The commercial duties of Iona were operated under the banner of Iona National Flying Services (INFS). Flight instruction for pilots was operated under the auspices of the National Aero Club (NAC). Commemorative souvenir badges were available to members of both organisations and became a treasured possession.

One of the best-known female aviators of the previous decade was Limerick woman Lady Mary Heath. Her first reported flight in Ireland was on Saturday, 22 April 1933, when Lady Heath left Baldonnel for Ballincollig. The weather would not permit a landing, so she diverted to Fermoy where she was well received by personnel of the 4th Battalion of the Irish Army, then stationed at Fermoy. Her Moth was placed in one of the hangars for the night. The following day she flew to Ballybunion and later to Ballincollig before returning to Dublin. From August 1933 she based the Moth at Kildonan. In September 1933, another well-known female aviator, Lady Cathleen Nelson, purchased a Stinson Junior, G-ABTZ. It was based at a field near Athboy, County Meath and was a regular visitor at Kildonan, initially using the aerodrome to clear Customs. Both of these women were to feature in the future of Kildonan. Their period at Kildonan is discussed elsewhere in this publication. At that time the only airfields in Ireland licensed for Customs clearance were Baldonnel and Kildonan.

The licence for the airfield at Kildonan was due for renewal at the end of 1933. Despite the unfortunate accidents referred to previously, there was still a considerable interest in aviation at Kildonan. In October 1933, Iona National Airways Limited applied to the Department of Industry and Commerce for the first renewal of the licence for the aerodrome at Kildonan. On 10 November 1933, Captain W. I. Hannon, administrative officer, Air Corps reported to his commanding officer on his inspection of Kildonan Aerodrome; some of his comments give an indication of facilities at a licensed aerodrome in the 1930s:

'The only fire-fighting apparatus on the aerodrome is of a hand-cart type, fitted with three minimax fire extinguishers. It is not of a type that could be moved rapidly and cannot be connected to transport of any kind. First-aid appliances: one minimax first-aid outfit, no splints available. From 4000 feet at a distance of 5 or 6 miles, the markings on the hangar are visible from the air.'

It was recommended to renew the licence.

While reports of activities at Kildonan were portraying an active airfield with plenty of flying taking place, the fact was that the operations at Kildonan were costing Hugh Cahill considerable amounts of money. This was the consequence of trying to bring low cost flying to as many people as possible. He felt he could not continue financing this venture and following successful renewal of the aerodrome licence, in November 1933, he decided to hand over the operations at Kildonan to Lady Nelson.

Hugh had expended a considerable amount of time and money in his attempts to bring aviation to as many of the population of Ireland as possible. In this it can be said he was successful. However, it was time for him to stand back and take a look at the venture from an economic perspective. It was by no means a paying enterprise and regrettably his conclusion was to cut his losses and return to his well-established engineering business at Cross Guns Bridge in Glasnevin. Hugh Cahill had only been involved in aviation for just over three years, yet he was to pioneer a lot of the developments in Irish aviation and most certainly left his mark on an industry that was to thrive well into the future.

On 2 September 1935, Iona's Accountant, Paul Callan, wrote to The Registrar, Companies Registration Office at Dublin Castle advising: '*In reply to your letter 30th, we have to inform you that the company is not carrying on business or in operation.*' In their reply 15 November 1935, The Companies Office advised, '*at the expiration of 3 months the company would be struck off.*' On 21 February 1936, The Companies Office wrote and advised '*Iona National Airways Limited was dissolved under Section 242(5) of the Companies (Consolidation) Act 1908, by notice in Iris Oifigiuil dated 21st February 1936.*' It was five years, to the month, since Incorporation.

In early 1939, Hugh Cahill decided that Pearse and he would travel to New York to the forthcoming World Fair and booked their passage on the liner *Athenia*. With the political developments in Europe and references to war clouds gathering, Hugh decided to cancel the trip.(*v) Pearse was elated at the cancellation as it allowed him to focus on his passion of motorcar racing. He entered his name as a contestant for the forthcoming races at the Phoenix Park, scheduled for 9 September 1939. The decision not to travel turned out to be a wise one, as war was declared on 3 September 1939 and the *Athenia* became the first British merchant ship to be lost in World War Two.

FOOTNOTE (*v)

At about 4.30pm, 3 September 1939, the *Athenia* was sailing westbound about 250 miles off the northern coast of Ireland. Lieutenant Lemp in a German U-Boat observed, what he later said, he thought was not a passenger ship but an auxiliary cruiser (a British armed merchant cruiser). He saw the large vessel with its high superstructure outward bound and zigzagging on a course that seemed to him to be well off the normal shipping routes. Lemp tracked the *Athenia* for three hours. At 7.40pm, while both vessels were between Rockall and Tory Island, County Donegal, Lemp gave the order to fire two torpedoes. The first scored a direct hit and the second misfired. At this time most passengers were at dinner. Witnesses that survived the tragedy estimated the submarine was a mere one thousand yards when it fired the torpedoes. Lemp then fired a third that survivor's claim struck the ship, that was contrary to naval operations. Other reports say the submarine surfaced and fired shells that brought down the wireless carrying mainmast. The ship remained above the water for 14 1/2 hours until 10am the next morning. A total of 1,418 were on board. 112 persons died - 93 passengers and 19 crew - most were killed by the torpedo while at dinner. 28 of the passengers lost were American citizens. Three nearby steamships picked up the survivors, *City of Flint* (USA) took 223 onto Halifax, the *Southern Cross* (Sweden) saved 300 and the *Knute Nelson* (Norway) rescued 450, taking them to Galway. On the morning of Tuesday, 12 September 1939, Galway witnessed the harrowing scenes as the 441 survivors were taken ashore from the *Knute Nelson*. British Destroyers also arrived on the scene and rescued the remainder. One ship recorded that as the lifeboats were being picked up a school of whales played around as if to ensure that no further harm might befall the victims. The *Athenia* entered the history books as the first British merchant ship to be lost in World War Two. Lloyds War losses for World War Two records the loss of the *Athenia* at the very first entry at the top of page one. As a result of the sinking of the passenger liner, without warning, both Allies and neutrals concluded that Germany had consigned the laws of naval warfare to the scrap heap and from the outset released her submarines from all restrictions.

The dissolution of Iona National Airways Limited was not the final involvement of the Cahill family and Iona in Irish aviation. Hugh's son, Pearse, would emerge in post-War years as another man who would leave his mark on aviation in Ireland. The seeds that Hugh Cahill had sewn were not in vain; flying continued at Kildonan, the first commercial airport in Ireland, and his son Pearse was to reactivate Iona National Airways, the first commercial airline in Ireland. His legacy would live for many years to come.

The *Athenia* with its stern in the water prior to it's sinking.
Photograph taken from one of the rescue ships 4 September 1939

Hugh Cahill booked passage for himself and 22-year-old Pearse to sail on the *Athenia* to the 1939 World Fair in New York. As the threat of war approached Hugh cancelled the bookings. The *Athenia* was the first ship sunk at the start of World War 2 when torpedoed off the coast of Donegal on 3 September 1939. Photograph shows *Athenia* (on right) shortly before it sank with a rescue ship alongside

Photograph courtesy Imperial War Museum

TABLE 3

Registration	EI-AAF
Aircraft Type	de Havilland DH60X Moth 2-seater bi-plane
Constructors Serial Number	1262
Place & Year of Manufacture	Stag Lane, London, 1930
Previous Registrations	G-ABAH
Registered to	Iona National Airways Ltd, 3 June 1931
Delivery date	circa 3 June 1931
Remarks	Registered as G-ABAH on 2 July 1930 to Brian Lewis and C. D. Barnard Ltd, Heston.

Registered as G-ABAH on 2 July 1930 to Brian Lewis and C. D. Barnard Ltd, Heston.

On 31 July 1931, EI-AAF was initiating a go-around at Bundoran, County Donegal, but collided with the thatched roof of a house. The aircraft never flew again and was subsequently removed from the register on 31 July 1932. Part of the airframe was used as a link-trainer at Kildonan to provide instruction to student pilots. The engine was placed in the Cirrus Moth, EI-AAG, thus converting this aircraft to a Gipsy Moth.

TABLE 4

Registration	EI-AAG
Aircraft Type	de Havilland DH60X Moth 2-seater bi-plane
Constructors Serial Number	648
Place & Year of Manufacture	Stag Lane, London, 1928
Previous Registrations	G-EBYV
Registered to	Iona National Airways Ltd, 2 June 1931
Delivery date	circa 2 June 1931
Remarks	First registered as G-EBYV on 23 June 1928 to Major A. A. Nathan, Stag Lane; Sold to Flight Officers K. E. & J. Parker, Gosport. Cancelled from UK register 7 June 1931. Built as a dH60G floatplane but converted to 60G landplane, on 2 July 1928, before sale to Ireland. Following the accident to EI-AAF the engine was placed in EI-AAG, thus altering it to a Gipsy Moth. EI-AAG was cancelled from the Irish register 17 August 1932 as sold in England and returned to its former registration G-EBYV on 16 September 1932. Newcastle upon Tyne Light Aeroplane Club, Cramlington, operated it. On 30 June 1936 it crashed at Medomsley, Durham and was cancelled from the UK register in December 1936.

TABLE 5

Registration	EI-AAP
Aircraft Type	de Havilland DH83 Fox Moth 5-seater bi-plane
Constructors Serial Number	4003
Place & Year of Manufacture	Stag Lane, London, 1932
Previous Registrations	New aircraft
Registered to	Iona National Airways Ltd, 20 July 1932
Delivery date	23 July 1932

Remarks

Operated by Iona until its operations were transferred to Everson Flying Services and the aircraft was registered to Caithleen Nelson 2 December 1933. When the aerodrome at Kildonan was occupied by Dublin Air Ferries Limited, the Fox Moth was transferred to them 22 March 1935.

On 31 August 1938, it was ferried to England and registered as G-AFKI to H. G. Aitcheson, Croydon near Shoreham. It was cancelled from the Irish register on 18 September 1938. The Royal Air Force impressed it for HQ No. 41 on 31 August 1941 for wartime duties. Its final fate is unknown, but was probably scrapped.

Chapter

3

LADIES' TIME AT KILDONAN

Activities at Ireland's premier aviation location during the mid-1930's. A romantic era in the years preceding the outbreak of World War Two

Chapter 3

LADIES' TIME AT KILDONAN

The enterprise and foresight that Hugh Cahill had put into developing Kildonan was not in vain. On 26 January 1933, Lady Mary Heath purchased a Gipsy Moth, G-ACBU, and brought it to Kildonan in August of that year. In September, a Stinson Junior, G-ABTZ, was purchased in England by Lady Cathleen Nelson and delivered to Kildonan in November. Both these ladies were to be highly influential in the future of Kildonan. In November 1933, following more than three years at the cutting edge of commercial aviation in Ireland, Hugh Cahill handed over the airfield, aircraft and staff of Kildonan, to Lady Cathleen Nelson(*vi).

Activities at the aerodrome indicated positive times ahead, including a considerable amount of instruction and training, in addition to the commercial side of operations.

On 24 September 1923 Cathleen married recently divorced Sir James Hope Nelson, 2nd Baronet of Knockbawn, Inch, (near Gorey) County Wexford(*vii). Sir James' family owned the Liverpool based Nelson shipping line. Transporting meat from Argentina to Britain was one of the many roles they performed, being the first shipping line to operate refrigerated ships for transporting meat in cold storage. The British Government later commandeered their ships for ferrying soldiers during World War One. Sir James

Lady Nelson's Stinson, G-ABTZ, clearing Customs at Kildonan. Left to right: Iona's taxi driver, Customs officer, Lady Nelson and pilot George Everett

Photograph via Pearse Cahill collection

and Lady Cathleen had a mutual interest in horses and continued the horse training industry commenced by his father in 1909 at Clonbarron House, Kildarkey near Athboy, County Westmeath. The lands contained a field about a mile long used for training horses. Lady Nelson also used this field as a landing strip. In 1934 Sir James Nelson's horse, *Poolgowran*, won the Irish Grand National. The jockey on the occasion was Robert Everett.

Cathleen learned to fly in London and obtained her pilot's 'A' licence on 29 December 1932. In September 1933 she purchased her first aeroplane, a Stinson, bearing the registration G-ABTZ. This aircraft was brought to Kildonan, in November 1933. Sir James' jockey, Robert Everett, had a brother George who held a pilot's licence.

FOOTNOTE (*vi)
The new owner was born Annie Cathleen Elizabeth Loftus Bryan on 28 May 1899 at Borrmount Manor, Enniscorthy, County Wexford. She was the youngest daughter of one the wealthy gentry families of County Wexford. Her father, Lt. Col. Loftus Anthony Bryan, J.P., Deputy Lieutenant, and High Sheriff of Limerick in 1892, was heir to large estates in County Wexford and served in World War One. On 2 January 1886 he married Annie Maria Ryan youngest daughter of Michael Ryan, J.P., Temple Mungret, County Limerick. Cathleen's father died on 2 September 1939 – the eve of the outbreak of World War Two. Cathleen's older brother, Lieutenant Anthony, served in the Royal Flying Corps during World War One.

FOOTNOTE (*vii)
This was Sir James' second marriage as he had previously wed Mary Isabel Vallel, on 26 September 1913; she was a daughter of Dr. Jules Vallel, M.D., St. Louis, Missouri. They were divorced in 1921. Sir James was the eldest son of Sir William Nelson, 1st Baronet, of Gartlandstown, County Westmeath. Sir William died at 16 Hill Street, Berkley Square, London on 7 July 1922.

Lady Nelson beside her Stinson G-ABTZ

Photograph courtesy Patrick Browne

'Owing to the greatly increased demand for instructional courses, it has been found necessary to enlarge the fleet of Everson Flying School at Kildonan, County Dublin. Above is seen Mr. Miles, designer of the Miles-Hawk monoplane, formally handing over a new dual-controlled Miles-Hawk aircraft to Mr. J. R. Currie, A.R.A.S.I., Chief Instructor, Everson Flying School at Woodley, Aerodrome, Reading.'

On 26 March 1934 Lady Nelson transferred it to the Irish register in her name as EI-AAX. It was to remain thus until 18 December 1934 when she sold it back to the UK and it returned to its previous registration, G-ACNX. Throughout World War Two it was to see active service when impressed by the Royal Air Force. Events at Kildonan became more upbeat during the summer of 1934. Everson Flying Services initiated plans for a twice-weekly service from Kildonan to Cork, using either the base at Fermoy or Ballincollig. Despite efforts the service never took off. The peak summer months bore witness to all sorts of aviation related activities – instruction, 'joy-rides', charters, air taxis etc.

When Hugh Cahill handed over operations at Kildonan to Lady Nelson, she joined with George Everett and formed a company called Everson Flying Services, using both their names to derive the company name. It officially commenced operations at Kildonan on 1 December 1933, operating with four aircraft. The two remaining of the original five aircraft registered to Iona, Gipsy Moth, EI-AAK and Fox Moth, EI-AAP were transferred to Everson Flying Services on 2 December 1933. The new company also had the use of the two recently acquired aircraft by Lady Nelson and Lady Heath, the Stinson G-ABTZ and the Gipsy Moth G-ACBU respectively. This latter aircraft was transferred to the Irish register on 29 May 1934 as EI-AAW. In its first four months of commercial operations it reported carrying almost one thousand passengers. Not bad, bearing in mind these were winter months.

Lady Nelson was confident enough of the development of the company that she purchased another aircraft. On 24 February 1934 a Miles Hawk, G-ACNX was delivered to Kildonan. A newspaper photograph of the time had the following caption accompanying it:

Lady Nelson's Miles Hawk, EI-AAX, at Kildonan, used for pilot training

Photograph via Pearse Cahill collection

The two aircraft purchased by Lady Nelson, Miles Hawk, EI-AAX and Stinson, G-ABTZ, at Kildonan after she formed Everson Flying Services.

Photograph courtesy Chris Bruton collection

A promotional leaflet distributed by Everson Flying Services, Kildonan aerodrome, Finglas, Dublin, telephone Finglas 5, advertised the flying club as follows:

'Entrance fee £1-1-0, Annual subscription £1-1-0
Instruction rates 40/= Solo, 30/= per hour
Tuition may be taken on either the well known
GIPSY MOTH or the latest MILES HAWK
monoplane
Expert staff of instructors and engineers
All machines fully insured
Aeroplanes can be chartered at any time for short pleasure trips or taxi work from 9d per mile.
Joy flights from 2/6.'

The Fox Moth, EI-AAP, carrying the logo of 'Everson Flying Services - Dublin' on the field at Kildonan, during summer 1934

Photograph John Duggan via Pearse Cahill collection

Promotional leaflet and price list for 'Everson Flying Services'

Copy leaflet courtesy Ronny Vogt collection

In early March 1934 an unusual one-off aircraft arrived at Kildonan. It was a two-seat tandem parasol monoplane, with large wheel spats, powered by a single Cirrus III engine and with the name *Spirit of Erin* proudly painted on its fuselage. It arrived at Kildonan by road as it had yet to make its maiden flight. Its builder had great plans for this, his invention. Charles Vincent Leo Foley celebrated his twenty-first birthday just days before arriving at Kildonan. He had been involved in at least two other attempts to build flying machines in his teenage years, but he expected this machine would put him on the historical records of great aviation pioneers. The confident young man had built the machine in his native Sligo, with the experience from his previous attempts and from the knowledge corresponding with and attending the London School of Aeronautics. The name *Spirit of Erin*, no doubt, was inspired by the *Spirit of St Louis* flight just six years earlier, thus reflecting his stated ambition to fly the Atlantic.

But this aircraft had a second purpose. It was to be the flying 'test-bed' for an invention Charles Foley had registered with the British Patent Office. He claimed that his invention would:

> 'Prevent loss of control of an aeroplane or airship due to disablement of the elevator, thereby, reducing the vulnerability of the craft by making it possible for the pilot to avoid disaster when the elevator has been destroyed by gunfire or put out of action by some other cause.'

His invention was a smaller second elevator in the horizontal stabilizer, immediately forward of the main stabilizer and would be operated by independent control lines. The full patent was granted to him on 6 April 1933. So, it was with great confidence, that Foley unveiled the *Spirit of Erin* to the public in the Gilhooly Hall, Sligo, on 3 February 1934. From there it travelled to Higgin's garage, Galway, where it was displayed for a week. Charles Foley had hoped this tour would extend nationwide. From the start, local newspapers had given much coverage to the project, but now national and weekly papers were joining in. The publicity encouraged lord mayors to hold civic receptions in his honour, county councillors wanted their airfields to be used for the Atlantic attempt and politicians wanted him to locate the factory to mass-produce his design in their constituencies. There was talk of Government funding for the entire project.

The mechanics and pilots of Kildonan and Baldonnel were eager to inspect this aeroplane which seemed so promising. Until its arrival at Kildonan, it would appear that Foley had carried out all the work on the aeroplane without consulting anyone with professional mechanical or flying expertise. Although the aeroplane looked quite smart, the old experienced hands were not at all impressed with what they saw. Pearse Cahill recalls John R. Currie's critical examination of the machine – *'with little bracing or supports and the whole plane wobbled when he shook the wing.'* Much of the construction was over-engineered, crude, and appeared to the experienced eyes at Kildonan, far too heavy. As part of its streamlining no bracing wires were used, which lead to an alarming amount of free movement of the wings! Charles Foley wasn't short of words to explain away all the criticism.

Charles Foley beside his *Spirit of Erin*. This aircraft was examined by Kildonan engineers in March 1934 and found questionable

Photograph via Ronan Lee

However, the observation that the fuselage was very similar to that of a Robinson Redwing was more difficult to explain away. He stuck to his guns claiming it to be an original design, but it would appear that he had bought parts from a crashed aeroplane during his time in the UK the previous year. Under this cloud the young Foley left Kildonan and returned with the *Spirit of Erin* to Sligo.

At Sligo he prepared it for a test-flight. He had taken a few hours flying instruction with Lady Nelson's Everson Flying Services and claimed to have started flying lessons in the UK. On the morning of the attempt he taxied the plane up and down the field several times before finally opening up the throttle and gathering speed for take-off. Almost immediately after leaving the ground the left wing began to drop and Foley closed the throttle. The result was a heavy landing, sluing around to its left. Damage was not great and a shaken, but uninjured, young aviator eased himself out of the cockpit. His shock soon turned to embarrassment and he removed the plane from the field as quickly as possible. He decided to call it a day and put his entrepreneurial skills to other tests. In November of that year he left Ireland for the United States, where he started an import business with South America making and loosing several fortunes. He never tried his hand at flying again. The *Spirit of Erin*, although not a Kildonan based aircraft, is worthy of its place in Irish aviation folklore.

The *Spirit of Erin* was not the only 'strange looking' aircraft to appear at Kildonan. Hugh Cahill's friend, Jim Malone constructed a homebuilt aircraft in the garage at his home in Malahide, County Dublin. In the early 1930s a French aircraft designer, Henri Mignet, produced plans on the construction of such an aircraft. He called it a *'Pou du Ciel'*, loosely translated as *'sky louse'* or more commonly referred to as a Flying Flea. Jim Malone's home-built was never registered and there is no evidence it ever flew. At the same time Pearse Cahill, replicating the efforts of Jim Malone, commenced constructing a *'Pou.'*

He succeeded in completing the fuselage and ribs of the wings until the French authorities issued a directive banning the flying of such machines due to the insecure nature of some of the models constructed. Both Jim and Pearse ceased further work on their homebuilt machines – Hugh ordered Pearse's effort to be demolished.

However, one of the other Fleas built in Ireland was discovered in a plumber's yard in Leeson Street, Dublin in June 1952 by Otto Reilly. He took it to his home at 105 Melvin Road, Harold's Cross, Dublin. In 1954 when Otto was emigrating to the United States of America he burned the Flea. It transpired this was the only *Pou du Ciel* to be granted an Irish Certificate of Registration. On 9 June 1936 it was registered as EI-ABH to William Benson, 46 Dufferin Avenue, South Circular Road, Dublin. From September 1935, Benson was assisted in the construction of the 'Flea' by J. Quinn (plasterer), J. Gallagher (driver) and V. J. Grace (electrical engineer). The red and silver aircraft is believed to be the only such aircraft to fly, when it took to the air at Kildonan about June 1936. On the rudder were the titles *'Dublin Amateur Flying Club.'* It crashed at Kildonan during one of these flights and was removed to a loft in a yard in Leeson Street, where Otto Reilly discovered it. It was formally removed from the register on 9 November 1948.

The *'Flying Flea'* registered to William Benson as EI-ABH, in June 1936. The only such aircraft to be registered in Ireland, and believed to be the only *'Flea'* to get airborne when it was flown at Kildonan about June 1936

Photograph via Leo Murray from Jim Masterson collection

The following is an extract from a talk given to the Old Dublin Society on 18 January 1984 by Sr. Katherine Butler, RSC. The talk was titled *'Kildonan 1933 – 1936: A Memory.'* It is selectively reproduced here as it portrays in vivid detail what one could expect to find at Kildonan in the days of Everson Flying Services. When reading this extract, try and cast your mind back in time.

Margery Bayley-Butler first visited Kildonan during a display by Sir Alan Cobham in July 1933. Her next visit was during the period of operation by Everson Flying Services in June 1934 when she went to Kildonan with her friend Denise Beattie. This visit is described thus:

'As we walked along the road from Finglas village, we noticed a small plane coming in to land. By hurrying we were able to reach the field as it touched down. Out jumped a man from the front cockpit and then, to our amazement, he was joined by a girl who appeared no older than ourselves who'd been having a flying lesson. Her name was Oonagh Scannell we later learnt. On entering the clubhouse we met another pupil, Ivan Hammond, who would later marry Oonagh. Ivan was subsequently to become Chief Pilot with Aer Lingus.'

Aerial view of Kildonan in summer 1934, showing the area available as runways on both sides of the avenue leading to Kildonan House

Photograph courtesy Chris Bruton collection

'We asked for our flight or 'flip' and requested that we go over Howth. I cannot recall who the pilot was on that occasion but the machine was the Fox Moth, EI-AAP, with a small cabin that seated three. Within minutes we were over home and coming down lower and lower until we were less than 50 feet above the ground. Round and round we circled, climbed and dived while the family waved excitedly, also the Sisters in the nearby convent, little guessing who it was. Later we learnt that this behaviour was a risk not only to life but to pocket, for if we were spotted low flying we could face a fine of £5.'

'We promptly paid our £2 subscription and became the proud possessors of a log book, then borrowing a helmet and goggles, had our first experience with John Currie. Her engine was of 85 horse power, she was so light she could be pushed along the ground when the tail was lifted. In the cockpit a switch turned on the engine but as there was no self starter the propeller had to be swung by hand. So to take-off, the throttle was opened, stick pushed forward, tail lifted and when sufficient speed had been gained a gentle easing back of the stick lifted her. Apart from the height indicator, and fuel gauge, spirit level, rev counter and compass, there was no other source of information available. Communication with the instructor in the front cockpit was by a speaking tube plugged into ones earphones. The landing was the most difficult, one had to learn how to judge just when the engine should be cut off and the plane allowed to glide earthwards. Two mistakes could be made here: to undershoot, meaning the touchdown would come before the field was reached, and to overshoot when it would come beyond the boundary hedge. Once the trouble was spotted, the remedy was simple: open the throttle and do another circuit making a fresh approach.'

Many pilots might agree some aspects of flying haven't changed in seventy years!

Margery Butler performed her *'first solo'* flight in Gipsy Moth EI-AAK, being cleared by her instructor, George Williams, on 14 April 1935. After three hours solo, application could be made for the 'A' licence. This she obtained on 16 January 1936. Four days later she entered the Order of the Religious Sisters of Charity, Milltown, Dublin. She died 8 August 2000, aged 86 years.

Fox Moth, EI-AAP, Gipsy Moth, EI-AAK and Miles Hawk, EI-AAX outside Kildonan hangar during the summer 1934. Along with Gipsy Moth, EI-AAW, these aircraft formed Everson Flying Services

Photograph courtesy Chris Bruton collection

Margery Bayley-Butler relaxes on the wing of Gratten Esmond's Gipsy Moth, EI-AAC, shortly after undertaking her flight test on 16 January 1936

Photograph via Pearse Cahill collection

During the two peak months of August and September 1934, Everson Flying Services leased a Percival Gull, G-ACJW. A Kildonan based Gipsy Moth, EI-AAR, owned by E. J. Dease, was also used by the company. At the conclusion of their first year in business they lost their Chief Pilot, John R. Currie, on his return to his native England. He was later to acquire fame for his development of the *Currie Wot* aircraft. Fred Griffith replaced him at Kildonan as Chief Pilot. In October 1935, Fred was injured while flying from Croydon, London to Marseilles, south of France. A native New

Zealander, Fred was the pilot responsible for many notable flights, including, bringing to Dublin, photographs of the Royal wedding in 1934, of the Duke and Duchess of Kent, on behalf of *The Irish Times*. Due to dense fog at Heston airport, London, on the day, Griffith was the only pilot to depart that airfield.

Lady Heath purchased her second aircraft, another Gipsy Moth, G-AASY. It was delivered to Kildonan 21 December 1934. The following day, 22 December, Everson Flying Services had its first serious incident. The Moth EI-AAR, while on lease from E. J. Dease, was chartered for a flight to Belfast. On route conditions became very foggy and the pilot, James Bell, ground engineer at Kildonan, elected to make a precautionery landing near Saintfield, County Down. The landing was successful and when conditions improved they decided to continue their journey. Unfortunately, on take-off they struck a bush, nose-dived, the plane turned over and was completely wrecked. Fortunately both occupants escaped serious injury. Not to imply this incident had any implications for the future of Everson Flying Services, but a

Group of men at Kildonan in 1934. Left to right: Andy Woods, Reginald (Jack) Williams, George Kennedy, John R. Currie and Nat Preston

Photograph courtesy Chris Bruton collection

Following the departure from Kildonan of Lady Nelson, the next operator of the field was a more world renowned aviator, Limerick native, Lady Mary Heath. She is photographed prior to embarking on her fateful tour of United States

Photograph courtesy Ronny Vogt collection

decision was made a few weeks later, in January 1935, to cease operations.

Lady Nelson and her husband, Sir James, later moved from Clonbarron House, near Athlone, to Lough Bawn House on the shores of Lough Bawn near Oldcastle, County Meath. Sir James died on 5 May 1960 and is buried in the Nelson family vault, Vault 29, surrounding the O'Connell Tower, Glasnevin Cemetery, Dublin. Following his death, Lady Nelson, an accomplished horsewoman, continued to enjoy her love of horses. There is no evidence to say she continued her interest in aviation matters. She moved to Dublin and due to a physical disability she became somewhat housebound and lived alone at 12 Brookfields, Anglesea Road, Ballsbridge, Dublin 4. There she died on 11 May 1989 – 17 days before she was due to celebrate her 90th birthday. She was buried with her husband in the Nelson family vault in Glasnevin Cemetery. There were no children from the marriage.

The next operator at Kildonan was, by far, a more extrovert and widely renowned individual; in fact she was world famous before ever she came to Kildonan. The lady in question, Lady Mary Heath, ARC, ScI, FRGS, was born Catherine Sophie Peirce in Newcastle West, County Limerick on 10 November 1896. She was daughter of Jackie Peirce and Teresa Doolan who were married 29 May 1895. What was to be the first of many sad events for the one-year-old infant, Sophie, was the death of her mother Teresa on 7 December 1897. In the coroner's report of the inquest, cause of death was *'exhaustion and result of injuries inflicted (undefined).'* Sophie's father was later arrested and charged with the murder of his wife, found insane and spent the rest of his life in Grange Gorman Asylum, Dublin.

Like several members of the Peirce family, the young Sophie wanted to be a doctor. Just before World War One broke out in 1914, she went to England to earn money to pay for her studies. During the War, she was a dispatch rider attached to the newly formed Royal Flying Corps. This was to be her first contact with aviation. During her dispatch riding days, she met, and after a whirlwind romance, married Elliott-Lynn, a young aviator. The marriage took place after the war and they moved to Kenya to seek fame and fortune, where they owned and managed a coffee farm. There the romance floundered and an impoverished Sophie returned to London; 1921 saw her studying for her BSc degree at Trinity College, Dublin. To make ends meet, she took up typewriting and shorthand. She then began lecturing at the University of Aberdeen. By 1922, she had saved enough money to obtain a legal separation from Elliott-Lynn.

Sophie developed an interest in athletics. She was a Vice President of the Amateur Athletic Association of England. At Aberdeen she helped to found the British Women's Amateur Athletic Association. On 6 August 1923 she broke the world record for the high jump, with a jump of 4 foot 11 inches. On 23 August 1923 she became British javelin champion. She was renowned as an all-round athlete. That year she produced a book titled *Athletics for Women and Girls*. She also wrote poetry and in 1925, she published a book of her verses *East African Nights*.

On 30 May 1925 Sophie made a presentation to the Olympic Congress in Prague on behalf of women seeking admission to compete in the Olympic Games. Her submission was successful. Sophie was selected as a British representative for meetings of the International Olympic Council (IOC). It was while returning from this Olympic Conference in Prague in May 1925, (where she was the only woman in attendance, acting in her capacity as a member of the medical sub-commission); she was sitting beside a Royal Air Force man named Reid. During a conversation she expressed an interest in flying and he promised to help her learn to fly. She joined the London Light Aeroplane Club immediately, being its first woman member and had her first flight in August 1925. The club was also referred to as the London Aero Club. It was based at Stag Lane, where the aircraft construction works of Geoffrey de Havilland was located. He leased a hangar to the Aero Club. Sir Philip Sassoon, Under Secretary of State for Air, officially opened the London Aero Club on 19 August 1925. Following his speech, Sir Philip enjoyed the

inaugural flight with the club's chief instructor, Captain G. F. M. Sparks. Following this inaugural flight, a ballot was conducted to determine the first pupil to receive instruction at the embryonic club. The winner of the draw was David Kittel, who chivalrously offered the honour to Sophie, thus making Sophie Elliott-Lynn the first student pilot at the London Aero Club.

Her instruction commenced immediately and the *Daily Mail* 20 August 1925 shows a photograph of Sophie receiving instruction from Alan Cobham, the renowned airman (on 1 July 1933, Sir Alan presented his first Air Circus in Ireland to the people at Kildonan). Another man responsible for assisting her attain her pilot's licence was J. M. St. John Kearney; later to instruct at Kildonan, Coonagh, Weston and other airfields in Ireland. She performed her *'first solo'* on 18 October 1925. She was granted her Pilot's 'A' Licence (certificate no. 7975) on 4 November 1925, the only female to obtain this licence type that year, and only the eighth woman to be presented with an 'A' licence. She showed an immediate aptitude for flying and proceeded to involve herself in competitive flying.

Sophie became very concerned at giving women the same opportunities at flying as men enjoyed. A ban existed since the April 1924 International Commission for Air Navigation that stated:

> 'Women shall be excluded from any employment in the operating crew of aircraft engaged in public transport.'

In November 1925, she wrote to the Commission, requesting to be examined to hold her 'B' (Commercial) Licence. She spent the first three months of 1926 living near Stag Lane and attended flight school, passing the required test, which involved not merely practical flight skills but theoretical examinations in navigation, meteorology, engine-fitting, rigging and the theory of flight. She successfully obtained support for her appeal from various governments and the ban was rescinded in May 1926 when the Commission met in Paris, thus creating another 'first' for Sophie when she became the first woman in Britain to hold a 'B' pilot's licence.

On 3 April 1926, Sophie was at Hereford, where she became the first woman to descend by parachute from an aeroplane at an altitude of 1,500 feet, landing on a football pitch while a match was in progress. The 14 September that year saw her winning a contest, in Paris, taking to pieces and re-assembling light aeroplanes. By the end of her first year with a pilot's licence, her reputation as a pioneering aviatrix was spreading far and wide.

In 1927, tragedy again came into her life when, on Sunday, 1 May, her ex-husband Major William Davies Elliott-Lynn was found in the River Thames off the Chelsea Embankment. Up to his death, he had continued to support her financially. Notwithstanding this tragic setback, Sophie carried on in public life. On 20 May, three weeks after his death, she made an attack on the altitude record. This attempt was unsuccessful, but on 2 June 1927, the *Daily Mail* carried a photograph of her along

Lady Mary Bailey having successfully obtained her pilots 'A' licence on 18 October 1926, aged 35 years. The following year she was awarded the title *'Lady Champion Aviator of the World'*

Photograph courtesy Ronny Vogt collection

with her passenger, Lady Bailey, following their success at Hamble, near Southampton, when they set an all-time light plane two-seater altitude record of 16,000 feet. On 5 July 1927, Lady Bailey increased that record to 17,283 feet while flying Geoffrey de Havilland's Moth with his wife, Louie, as her passenger. On 18 July 1927, Sophie entered the Birmingham Air Pageant, at which her friend and fellow aviatrix, Lady Bailey, beat her into second place.

Commencing before dawn from Woodford Aerodrome on the 20 July 1927, Sophie made a record flight round England. In a total flight time of 13 1/2 hours she landed at 79 airfields covering 1,300 miles and completing the attempt at 9.27pm in her Avro Avian, G-EBRS – a highly commendable achievement at the time, considering the poor state of development of many aerodromes in the 1920s. Ten days later she entered the King's Cup Air Race at Hucknall, Nottingham, however, due to a mechanical problem, she was unable to participate. On the same day, she entered the Grosvenor Cup Contest that was around a course of 15 miles, with three heats and a final race. This she won and created further history by becoming the first woman to win an 'Open-to-all' air race. The 18 August of the same year saw her participate in the Flying Club Meeting in Zurich, at which she had a number of successes. The 12 October 1927 marked the occasion of Sophie Elliott-Lynn's second marriage. This time it was to Sir James Heath, of Staffordshire, a wealthy industrialist then in his seventies. She was thirty-years-old and took the title Lady Mary Heath.

Lady Bailey was also an aviatrix who achieved world acclaim around the same time as Sophie. Born on 1 December 1890, Mary Westenra was the first daughter of the Fifth Baron of Rossmore, County Monaghan. In 1911 she married Sir Abe Bailey, a wealthy South African businessman, and became Lady Bailey. Her first flight was on 7 June 1926 in Sophie Elliott-Lynn's aircraft. Lady Bailey obtained her 'A' Licence on 18 October 1926. In April 1927, both women were racing against each other at Bournemouth.

In August 1927, Lady Bailey became the first woman to fly solo across the Irish Sea. In the event of her being forced to ditch, she had some inflated motorcycle tyres around her waist – rather undignified, but very practical. She arrived at Baldonnel to attend the Horse Show. On her return to the UK, Colonel James C. Fitzmaurice gallantly escorted her to the coast.

At the Meeting of the Committee of the International Union of Aviators in Paris, it was decided to award the International Trophy for Men for 1927, which carries with it the title *'Champion Aviator of the World'* to Charles Lindbergh, and, for the first time, the title *'Lady Champion Aviator of the World'* was also awarded. The Committee singled out Lady Bailey for the Honour.

Both women were to undertake epic pioneering flights in 1928. In 1926, Sir Alan Cobham flew from London to Cape Town, South Africa. It had frequently been an aspiration of Lady Heath's to fly from Cape Town to London. On 29 October 1927 an Avro Avian III was registered to her as G-EBUG. On 18 November 1927, she sailed with her husband to Cape Town with her Avro Avian aeroplane in a crate. She told few people of her plans to return solo. At 4.30am on 5 January 1928, she took off from Cape Town for Johannesburg, where she arrived 22 January. She spent a month in the area, giving demonstrations, 'joy-rides', lectures and promoting flying in any way she could. At 7.30am on 25 February, she departed Pretoria on the second leg, arriving at Nairobi 14 March. While approaching Bulawayo, she developed sunstroke, quoting a cockpit temperature of 120 degrees Fahrenheit. She courageously made a successful landing in hostile terrain causing minor damage to her aircraft, but lapsing into unconsciousness for four hours until rescue arrived. She recovered in a few days and continued her journey.

On 22 March her third leg began at Nairobi where her destination was Cairo. She arrived 4 April, a distance of 5,132 miles and a total flying time of 72 hours. On 15 April, she departed Cairo for Sollum in the Libyan Desert; from there on 23 April she departed for Tripoli. On 5 May she left Tripoli for Tunis - where mechanics discovered holes through one of her wings! She did not realise it, but evidently she was shot at somewhere along the North African coast. On 6 May she took off from Tunis to fly the Mediterranean against a very strong head wind, crossing the 95 miles of sea between Cape Bon, the most northerly point of Africa, to Sicily. For this journey, she had blown up some motorcycle tyres and wrapped them around her waist as a life belt. She travelled up through Italy, to Naples and Rome (where she stayed for a week). At 8.30am on 14 May she left Rome for Marseilles, eight hours non-stop.

Weather over Europe was a lot worse than she had encountered through Africa. Landing at Dijon four hours later she was more tired than on any of her long sojourns over Africa. Next morning she took off and flying over Paris, touched down at Le Bourget four hours later. At 11am the next morning, she said good-bye to France on the last lap of her journey. She encountered a storm over the English Channel and landed at Lympne before going on to Croydon on 17 May 1928 - having left Cape Town on 5 January. She had thought the journey would take about three weeks and that was what she had told her husband. Even though the distance was less than 9,000 miles, she flew about 10,000 miles, due to all her diversions and delays, firmly carving her name in the record books as the first woman to fly solo from Cape Town to Croydon. This flight brought her world acclaim. The Avro Avian III, G-EBUG, used for this pioneering flight was bought in June 1928 by Amelia Earhart. It was shipped across the Atlantic and Amelia used it for a solo return flight across the United States. The two ladies became acquainted, and though rivals on different sides of the Atlantic, they campaigned together for the advance of aviation in general and for the equality of women, especially in the air, in particular. Lady Heath's courage and determination caused her to be elected *'Lady Champion Aviator of the World'* in the USA, - a title she accepted from the receipient of the award the previous year, her friend and flying companion, Lady Mary Bailey.

While Lady Heath was making her way back, somewhat leisurely, to England, Lady Bailey was embarking on the epic journey in the opposite direction. Lady Bailey took-off from Stag Lane, north London on 9 March 1928, bound for Cape Town. On 1 April both ladies met at Khartoum, in Sudan, where a dinner was hosted in honour of these brave aviatrixes. On 30 April Lady Bailey reached Cape Town, while Lady Heath did not reach Croydon, London until 17 May 1928. Later in 1928, Lady Heath established a Woman's British Seaplane altitude record, reaching 12,833 feet. In September 1928, she returned to Ireland, where she landed on the beach at Renville, Galway among other places.

In March 1929, Lady Bailey replaced Lady Heath as chairperson of the Ladies Committee of the Air League. On 1 January 1930 Lady Bailey was the first woman flyer to be honoured the D.B.E. (Dame Commander of the British Empire) for her *services to aviation.* In December 1932 she obtained her 'B' licence (Commercial). During the course of her studies she befriended Amy Johnston. Despite the numerous occasions both 'Lady's' paths crossed, there is no evidence Lady Bailey flew to Lady Heath's aerodrome at Kildonan. Nonetheless, it is interesting to diversify and briefly record the aeronautical achievements of another Irish aviatrix of the pioneering days of aviation.

1929 was to be an eventful year for Lady Heath; she became second pilot with the Royal Dutch Airline, KLM, having joined the airline in August 1928, and flew all over Europe. She was, therefore, the first female commercial pilot in Europe. In the summer of 1929, she went on a well-paid lecture tour of USA, earning (she later said) about £10,000 a year – an incredible amount of money at that time. While on this tour, she heard of and entered the National Air Race at Cleveland, Ohio, in August. During the final lap she was seen to lose altitude and, failing to bring the nose up, she careered along the roof of a factory and crashed into its large chimney. She remained unconscious for three weeks. Mr. Elliott C. Cutler, Professor of Surgery at Lakeside Hospital, wrote on 16 Sept 1929:

'She has made an excellent recovery. Everything is now healed and she gets out of bed today or tomorrow. She sustained a compound fracture of her skull.'

As a consequence of this serious accident she had a silver plate inserted in her skull.

This accident was to mark the tragic turning point of a potentially wonderful flying career, coming as it did at the tender age of 32 years. Her endeavours to create further records receded and she made no more ambitious flights. She did, however, continue her lecture tour following her recovery.

While in America, Lady Heath's marriage was in difficulties - her husband once said, *'my wife has flown away in the clouds.'* She obtained a divorce from him in Reno, Nevada. However, the divorce was not recognised on this side of the Atlantic. In 1932, Sir James Heath sought for the dissolution of the marriage on the grounds of adultery. The petition was not defended and a *'decree nisi'* was granted to Sir James. On 18 August 1930, Lady Heath arrived at Plymouth, England on a liner from USA. She was still recovering from the Cleveland accident and was en-route to Paris. She expected to be in Europe for several months forming aeronautical and athletic societies for women.

Around the time she lectured in America, she met a fellow flyer, George Anthony Reginald (Jack)

Lady Heath's Gipsy Moth, G-ACBU, at Kildonan in February 1934, prior to becoming EI-AAW

Photograph via Pearse Cahill collection

Williams, son of Sir Joshua Williams, Governor of Antigua in the West Indies. Jack was born 15 October 1900 and was four years her junior. They fell in love and were married in South Africa where they had gone to fly mail up country. Business was poor and they returned to England and then Ireland in March 1933.

She soon discovered the aviation activities at Kildonan. In August 1933 she based her Moth, G-ACBU, at Kildonan. She became involved in the activities at the airfield, offering her services as a pilot and providing instruction. She also organised several air shows at Kildonan, Phoenix Park

Lady Heath and her husband Reginald Williams beside her Gipsy Moth, G-ACBU, affectionately known as *The Silver Lining*, prior to its transfer to the Irish register as EI-AAW

Photograph courtesy Chris Bruton collection

and throughout Ireland. Hugh Cahill gave up his interest in Iona in November 1933 and Iona National Airways faded into obscurity. The airfield at Kildonan had been taken over by Lady Cathleen Nelson and George Everett and operated by their company Everson Flying Services. In February 1935, the company was re-organised and renamed Free State Air Ferries. This name was quickly changed to Dublin Air Ferries on 19 March 1935. Lady Mary Heath and her husband, Reginald Williams, became directors. As both of them could fly the company aircraft, this dispensed with the requirement for additional pilots, thus reducing the overheads considerably.

Dublin Air Ferries continued with the use of the two original Iona aircraft – Gipsy Moth, EI-AAK and Fox Moth, EI-AAP. Lady Heath also used her own two machines, Gipsy Moths, EI-AAW and EI-ABE. The latter being the aircraft G-AASY she purchased on 21 December 1934 and had it

placed on the Irish register on 1 March 1935.

Kildonan was to enjoy its third formal opening ceremony in less than four years. The date was 2 March 1935. On this occasion the official ceremony was performed by the Lord Mayor of Dublin, Alderman Alfie Byrne TD, (*viii), who delivered a speech to the large crowd that gathered. In addition to the company's own four aircraft, the occasion attracted six other aircraft. Lady Nelson's Stinson, G-ABTZ, never graced the Irish register and returned to England in May 1935. Ruth Hallinan's Gipsy Moth, EI-ABB travelled from its base in Cork, having only entered the Irish scene the previous day. It was subsequently sold to India, where it saw wartime service with the Royal Air Force. Major E. J. Dease brought his Klemm Swallow, EI-ABD. Also from Cork was C. H. Gates in his Spartan, EI-AAT. Unfortunately, this aircraft was written-off in a crash three days later. Grattan Esmond, TD, brought his Gipsy Moth, EI-AAC.

FOOTNOTE (*viii)
Alfie Byrne was Dublin's longest serving Lord Mayor, with nine consecutive years of service between 1930 and 1939 and a further term 1954 to 1955.

Mick Brady, John R. Currie and Dermot Duffy pose in front of Everson's Gipsy Moth, EI-AAK. Note the push-in Gosport speaking tubes linked to student and instructor helmet

Photograph via Pearse Cahill collection

This aircraft was only the third aircraft on the Irish civil register, being registered on 11 April 1929. In two years time it would become part of the Dublin Air Ferries fleet. A visiting aircraft from England was a twin-engine Monospar. The Kildonan based Moths gave the crowd a display. On the field at the time undergoing its Certificate of Airworthiness was Robinson Redwing, EI-ABC.

Four mechanics and three pilots were employed to maintain and fly the four aircraft. During its first month of operations, company aircraft flew 63 hours. George Williams earned some recognition for the fledgling airline on 24 April 1935. A fire in the Plaza building, Abbey Street, Dublin, attracted many reporters from the UK. Using Fox Moth, EI-AAP, George flew photographs of the disaster across the Irish Sea in time for publication in the evening newspapers in Manchester.

In May 1935, Lady Heath formed the *National Irish Junior Aviation Club*. To attract more interest to Kildonan, Lady Heath arranged an Irish Aviation Camp for two weeks in May 1935. Tents were erected at Kildonan where the students billeted for the two weeks. It involved lectures and discussions on various aspects of aviation. One of the lectures on Air Navigation was delivered by Captain J. P. (Paddy) Saul. On 23 June 1930, Paddy was navigator for the Australian aviator, Sir Charles Kingsford-Smith on their epic crossing of the Atlantic in the *Southern Cross*. The aircraft left Portmarnock beach at 4.30am that morning and arrived at Harbour Grace, Newfoundland – thirty and a half hours later. The following day they continued to Roosevelt Field, New York, to become the first to fly from Europe to New York, and the second to cross the Atlantic (The *Bremen* was the first in April 1928). For the duration of the camp, flying would be reduced to 30/= per hour. In the evenings, dances and other forms of entertainment were arranged. The aerodrome was earning a reputation for its ability to produce pilots. *Aviation* magazine, first produced by Colonel Charles Russell in January 1935, reported in the May 1935 edition:

'The Ground Engineer, Mick Brady, performed his 'First Solo' after 6 1/2 hours. A deaf and dumb student Mr. Peacocke, who is learning to fly, is showing great aptitude, and is nearly ready for his 'First Solo'. He has to be trained entirely by signs, as he knows no deaf and dumb hand language.'

Mick Brady went on to obtain Private Pilot's Licence No. 50. He remained at Kildonan from 1931 to the cessation of flying there in 1938. He was ground engineer for all three companies that operated from the aerodrome. Another engineer employed at Kildonan was Kevin Sheridan.

During July 1935 the four aircraft of Dublin Air Ferries flew 105 hours 20 minutes, making a total to date since inception on 1 March 1935 of 380 hours and 50 minutes. Charters were flown to Belfast, Birmingham, Cork, Fermoy, Galway, Liverpool, Manchester and Tramore. Probably, in response to the increased volume of aerial crossings of the Irish Sea, a further Civil Aviation Notice, No.3 of 1935 was issued titled *'High Gasholder at Dublin.'* It referred to the erection of a gasholder 3 3/4 miles west of the Poolbeg Lighthouse on the south side of the river Liffey. It included the clause: -

'White direction arrows have been painted on the top surface of the gasholder, pointing respectively to KILDONAN and BALDONNEL aerodromes, as indicated on the sketch overleaf. It should particularly be noted that the angles shown are from True North not Magnetic North.'

DEPARTMENT OF INDUSTRY AND COMMERCE.

CIVIL AVIATION NOTICE.

No. 3 of 1935.

HIGH GASHOLDER AT DUBLIN

A. Obstruction to Air Navigation.
B. Direction signs for aircraft.

It is hereby notified:—

A. 1. A high gasholder has been erected at DUBLIN, and constitutes an obstruction to air navigation. The following are particulars :—

Position			Height	Description
Lat.	Long.	Local		
53° 20′ 44″ N	6° 14′ 22″ W	3¾ miles W. of the Poolbeg Lighthouse, on S. side of River Liffey.	260′	Circular, 136′ in diameter, dark grey in colour.

2. Pilots should exercise caution when flying in the neighbourhood of the gasholder in conditions of bad visibility.

B. 3. White direction arrows have been painted on the top surface of the gasholder, pointing respectively to KILDONAN and BALDONNEL Aerodromes, as indicated on the sketch overleaf. It should particularly be noted that the angles shown are from True North, not Magnetic North.

By direction of the Minister for Industry and Commerce.
JOHN O'BRIEN, *Director*.

TRANSPORT AND MARINE BRANCH,
14 St. Stephen's Green, N.,
DUBLIN, 11*th April*, 1935.

(65197).N580.W1.387/P107/35.3.250.5/35.W.P.W/Len.22.

Civil Aviation Notice No. 3 of 1935, issued following a proposal put forward by Lady Mary Heath

Copy notice courtesy Military Archives, Cathal Brugha Barracks

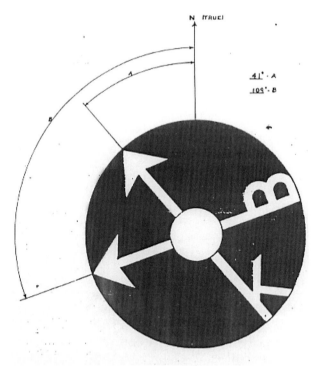

Sketch of directional arrows painted on top of the Dublin Gasometer, pointing respectively to Kildonan and Baldonnel

Copy notice courtesy Military Archives, Cathal Brugha Barracks

The sketch showed an arrow with a 'K' on it's tail pointing towards Kildonan, 041 degrees (true). Another arrow with a 'B' on the tail pointed towards Baldonnel, 109 degrees (true).

The Notice was the result of a proposal, dated 30 July 1934 from Lady Heath to Alliance and Dublin Consumers Gas Company; she proposed a direction sign be painted on the roof of the Gasometer. The military authorities had no objection to the proposal and it was referred back to the civil authorities, the Department of Industry and Commerce, on 3 September 1934. At that time any proposals or suggestions regarding aviation were referred to the military for consideration.

In an effort to segregate commercial activities from flying training, the flying school was formed into a club in August 1935, called the Dublin Aero Club.

On 22 September 1935, a Lockeed Vega, flown by Felix Waitkus, crashed at Ballinrobe, County Mayo. It was undertaking an attempted flight from New York to Lithuania. Gipsy Moth, EI-AAW, flew to Ballinrobe to visit the transatlantic aviator, but was itself damaged on landing in the field. It was taken back to Kildonan by road, repaired and returned to service. Unfortunately, following repair and return to service it had a short life. On Tuesday, 26 November 1935 it took off from Kildonan on a charter flight to Croydon. The pilot was George

The remains of the fuselage of EI-AAF was used by members of the *National Irish Junior Aviation Club* as a 'link trainer'

Photograph via Pearse Cahill collection

Lady Heath and George Weston, club President, give a talk on aeronautics to members of the *National Irish Junior Aviation Club*

Photograph via Pearse Cahill collection

Lady Heath, in her KLM uniform, indicates the controls and instruments of her aircraft, EI-AAW, to young aviation enthusiasts at Kildonan

Photograph via Pearse Cahill collection

Williams, and his passenger, Nora Wilson, a pupil with the flying school, were flying to London to see her brother. The Moth landed at Liverpool's Speke airport to fuel and then continued on for Croydon. Over Stone, Staffordshire, the pilot noticed smoke coming from the engine. He immediately sought a landing ground and managed to land in a field. Shortly after evacuating the plane, it burst into flames and was totally destroyed. This was the first serious incident to befall Dublin Air Ferries.

Obviously, Nora Wilson was not to be deterred from her pursuit of aviation. The following month along with her sister, Kathleen, they obtained their 'A' licences to become the first family to possess two such licences. The two Wilson sisters were from Shankill, County Dublin and were first introduced to flying by John Duggan. They travelled to Baldonnel where initially Lady Heath was conducting some instruction prior to her move to Kildonan; there the sisters continued flying until the demise of Dublin Air Ferries in 1938. On 7 April 1936, Gipsy Moth, EI-AAK was ferried to Hanworth by Nora Wilson for overhaul and sale. This was the first aircraft purchased by Hugh Cahill in July 1930 when it bore the marks G-ABBV. Following its return to England, it reverted to its original registration of G-ABBV. It had a few owners in the UK until it crashed at Churchdown, Glostershire on 15 July 1939, after nine years of service. With EI-AAW burnt following its incident and EI-AAK sold in England four months later, Dublin Air Ferries were reduced to two aircraft - Gipsy Moth EI-ABE and the Fox Moth, EI-AAP.

In December 1935, a report by the Departmental Committee established by the Minister for Defence to enquire into *'Civil Aviation in Saorstat Eireann,'* concluded that: -

> 'Either Collinstown or Kildonan could be developed as the Terminal Airport of Dublin, though neither would be quite suitable in view of their distance from the centre of the city.'

Kildonan is 8 kilometres north of the centre of the city, and similar distance as present location of Dublin Airport.

Pictured at Kildonan in 1937 in front of Fr. Furlong's Aeronca. Left to right: Ivan Hammond, John Duggan, Johnny Maher, Fr. Furlong, George Kennedy, Mrs. Maher and her son, John. In front is Una Scannell (later Mrs. Ivan Hammond)

Photograph courtesy Ronny Vogt collection

An addition to the field at Kildonan, but not to the fleet of Dublin Air Ferries, was an Aeronca C-3, registration G-AEFU. A priest attached to Finglas parish, Rev. Fr. Joseph Furlong, purchased it in England. It was delivered from Hanworth to Kildonan in May 1937. Father Furlong formed a flying club at Kildonan called Tramway Aero Club, for which the Aeronca was used for instruction and pleasure flying. On 16 June 1937, the Aeronca was transferred to the Irish register as EI-ABN. It was the first Aeronca C-3 on the Irish register. Unlike many other training aircraft the student sat alongside the instructor, and had many advantages over previous fore and aft seating arrangements. Fr. Furlong became a popular figure at Kildonan, with his fearless dog 'Bruno' accompanying him on his flights. On the outbreak of hostilities in September 1939, the Air Corps at Collinstown decommissioned the Aeronca. In post war years it was observed at Weston and is believed to have been scrapped there about 1955 and formally cancelled from the register 22 November 1955.

At the *National Irish Junior Aviation Club*, Lady Heath arranged lectures. The lecturers included Michael A. Doyle, Aeronautical Engineer to the Free State Government, Captain J. P. (Paddy) Saul, John R. Currie, club engineer and manager at Kildonan, and Lady Heath herself. The club's first Annual General Meeting was held in the Mansion House, Dawson Street, Dublin on 5 June 1936. The Lord Mayor of Dublin addressed the meeting. The club fixed an entrance fee of 2/6d and annual subscription of 1/=. The year ended for the club with a very successful dance at the Shelbourne Hall, Merrion Row, Dublin.

Meanwhile, matters had deteriorated at Dublin Air Ferries during the second half of 1936. On 27 May 1936 the Irish Government, commencing with a flight from Baldonnel to Bristol, inaugurated Aer Lingus. The pilot on this auspicious occasion was Oliver Armstrong, formerly Chief Pilot at Kildonan. The national carrier extended its range of routes throughout Ireland and to mainland Great Britain. This was to have a consequence for the charter flights undertaken by Dublin Air Ferries to similar destinations. In September 1936, the company announced it was closing down temporarily *'for change of direction and re-organisation.'* The flying school, Dublin Aero Club, also ceased to function. Members that wished to continue their tuition transferred to the Irish Aero Club at Baldonnel. The company remained closed throughout the winter months of 1936 / 1937. In January 1937, Fox Moth, EI-AAP, affectionately known as the *'Honeymoon Express'*, was ferried to Hanworth for its Certificate of Airworthiness check. Following the death of Grattan Esmond, TD, Dublin Air Ferries purchased the Gipsy Moth, EI-AAC, that had been available to them and the change of ownership was registered on 26 February 1937. The Gipsy Moth, EI-ABE, was transferred from the ownership of Lady Heath to Dublin Air Ferries on 20 February 1937. With three aircraft registered to them the company completed its re-organisation and were back in business in March 1937. The flying school also resumed. A one-third-page advertisement appeared in the April 1937 edition of *Aviator* announcing its change of management. Air Taxis within the Free State would be charged at 1/6d per mile.

The anticipated, and longed for, return to previous business levels failed to materialise. The recently purchased Gipsy Moth, EI-AAC, was cancelled from the Irish register on 5 April 1937 and stored before being ferried to England following sale there on 1 September 1938. It became G-AFKA before being impressed for service during World War Two with the Royal Air Force on 25 January 1941. It served with many units and finally became an instructional airframe before being scrapped in November 1945. To further compound matters for the company, the two remaining aircraft were damaged in separate incidents.

The National Irish Junior Aviation Club held its second Annual General Meeting on 6 May 1937. At this meeting it was passed that the club change its name to the Irish Junior Aviation Club. The annual subscription was increased fivefold to 5/=. Members may remain in the club until they reach the age of 25 years, but they cannot join after 21 years-of-age. Colonel Charles Russell was elected President and Chris Bruton was elected Honorary Secretary. Members showed a keen interest in model aircraft. As a consequence, a model-flying day was scheduled for the 15 acres at the Phoenix Park, Dublin. On Sunday, 12 September 1937, the club organised a social to Greystones, County Wicklow. 50 members attended. The fee for the day was 6/=, to include the return rail journey from Dublin, tea, dancing and a pleasure flight. Captain James M. St. Kearney gave a lecture on 7 October 1937, at which 60 members attended. The club also rendered assistance to the Tramway Aero Club, who held their first annual dinner dance in the Hibernian Hotel, Dawson Street, Dublin, on St. Stephen's night, 26 December 1937. Admission was 9/=. In post-war years the word 'Junior' was dropped and the organisation became the Irish Aviation Club. In later years it evolved into the Irish Aviation Council.

Dublin Air Ferries continued their training operations. In October 1937, three engineers, Ivan Hammond, G. C. Toye and George Williams, qualified for 'A' and 'C' licences. Ivan Hammond (later an Aer Lingus Captain) was undergoing training by Captain O. E. Armstrong as an airline pilot. The company struggled with its efforts to keep going through the winter months 1937 / 1938. Meanwhile, over at Baldonnel, the Irish Aero Club was experiencing similar operational and financial difficulties. In September 1937, they hosted a stage of the King's Cup Air Race. The event was a highly prestigious occasion for the club and they received accolades for their organisational skills in the role they played. When the dust finally settled and the visitors were long gone from Baldonnel, the Irish Aero Club was deeper in debt than prior to the event. On 29 May 1937, club Moth EI-AAJ crashed into the Sugar Loaf Mountain, killing the pilot. This was the third fatal crash in the club's history, and left them also with only one aircraft. At a meeting of the Irish Aero Club on 26 November 1937, it was resolved to cease trading and a Liquidator was appointed to wind up the company.

Almost simultaneous was the demise of the publication *Aviation*. The magazine ceased production in December 1937. Dublin Air Ferries managed to carry on until 1938. The final act was to dispose of the assets. Gipsy Moth, EI-ABE was cancelled from the Irish register on 2 February 1938. It was restored to the UK register using its previous registration, G-AASY, going to London Air Park Flying Club, Hanworth. It too was impressed by the Royal Air Force and had many uses, until it became an instructional airframe, ending its days toward the end of the War at Cosford.

On 9 July 1938, a young Irish-American touched down at New York from Los Angeles in his Curtiss Robin single-engine monoplane. Eight days later the intrepid aviator left New York and after a flight of 26 hours he landed at Baldonnel, claiming he departed New York to return to the west coast of America. For his navigational 'misjudgement' he earned the immortal title Douglas 'Wrong Way' Corrigan. The huge media interest resulting from this epic flight did little to rejuvenate the flagging interest in general aviation in Ireland.

The Fox Moth, EI-AAP, was the sole surviving aircraft for Dublin Air Ferries, continuing to serve the company throughout the summer of 1938. On 31 August 1938, it was ferried to England and registered as G-AFKI to H. G. Aitcheson, Croydon near Shoreham. It was cancelled from the Irish register on 18 September 1938. Hugh Cahill had purchased it new in July 1932. Like the fate of its predecessors, the Royal Air Force impressed it on 31 August 1941 for wartime duties. Its final fate is unknown, but was probably scrapped.

The departure of EI-AAP marked the end of operational functions at Kildonan. Following the conclusion of operations, the Department of Industry and Commerce formally announced, by Notice, that appeared 20 December 1938, that the aerodrome at Kildonan was closed. *The Irish Times* in an epitaph wrote: -

> 'During the past seven years, the various organisations operating from Kildonan trained a number of pilots and carried out many charter flights without any accident causing loss of life.'

A claim the owners and operators can be distinctly proud of. Fate would probably have delivered a blow to most operators within a year. War clouds were gathering over Europe and World War Two was declared on 3 September 1939. During this period Ireland was in a state of 'Emergency.' Part of the prohibitions was the banning of civilian private flying in the Free State. The Air Corps immobilised all private aircraft. Many never returned to active flying roles after the six years of war were over.

Finglas village in 1932 at the time Kildonan was in operation. The airfield was located off the Ashbourne road but out of photograph at top left hand corner

Photograph via Pearse Cahill collection

The final physical act for Dublin Air Ferries was the sale and removal of the hangar. In the post war years the McMahon family of Milford, County Donegal were involved in the development of a military airfield at Ballykelly, County Derry, and the hangar was dismantled at Kildonan and transported to Milford where it was re-erected and used to maintain and garage the fleet of 20 trucks then operated by McMahon's. A son of this developer, Derek McMahon, the rally driver of the 1970s, used it as a garage when he was involved in the motor trade in Milford. It was finally dismantled and destroyed in 1995 to make way for premises acquired by the North Western Health Board for a Health Centre, in Milford. For many years while in Milford the lettering 'KILDONAN' were to be distinctly legible on its roof – showing its determination that it might be gone but not forgotten.

Lady Heath and Williams set up a butcher's shop in Finglas and for a while it prospered. However their marriage broke up and they went their separate ways. Lady Mary returned to London. Her career started in sadness, there was sadness throughout her life and she died tragically when she fell down the stairs of a tramcar in London. She died within a day at St. Leonard's Hospital, Shoreditch, of the head injuries she sustained and the complications of the silver plate in her skull. This occurred on 9 May 1939 - four months before the outbreak of World War Two, during which, no doubt, she would have added further to her glorious achievements. Her ex-husband, Sir James Heath, though over forty years her senior, was to outlive her by over three years; his death is recorded as occurring on 20 December 1942. The real tragedy was not the tramcar accident, but the crash in Cleveland almost ten years prior to this. An inspiring career was ended at the early age of forty-two years.

Chapter

4

THE SPARK REKINDLED

From pre and post War motor racing to the purchase by Pearse Cahill of his first aircraft. Then came the establishment of an aviation business at Dublin airport during the 1950's

Chapter Four

THE SPARK REKINDLED

During the 'Emergency', and for many years after, Iona took a back seat in the world of aviation. The charismatic Pearse Cahill, who was ultimately to revive the family interest in flight, concentrated, in the meantime, on another series of adventures, this time on four wheels. When Hugh Cahill informed his son that their trip to the World Fair in New York in September 1939 was off, Pearse was not too disappointed. He had his heart set on continuing to build the relatively successful reputation he was earning as a motoring competitor. This interest had been firmly ignited when he borrowed his mother's Hillman Minx and entered it in the St. Patrick's Day Trials organised by the Irish Motor Racing Club in 1936. This was the 19-year-old Pearse's first competitive event and involved a Terenure start, continuing for 110 miles and finishing in Greystones, County Wicklow. There were 19 entrants and only 11 succeeded in completing the event. Pearse finished a very credible 2nd place. His next event was the Leinster Motor Cycle and Car Club, National Championship Trial. It was held in appalling weather conditions on 13 April 1936 with a start at St. Stephen's Green, Dublin. Pearse received the First Class Award. He did not partake of any further competitive event until the Leinster Motor Club Trial on 2 October 1937, comprising four laps of a 55 mile course in south County Dublin. He finished 7th in the Hillman. On 30 October he entered the Hillman in the Irish Motor Racing Club Autumn Trial starting in Dundrum and continuing for 45 miles ending in Tallaght. In this trial he was awarded First Class Awards for his third place finish.

A night trial was organised by the Leinster Motor Club for 6 November 1937 with a 7.30pm start at Tallaght and, travelling in the dark for 60 miles, the course finished at the Glenview Hotel, Glen O' the Downs. Yet again Pearse achieved the First Class Award. The final motoring event of 1937 was the Boxing Day Trial on 27 December. With a start at Rathfarnham it wound its way over the Dublin and Wicklow mountains to finish at Ashford, County Wicklow. Various tests determined the skill of the drivers. His finish in this event, again in his mother's Hillman, earned him a Second Class Award.

The Hillman Minx borrowed from Pearse's Mother, Caroline, (pictured behind the wheel) to enter his first Trials event, 17 March 1936 when aged 19 years

Photograph courtesy Pearse Cahill collection

His participation in various events throughout 1938 increased. On 5 March the Hillman entered the Grafton Cup Trial, and, during the following week, a Night Trial where he was awarded the Premier Award. On 14 May 1938 he entered the 1185c.c. Hillman Minx in the Speed Meeting at Turvey Avenue, Donabate, in north County Dublin. He came second in the 'cars over 1100 c.c.' event and first in the 'cars, unlimited c.c.' event. This success convinced Hugh that Pearse was achieving remarkable results in an ordinary saloon car. What was not revealed at the time was Pearse had managed to install an aircraft cabin blower, which enabled the Minx to go faster, so fast; it clocked 84mph from a standing start. *'It went like a bomb'* according to Pearse, for a car that was entered as *'the mother's saloon car'!*

Sligoman, Alex MacArthur was a member of the Irish Motor Racing Club and competed in a few motoring events in his 1935, N-type MG Magnette, with the County Sligo registration EI 3332. The car was purchased in chassis form from the MG factory and delivered to Bellevue Garages in London, then owned by the Evan's family, where a four seat body, with bulbous single-hump cowling, was added. Alex purchased the car from them. In the summer of 1938 he sold this car to Tracey's. Pearse successfully encouraged Hugh to purchase the car for him. Without making any changes to the car, Pearse entered it in the Handicap Race for the Wakefield Trophy organised by the Irish Motor Racing Club as part of the Phoenix Park Grand Prix Meeting, on 10 September 1938. Thirty two cars started the 18 laps of the course, totalling 77 miles. The report of the race appeared in the *Irish Motor News* including the comments:

'At the finish eighteen cars were on their last lap at the same time and the flagging-in squad had some busy moments. Thirty four seconds separated first and second and then fifteen of the remainder crossed the line in 99 seconds. This is the closest finish of the field in any race ever held in Ireland and, possibly, anywhere.'

Pearse, in the newly acquired 1287 c.c. MG was among the bunch of fifteen – being credited with 14th of the 26 that completed the race, having been placed an amazing 6th at the half way stage. Pearse entered one further race that year, the Reliability Trial on 29 October 1938 where he achieved a Second Class Award.

Pearse began making modifications to the car. He was ably assisted by one of the engineers from the Iona workshop – Paddy Kavanagh. Paddy was to assist Pearse with the maintenance of his cars for many years that followed while remaining as an engineer for Iona. For the MG, Paddy made a beautiful balanced 'bunch of bananas' exhaust that came out and as the exhaust extended the diameter kept increasing. According to Pearse the: *'engine used to sound beautiful when she was at full shaft.'* In an interview with Pat Sweeney in October 1990,

Pearse describes in vivid detail all the modifications made to the MG to bring it to the standard he required to enter it for some serious events. Components from aircraft were used in the rebuilt version – anything to improve the performance of the car. The car was painted dark green – to coincide with that of the Irish Racing Club colours. The work on the 1287c.c MG transformed the car – both in appearance and performance. It was now a single-seat racing car and was affectionately to be known as the *Iona Special,* – it was a car to be reckoned with.

The threat, and later the onset, of war caused many car and motor cycling race meetings to be abandoned on these islands, until at last the only one left was the Irish Motor Racing Club's Phoenix Park races on 9 September 1939.

Pearse entered the MG in the Grand Prix Car Handicap race of 24 laps totalling 100 miles. A field of fifteen competitors faced the starter. On the third lap, Pearse took the lead and remained in that position for a considerable time. He was lapping at the remarkable speed, for such a car, of 80.7 mph The *Irish Motor News* reported as follows:

'Cahill, however, looked an out and out winner; but 'there's many a slip...', and so it proved. After three consecutive laps at over eighty miles an hour, his clutch began to slip badly and he lost 22 seconds on his seventeenth lap. A pit stop cost him another 70 seconds and Thompson got by him a lap later, so his excellent chance of victory had gone. He had then to fight hard even to secure second place, for he was only two minutes ahead of MacArthur with five laps to cover, and losing about half a minute a lap. Then the clutch slip became worse, and his lap speed fell to 70 mph, with the result that MacArthur passed him with two laps still to go. At the start of the last lap he slowed down and signified his intention of again visiting the pit; but an excited official waved him on and he completed his final lap over a minute ahead of the fourth man.'

MG Magnette, EI 3332, purchased by Pearse. The car was previously owned by Alex MacArthur. As car number 41, it was entered in the 1938 handicap race in the Phoenix Park

Photograph courtesy Pearse Cahill collection

Only six cars completed the course. Despite providing some excitement to the thousands of spectators, when he shot off the road behind the trees at Mountjoy Corner. Pearse managed to secure third place in a total time of 70 minutes 32 seconds at an average speed of 76.27 mph. Another race was held on a fine summers evening on the 'short-circuit.' A female spectator, wearing a very fine see-through dress, was viewing the race from a spot near the 'Furry-Glen.' Owing to the position of the evening sun behind her, many drivers were distracted by the vision before them, with a few admitting to have almost lost control of their cars. Pearses' descriptive comments on the sight of the attractive lady are not for printing in this book! Following the race Pearse made reference to Wilf Fitzsimmons about *'nylon, ninon or none-on'* !! This was the last competitive motor race in Europe until the end of World War Two.

Army Transport Certificate issued on 27 November 1940 to Second Lieutenant Pearse Cahill, authorizing him to drive *'Light saloons and trucks'*. Pearse's military driving experience went beyond these vehicle types!!

Copy certificate courtesy Eric Hopkins

Pearse in control as the MG Magnette (No. 19) rounds a corner during the short-circuit race in the Curragh

Photograph courtesy Pearse Cahill collection

During the 'Emergency' period in Ireland between 1939 and 1945, petrol was rationed; this effectively caused the cessation of motor racing throughout the island. Pearse enlisted for military service. On 4 September 1940, one year and one day following the declaration of World War Two, Pearse commenced his duties as a Commissioned Officer in the Army. He was involved in the Transport Section and drove anything from a motorcycle to a tank!

Lieutenant Pearse (on right) as Officer-in-Command of a group of soldiers during the 'Emergency'. The occasion was the changing of the guard, at Croom, Co. Limerick in September 1943

Photograph courtesy Pearse Cahill collection

It was during the war years that Pearse met and married Constance Duncan from Clontarf, a Scottish born niece of Sir Andrew Duncan, Minister for Industry and Commerce during Winston Churchill's wartime Government. Constance was born on 19 September 1919 at 7 Havelock Street, Partick, Glasgow. The groom, dressed in Irish Army uniform, married Constance in St. Anthony's Church, Clontarf on 12 October 1943. Prior to his marriage, Pearse was still living in Prospect Villa. The couple then moved to 5 St. Mobhi Road, Glasnevin. They had two sons, Hugh and Peter and one daughter, Enda. Pearse's military service concluded on 31 October 1946, having attained the rank of Lieutenant.

Pearse remained both a member of the Irish Motor Racing Club and the Leinster Motor Club. Petrol rationing was to continue until 1950 and consequently few motoring events occurred in the immediate post-war years. After the war he purchased another second-hand N-type MG Magnette, bearing County Carlow registration CI 2066, for spares for the *Iona Special*. However, he began using it for his personal daily use and eventually entered it for hill-climbs, reliability trials and speed events. This left him with the *Iona Special* for races.

The first post-war event featuring the *Iona Special* was the Kilcroney races in 1946. He entered three events finishing 2nd in the over 1100c.c. handicap,

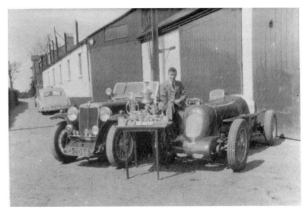

Pearse with both MGs. On left is MG registration CI 2066 and on the other side of Pearse and his trophy table is the MG EI 3332 - later to become the *'Iona Special'*

Photograph courtesy Pearse Cahill collection

1st in the 1500c.c. scratch and 1st in the unlimited scratch (fastest time of the day). He also drove an Austin 8, with Dublin registration ZO 6147, that he entered in the Circuit of Ireland as a member of the manufacturer's team, finishing in third place. Most of the competitors were in it for the fun and enjoyment with many stages won by the person that could reach the pub the quickest! The following year he entered the Circuit of Ireland in the *Iona Special*. At that stage he had enlisted a couple of Aer Lingus sheet metal workers to make up a light angle iron frame and sheet it with aluminium to shape the radiator cowlings. The shaping was done on a bag of sand with the two men beating it out and putting it into shape. Machining the head and increasing the compression ratio to 9:1 tuned the engine.

The now well known MG was featured in the Kilternan Hill Climb, County Dublin. Pearse had been unwell for a few days prior to the race, nonetheless, in typical Cahill dogged and determined style he started the event. While alternating 1st place with his good friend and opponent, Wilf

Pearse Cahill, with his bride, Constance Duncan, receives a military guard of honor outside St. Anthony's Church, Clontarf, following their nuptial ceremony, 12 October 1943

Photograph courtesy Pearse Cahill collection

Austin 8, ZO 6147, driven by Pearse in the Circuit of Ireland

Photograph courtesy Pearse Cahill collection

Leaving the 'refueling-stop' at Bridget Burkes (now the Old Mill pub), Old Bawn, Tallaght en route to the Hell Fire Club are, left to right: Pearse Cahill, 'Bill' Poole and Jimmy Millard

Photograph courtesy Bob Montgomery / Royal Irish Automobile Club archives

Fitzsimmons, at the last attempt, Pearse 'blacked-out' and crashed on the final corner at the top of the climb. The car rolled over and Pearse suffered injuries that necessitated his removal to the Meath Hospital, near Dublin city centre; with Pearse giving directions to the ambulance crew. He broke both his index and middle fingers on his right hand – as well as his pride! The car was not seriously damaged. That was the last occasion the hill at Kilternan was used for hill climb events.

Another major trophy in Irish Motor Sport was the Hewison Memorial Trophy, established in 1938; it was based on the results of Trials held during the year. In 1947 Pearse won it. The following year Wilf Fitzsimmons was the winner with Pearse placed third in 1949. In 1950 he was placed 4th overall, marginally beaten by Sligoman Kevin P. Murray. Kevin was awarded the trophy consecutively in 1951 and 1952, the first time this feat had been accomplished, though Wilf Fitzsimmons had been a dual winner (1938 and 1948) before.

On the 12 July 1947, The Leinster Motor Club organised the first ever motoring event held on the 'Short' circuit at the Curragh, a distance of 1.67 miles. Pearse entered this event the following year, on Saturday, 28 August and finished in 2nd position in the Consolation Race in the MG.

The Walter Sexton Trophy was an important contest as it produced the champion driver overall for the year, based on points scored in races and other speed events, on a sliding scale depending on the importance of the event in the year's Irish speed events. In 1949, Pearse finished in third place. In 1950 he was the Trophy winner and was 2nd in 1951, having made a strong bid to hold the Trophy, but retirements in Wicklow and the Curragh races put paid to his chances. In 1952 he was placed 5th, with only six points separating third and fifth place.

The year 1950 was to prove one of Pearse's most successful years in Irish motoring. On 8 July he entered the *Iona Special*, in the Leinster Trophy handicap race held over one hundred miles. The race was organised by the Leinster Motor Club. The course was twelve laps of a circuit eight and one third miles, and located near Wicklow town. The following extract from a newspaper article of the race states:

'Cahill, a well-known member of the motor trade in Dublin, is one of the most consistent supporters of motor speed competitions in the Dublin area, and, it may be added, one of the most consistent prize-winners in trials and speed tests.

Yesterday's win may be regarded as his biggest success to date, and it was a very popular one, as he is one of the most active members of the Committee of the promoting club.

Cahill took the lead in the eighth lap and was five seconds ahead of the second place man when he entered the final lap, and ran out a winner by three-fifths of a second after one of the most exciting finishes that any Irish motor race has produced for many years.'

The Chief Flag Marshall that had the honor of waving the chequered flag as Pearse roared across the finish line was Joe O'Neill, manager at the Iona Engineering Works at Cross Guns Bridge.

Pearse's time for the one hundred mile race was one hour 22 minutes and 25 seconds. His average speed was recorded as 68.87 mph. This was the first occasion the Leinster Trophy took place in Wicklow, following many years at Tallaght. On 7 October 2000, to mark the 50th anniversary of this event a commemorative stone was erected at the entrance to Wicklow town, listing the successful drivers during the period the event was staged in the county. Pearse Cahill is the first name inscribed on the stone. The following year the event was won

by Mike Hawthorn, who went on to achieve world acclaim in both motor car and motor cycle racing. In 1968 the venue was transferred to its current location at Mondello Park, County Kildare. Other notable winners of the same Leinster Trophy since Pearses' victory were John Watson (1966 and 1971),

Pearse acknowledging the congratulations of Jack Lewis, following his win of the 1950 Leinster Trophy

Photograph via Pearse Cahill collection

Eddie Jordan (1978), Ayrton Senna (1982), Mika Hakkinen (1988). Could Pearse have had a career in Formula One? During his period in competitive motor sport, Pearse raced alongside Mike Hawthorn, Stirling Moss and other 'greats' of the fast car world.

The second international meeting in 1950 organised by the Irish Motor Racing Club was held at the Curragh, County Kildare on 9 September 1950. The 74 mile O'Boyle Trophy Handicap Race attracted an entry of 32 starters. The best average speed was awarded to Pearse at 69.04 mph and he was placed second overall. In 1951 the same event was won by the 22-year-old Stirling Moss. Moss also took the Wakefield Trophy that year.

Pearse crossing the finishing line to win the 1950 Leinster Trophy, on the occasion of it's first visit to Wicklow, 8 July 1950

Photograph via Pearse Cahill collection

On 13 September 1950, Pearse, then living at 5 St. Mobhi Road, Glasnevin, was appointed a Peace Commissioner. He was a committee member and competitor of the Irish Motor Racing Club. Throughout the years there was an excellent degree of camaraderie between all competitors, both on and off the track. When members were not competing in an event they would volunteer to act as marshal or offer assistance otherwise. This goodwill and enthusiasm extended to two-wheel racing as well as four-wheel competitions.

Motor sport in 1951 attracted increased attention and enjoyed greater support than in any year since the war, despite a worsening economic situation. Pearse's first achievement that year was in the Dungarvan hill climb on 29 April, where he attained best time in the *Iona Special*. In 1953 the 35-year-old Cahill was honoured to be elected President of the Irish Motor Racing Club. That year he was offered a Gordini in which to race. Pearse could not resist another challenge. He entered it for the Tourist Trophy 800 mile Race hosted by the Ulster Automobile Club at Dundrod on 5 September 1953. A large continental entry was evident with Redmond Gallagher and Pearse Cahill, in the 1.5 litre Gordini, scoring class wins. Redmond Gallagher, Managing Director of Urney Chocolates, was a regular entrant to motor races in his motorcycle-engined Leprechaun Special. Pearse entered the Tourist Trophy event the following year with Don Beauman as co-driver. 1953 saw Kevin P. Murray win the Hewison Trophy for the third successive time based on his results in the Trial events that year. Tragically, Don Beauman was killed instantly when he was thrown from his car during the 1955 Leinster Trophy race at Wicklow. This, along with other fatal accidents that year, caused the cessation of all future motor car racing events at the Curragh.

For his involvement in motoring, spanning the years 1936 to 1953, with the exception of the intervening War years, Pearse was elected an Associate Member of the Institute of the Motor Industry. This presentation was made to him on 2 July 1959.

The Gordini entered by Redmond Gallagher, Urney Chocolates, and driven by Pearse in the 1954 Tourist Trophy Race at Dundrod. His co-driver was Don Beauman

Photograph via Pearse Cahill collection

In a Royal Irish Automobile Club Archive publication *The Curragh Motor Races 1947-1954* by Oliver McCrossan, he refers to the following:

'In September 1999, the Curragh Local History Group and the Irish Motor Racing Club came together to mark the 50th anniversary of motor racing at the Curragh. A triangular granite monument was unveiled. It depicted the winners of the Wakefield and O'Boyle Trophy Races from 1949 to 1954. Two of those winning drivers, Dickie Odlum and Pearse Cahill were happily present.'

Pearse enjoyed his passion for motor racing right into the early 1950s and had been racing competitively for 18 years – except for the intervention of the 'Emergency.' He then felt it was time to hang up his helmet. He had retained the *Iona Special* to the end of his competitive career. According to Pearse, he sold it to Dr. Gleeson in County Wexford for £100. Around 1957 the MG Magnette racing car, chassis number NA 0774,

Pearse beside his Motoring Trophy cabinet, containing some, but not all, of the trophies he was awarded

Photograph courtesy Pearse Cahill collection

returned to the UK and was owned by a Mr. Wild – who continued to race it at events at Silverstone, Castle Coombe and other circuits in England. He retained it for about 10 years and sold it to John May, 21 Oxford Way, Warden Hill, Cheltenham, Gloustershire. About a year later, he sold it to Dudley Gahagan, 'Malden', Seale, near Farnham, Surrey. Dudley was acting on behalf of Horace Caraldi, 2 Station Road, Aldershot, Hampshire. The car was exchanged many times with dealers in the motor trade until it reached Paul Weldon, at Fine Motor Cars, Stalbridge, Sturminster Newton, Dorset. In August 1971 he sold it to William M. McCarty, MD, Pheasant Lane, Troy, New York 12180, for a figure believed to be around US$ 3,000. It was shipped in a container to the United States. The car was registered under number 866 with the MG Car Club Limited, Abington, Berkshire. Bill McCarthy sold it to LeRoy Jacobson, of Upton,

Massachusetts. Around 1977, it eventually found its way into the ownership of Dave Raymond, Abingdon Classics, 12 Old Redding Road, W. Redding, Connecticut 06896, about 50 miles from New York City. He has lovingly restored the car to its former glory and splendour and is very proud of and passionate about its heritage. Dave raced the car for many years, often up to fifteen events a year. In 1981, the *Iona Special* won the race for pre-war entrants at Sebring, Florida. In 1990, Dave turned down an offer of £75,000 Sterling, for the *Iona Special*. The car has proved to be very popular with the vintage car fraternity in the United States, featuring on several occasions in publications such as *The Vintage Sports Car Club of America*.

Until recently Dave still drove the car for leisure purposes regularly and even entered it for the 'Through the Streets Race' in Alexander Bay, New York State in September 2000. A conservative estimate value of the almost 70-year-old car would be US$125,000. On 11 June 2003 it arrived from New York in a crate at Dublin Port. On Saturday, 14 June 2003 it was delivered to Pearse's home in Skerries and 3 days later it was transported to Newtownards where it was a 'celebrity' in the 75th anniversary commemorations of the Tourist Trophy events at the Northern Ireland venue. During this historic event, Pearse was honoured and thrilled to drive the *Iona Special* around the former circuit at Newtownards. Following this event the car did not return across the Atlantic, instead, it crossed the Irish Sea where Dave Raymond placed it on the market for sale in the UK.

In the post-war years, Pearse never quite lost sight of aviation; his interest was revived with the help of his fellow motoring competitor, Sligoman, Kevin P. Murray, who was also an aircraft owner. Kevin was a business man and a director of Builders Providers, D. M. Hanley and Co. Ltd. In 1949 he purchased a B.A. Swallow, G-ADMF, which was registered to him as EI-AFF on 18 May 1949 and was based near his home at Rosses Point, County Sligo. On visits to Kevin in Sligo, Pearse had a few flights in the Swallow. He also had some additional flights at Weston with Kevin in the early 1950s. According to Pearse:

'A trip in this Swallow was enough to rekindle my aviation instinct. From that day I knew what my future would be and I set about developing Iona once again.'

This appeared to rekindle the spark of aviation that was still in Pearse's blood. In 1952 the Leinster Aero Club was formed. Among its founder members were Captain P. W. 'Darby' Kennedy, Kevin Murray and Pearse Cahill. On 23 May 1952 Pearse recommenced his flight training – after a 19 year absence – with an instructional flight in the dH82A, Tiger Moth, EI-AFJ, under the supervision of 'Darby' Kennedy at Weston. He obtained his Students Pilot's Licence, number 30, on 6 March 1953. He continued to improve his experience and knowledge by flying some of the many Tiger Moths then based at Weston. He obtained his Private Pilot's Licence, number 142, on 11 July 1960.

Hugh Cahill had not severed his links with aviation when he vacated Kildonan during November 1933. In post war years he had continued to perform some light engineering repairs for Aer Lingus. Pearse qualified as an engineer obtaining his A, B, C, and D licences, which are still current over fifty years later. He decided he would extend the work they had been doing for Aer Lingus by looking to the general aviation market to perform maintenance on light aircraft. The engineering company that was operated by his father was never formally registered. As Pearse was now formalising his affairs he registered the name Iona Garage and Engineering Works Limited on 22 April 1955 under Certificate of Registration number 015620. This name was to remain on the register long after its demise and not formally dissolved until 26 March 1999.

By the middle 1950s, ten years after the war, many Royal Air Force aircraft became surplus to requirements and were offered for sale to the civilian market. One lot of seven Chipmunks was purchased and placed on the Irish register on 31 May 1956 by David Montgomery, and delivered to Weston at various dates during June 1956. Pearse attended a motor show in the company of his fellow motor racing comrade, and former President of the Irish Motoring Racing Club, Wilf

Fitzsimmons. Wilf had a friend in the Royal Air Force, Air-Vice Marshall Ben Ball who had direct contacts with the person who was involved with the disposal of several hundred surplus machines. On Pearse's behalf, Wilf established contact and as a result Pearse put in a bid of £200 each for some Chipmunks. He got the fright of his life when the Air Ministry wrote to him seeking information on the number of aircraft he required as his tender price had been accepted. Not having any resources himself at the time, Pearse approached his father for a loan of £1,000 to purchase and make airworthy four of these Chipmunks. When his father learned that the loan was to buy aeroplanes he was none too pleased, nevertheless, Pearse succeeded in persuading Hugh to part with enough money to purchase the aircraft.

Most of them required little maintenance to make them airworthy and arrangements were put in place to have them flown from the various locations throughout the United Kingdom. Between 16 and 21 July 1956 all four dH Chipmunks were placed on the Irish register in the name of M. P. Cahill. They were transferred from their Royal Air Force markings WB620, WB630, WB764 and WD336 and received Irish civil registration marks EI-AJC, EI-AJD, EI-AJE and EI-AJF respectively (see Tables 6-9).

The Air Ministry received the payment of £800 on 29 June 1956. On 27 August 1956, EI-AJC, EI-AJD and EI-AJF were ferried to Dublin airport. Most of the ferry pilots were from Weston. On 21 September 1956, Pearse himself, still only a holder of a Student Pilot Licence, flew EI-AJE from Silloth, south of the Scotland-England border, stopping for fuel uptake at West Freugh, near Stranraer, and then routing via Belfast to Dublin. Modifications were required to convert the aircraft from military to civilian configuration. At Dublin airport the wings were removed from the four aircraft and they were removed by truck to the engineering premises at the rear of the *Brian Boru* public house in Glasnevin. There they were dismantled and Pearse did the necessary work to obtain a civilian Certificate of Airworthiness for the four of them. While at Glasnevin, one of the completed Chipmunks was placed in the front window of the

Chipmunk EI-AJC photographed at Shannon airport 26 May 1957 - eight months after acquisition by Pearse Cahill from the Royal Air Force

Photograph courtesy George Flood

Chipmunk EI-AJC later became Air Corps number 200. It crashed on a training flight from Gormanston, Co. Meath on 24 April 1980

Photograph courtesy Paul Duffy

EI-AJD, one of four Chipmunks purchased by Pearse Cahill from the Royal Air Force in September 1956

Photograph via Leo Murray from Jim Masterson collection

EI-AJE was the third in a series of four ex-Royal Air Force Chipmunks that established Pearse Cahill with aircraft acquisitions

Photograph via Leo Murray from Jim Masterson collection

A Chipmunk in the showroom window at Cross Guns Bridge (now Des Kelly carpets), Christmas 1956. Life size mannequin of Davy Croket, with lantern, 'stands guard'. Model aircraft are displayed along starboard wing

Photograph courtesy Pearse Cahill collection

engineering works (currently the premises of Des Kelly carpets) during the 1956 Christmas festivities. Much to the bemusement of the onlookers, Santa Claus was seated in the pilot's seat and a life-size figure of Davy Crockett was placed beside the

The fourth Chipmunk purchased in 1956 by Pearse Cahill was EI-AJF

Photograph courtesy Paul Duffy

aircraft. Model aircraft decorated the wings. It proved a great novelty attraction and families travelled far and wide to see the spectacle in the window.

The necessary maintenance work was carried out and they were removed to Dublin airport for final re-assembly at one of the Aer Lingus hangars. Two of the Chipmunks were test flown at Dublin airport. A third aircraft was removed to the old defunct aerodrome at Kildonan in a partly disassembled state, having obtained the permission of the current owners of the field, the Byrne family. There the various components of the mainframes and wings were left on the ground while the engineers were away. When they returned they were horrified to discover that cattle had got into the field and were curiously examining these strange artefacts. One of the cattle walked across one of the wings, fortunately for all concerned he only pierced the fabric and caused no damage to any spars. Pearse did the test flight on this aircraft. Using the old runway that ran on the southern side of the avenue leading to Kildonan House, and taking off from the same field vacated by Lady Heath almost twenty years previously, he flew the aircraft to Weston. This was the last recorded flight from the field at Kildonan that had been acquired by his father in 1931 as Ireland's first commercial aerodrome.

The fourth of the Chipmunks was transported to the Urney chocolate factory site at Tallaght (across the Belgard Road from Jacobs Biscuits). Three years previously, Pearse was co-driver in the 800 mile race at Dundrod with the owner of the Urney factory, Redmond Gallagher. The factory stood on the site of the old Tallaght aerodrome operated by the Royal Flying Corps. The Royal Air Force vacated the site in 1920 and, while the new Irish Government retained it for military reasons, they did not use it for aviation purposes. The Department of Industry and Commerce required the aircraft to be weighed. Suitable scales were available for the purpose of weighing the aircraft at the location. There, Pearse assembled the remaining Chipmunk and it was test flown by Commandant James Liddy, Irish Air Corps. Pearse's Chipmunk was the last aircraft to be flown at Tallaght aerodrome, now forming part of the site of the Cookstown Industrial Estate.

Air Corps Commandant James Liddy was tragically killed on 18 August 1970. On this Tuesday evening thousands of holiday makers on the shore of Wicklow Bay watched in horror as one of the SE5A replicas, EI-ARB, involved in the making of the film *Zeppelin* collided with the camera ship, an Alouette II helicopter G-AWEE. The SE5A came in on a double loop, but hit the hovering helicopter, which disintegrated and both aircraft crashed into the sea. Three on board the Alouette, the pilot, producer and cameraman were killed instantly, and Liddy, the pilot of the bi-plane, was also killed. The aircraft for these films were based at Weston and some were Currie Wots, designed by John Robert Currie, who had served as Chief Engineer at Kildonan. EI-ARB was not a Currie built aircraft.

On 23 May 1957, EI-AJC was registered to Desmond Hogan, a member of the Aero Club of Ireland. It was complete with Certificate of Airworthiness and was exchanged by Pearse for another Chipmunk, EI-AJA, that had been registered to Desmond Hogan on 31 May 1956 (see Table 10). He had been unsuccessful in completing the Certificate of Airworthiness on this machine. Pearse subsequently succeeded in completing the necessary maintenance to obtain a Certificate of Airworthiness. This was completed at the Aer Lingus hangar at Dublin airport, from where it was test flown. Its registration was crudely painted on the fuselage for the delivery flight.

Chipmunk EI-AJA, outside the Aer Lingus hangar at Dublin airport prior to completion of Certificate of Airworthiness by Pearse Cahill

Photograph via Pearse Cahill collection

The five Chipmunks owned by Pearse had varying fortunes under future ownerships in three continents. These aircraft represent the re-birth of an affiliation with Irish aviation by the Cahill family that was set to continue for many years to come. It was in Chipmunk EI-AJF that Pearse successfully underwent his Private Pilot's Licence flight test with Captain Robert Cusack on 24 March 1960; almost 29 years after his first flight. Ten weeks later, he flew EI-AJF to Newtownards, County Down to undertake his UK, PPL flight test with Mr. Dash in Tiger Moth, G-ANLS on 10 June 1960.

One of the first aviation companies to locate at the Iona hangar after its construction was Aircraft Associates Limited. Its second aircraft was Bellanca 14-19-3, EI-AKR. Photographed at Iona in September 1960

Photograph courtesy Paul Duffy

During the late 1950s and early 1960s, Iona worked closely with three different companies: Aircraft Associates Limited, Irish Air Charters Limited, and Skycraft Services Limited; companies that did much to establish Iona in the business of maintaining and servicing a wide variety of aircraft.

Around the time Pearse's four Chipmunks arrived at Dublin airport, a company was established to act as UK and Irish agents for Beechcraft and Bellanca aircraft. The company was Irish Sales and Commodities Limited. The first aircraft they placed on the Irish register was a new Beech G35 Bonanza. This machine was registered to them on 20 August 1956 as EI-AJG. It was also the first Beech aircraft on the Irish register. On 17 January 1957 they changed their name to Aircraft Associates Limited. The aircraft was principally a demonstration model and spent most of its time at Liverpool. It was sold in the UK as G-APTY on 29 May 1959 and was replaced with a new Bellanca, EI-AKR. It arrived at Dublin airport, following a transatlantic ferry flight via the Azores, on 12 August 1959. Its base alternated between Liverpool and Dublin. On 10 March 1964 it was cancelled from the Irish register following its sale to the UK as G-ASRD. It was 'written-off' following a crash at Wolverhampton

on 17 August 1966. Their third aircraft on the Irish register was another new Beech Bonanza, EI-ALL, registered to them on 30 October 1959 and delivered 16 December 1959. It remained with the company until it was transferred to the UK register as G-ATSR on 23 March 1966. The next new aircraft registered to them was on 11 August 1960, when a new Beech Debonair received marks EI-ALI. On 20 April 1963 it was sold, also to the UK, as G-ASHR. In a subsequent registration, G-DEBY, it crashed into the sea off Frejus, French Riviera, on 29 July 1986. All onboard escaped unscathed. The fifth, and final, aircraft registered in Ireland to Aircraft Associates Limited was a new Beech Travelair, EI-AMC, on 18 April 1962. It too was sold in the UK in 1966, one month before EI-ALL, on 23 February 1966, as G-ATRC. In March 1963 this aircraft became the first aircraft used for an airborne company board meeting, with Dennis Greene, Wayman Heles and Maurice Cronin, all the Aircraft Associates directors, on board.

In January 1957 Tim Vigors, A. C. 'Monkey' Morgan and the Marquess of Kildare formed a company called Irish Air Charters Limited. The company chairman was Dennis Greene, principal in a prominent firm of Dublin solicitors. The

The first aircraft purchased by Iona based Irish Air Charters was Piper PA 23, EI-AJL. Photographed at Dublin airport 8 March 1957 – 10 days after becoming the first Irish light aircraft to be ferried across the Atlantic. Left to right, Esso representative, Aer Rianta w/keeper, Mrs. Vigors, Captain A. C. Morgan, Wing Commander Tim Vigors. Tragically, this was the aircraft that claimed the life of Irish Air Charter Chief Pilot 'Monkey' Morgan in January 1958

Photograph courtesy Liam Byrne via Ronny Vogt collection

purpose was to carry on an air-taxi business in association with the Piper sales agency run by T. A. Vigors & Company Limited. They were based at Dublin airport and office space was later provided by Iona. Operations commenced almost immediately with the purchase of their first aircraft, a brand new Piper PA23 Apache 160, EI-AJL, registered to them 30 January 1957. It was the first of this type to grace the Irish register. This aircraft was ferried across the Atlantic from Lock Haven, Pennsylvania to Dublin on 26 February 1957 by Irish Air Charters' chief pilot, A. C. 'Monkey' Morgan and Max Conrad. It was the first transatlantic delivery of an Irish registered light aircraft directly into Dublin.

Apaches first started to filter over to Europe in the mid 1950s and Max Conrad's first transatlantic ferry was in a Piper Apache from New York to Paris in 1954. The ferry flight of EI-AJL was his twenty-fourth such crossing. The Apache was a familiar sight in the UK and Ireland as it was primarily used for demonstration purposes. Most other aircraft purchased by Irish Air Charters were brought to Ireland in crates, arriving by ship at North Wall,

Dublin. They were assembled at the Iona Engineering Works, located at the rear of the *Brian Boru* public house, where Iona engineers did the partial assembly of the Piper aircraft, in advance of them being transported by road to Dublin airport for final assembly at the Aer Lingus hangars and then test flown. This was clearly unsatisfactory from all perspectives.

Hugh Cahill purchased some land on the west side of Dublin airport across the road from the *Boot Inn*. On this land he proposed to erect a hangar for the purpose of assembling the Piper aircraft and carrying on other aircraft maintenance works. This would have involved the aircraft being taxied across the road using gates, similar to the system employed at railway level crossings. Pearse approached the authorities for permission to implement their proposal. Instead, the Department of Industry and Commerce offered them a ten-year lease on a site on the airport itself adjacent to the *Boot Inn*. The framework for a blister hangar, capable of holding about eight aircraft, was manufactured at the Glasnevin engineering workshop and transferred to the new location at Dublin airport where the hangar was completed by Iona engineering staff. The business of assembling Piper aircraft was moved to Dublin airport towards the end of 1957.

Aircraft engineering was steadily developing and additional engineers were required. Initially, there

Lattice framework for blister hangar constructed at Cross Guns Bridge and assembled at Dublin airport for Iona at end 1957

Photograph via Pearse Cahill collection

was a loose relationship between Iona and Aer Lingus, whereby some engineers worked for both companies. Examples included Danny Stapleton, an aero-engine engineer, Des Tighe, an airframe engineer and Michael Murphy, a radio specialist. Eventually, it became necessary to employ full time qualified personnel. These three engineers would also oversee the work carried out by Paddy Kavanagh, Paddy Dowling and Pearse Cahill, some of whom were granted engineers licences to work under supervision. The services of George Barton, an Air Corps engineer, were also available on request.

Rudi Bracken an ex-Air Corps licensed engineer was employed. He had previously been employed by Iona at their engineering works in 1931. Brendan Young, (a brother of Tom Young who was airport manager at Kildonan), was recruited from the Air Corps. Brendan was an expert on wooden airframes as well as being a licensed engineer. Brendan Young was followed as Iona's Chief Engineer by Paddy Geoghan. Following from this, Pearse Cahill obtained the necessary engineering qualifications and experience to carry the mantle as Iona's Chief Engineer. The overall maintenance schedule increased and this led to the recruiting of apprentices to the light aircraft engineering business. In the mid-1950's one of these apprentices

was Dessie O'Brien. Dessie later qualified as a licensed engineer. Pearse stepped aside as Chief Engineer and Dessie was appointed to the position - a role he would fulfil until the demise of Iona in 1994. In the interim years Dessie oversaw the work of many engineers, too many to mention and excluded here at the risk of omitting anyone that may be offended by such an oversight. Their work was invaluable to ensuring the well-oiled machinery at Iona was moving all day - and often throughout the night, on behalf of the commercial operations and club activities.

By this time, Iona was gaining recognition as the principal establishment for the servicing and maintenance of light aircraft in Ireland. It proved necessary to extend the original hangar and include engineering workshops at the rear. This work was undertaken in 1961 and the extended hangar could accommodate up to 20 light aircraft. Club members will recall the difficulties in moving an aircraft from the back of the hangar - this was somewhat overcome with the installation of a rear access gate.

In an effort to promote the aircraft manufacturing business in the United Kingdom, import restrictions were imposed on newly manufactured foreign aircraft coming to the UK; a high rate of excise duty was applicable to such aircraft. This

The completed Iona hangar in 1958, then catering for up to 8 aircraft. The building, near the road, was used by Irish Air Charters and Iona for storage. The *Boot Inn* is located to the rear

Photograph via Pearse Cahill collection

effectively placed an embargo on imports of new aircraft from the United States of America to Britain. Irish Air Charters Ltd circumvented these duties by importing aircraft to Ireland first, registering them here and then re-exporting them as used aircraft to the UK. Single engine Pipers were brought in crates across the Atlantic by sea to the North Wall. Any twin-engine aircraft purchased by Irish Air Charters Ltd were ferried across the Atlantic and stored at the Iona hangar at Dublin airport prior to resale.

On behalf of Irish Air Charters, Iona kitted many aircraft with spray gear for work in Egypt. The gear was prepared at Iona's engineering works at Cross Guns Bridge. Two of the aircraft, Piper PA-18 Super Cubs, G-ARSR and G-ARSS were photographed at Dublin airport

Photograph courtesy Paul Duffy

On 15 January 1958, Pearse Cahill had lunch in Jury's Hotel, Dublin with A. C. Morgan, General Manager, Irish Air Charters Ltd, to discuss maintenance and hangar terms for Irish Air Charters at the Iona hangar. That day an auction was taking place at Carmody's Hotel, Ennis, County Clare, during the course of which a floor collapsed killing eight and injuring 34 attending the auction. 'Monkey' Morgan was dispatched to Shannon to collect photographs of the tragedy. On take-off from Shannon airport his Apache, EI-AJL, crashed into the River Shannon unfortunately with the tragic loss of life of 'Monkey' Morgan. The company was only one year in existence when it suffered its first and only fatal accident.

Throughout 1958 and 1959 in excess of thirty Piper aircraft were brought to Dublin, assembled and prepared for sale by Iona. Thirteen appeared on the Irish register with a similar number that were not registered here. However, they were kitted out by Iona with spray gear that was prepared at the Iona Engineering Works at Cross Guns Bridge and the aircraft were ferried to Egypt for use in locust control work.

On 14 January 1960 Irish Air Charters Limited announced their intention to move their operations from Dublin to Kidlington, Oxfordshire. Being Piper agents for Britain and Ireland, the company decided to relocate after the British government removed its import restrictions. In England they changed the company name to Vigors Aviation Limited, after acquiring the Oxford Flying Club. This company later evolved into CSE at Kidlington. (The initials for the name CSE Aviation are the initials of the surnames of the founder members - Channon, Svejdar and Erlanger).

At the time of transfer of the company they had three aircraft registered to them on their books. The two Piper PA-24 Comanche's, EI-AKV and EI-AKW, were cancelled on 18 January 1960 and 16 January 1960 respectively, both aircraft going to England and registered to Vigors Aviation Limited. EI-AKV became G-APZF and EI-AKW became G-APZG. EI-AKY, a Piper PA-22 Tripacer, was re-registered to Lady Antonia Wardell on 22 January 1960. It went to England in February 1962 as G-ARXK, but crashed in the sea off Alderney, Channel Islands on 26 August 1966. During the three years Irish Air Charters were located at Dublin airport, they helped to establish Iona as a formidable company dealing in light aviation in Ireland. The new Piper agents for Ireland, Wardell and Company, held a demonstration at the Iona hangar in June 1961, at which two Aztecs, two Comanches, a Cherokee, a Colt and a Super Cub were on view.

Two ex-Aer Lingus DC3s, Wigeon helicopter, G-APTE, and Skycraft Rapide, EI-AKH, at Iona ramp, November 1960, prior to arrival of clubhouse

Photograph courtesy Paul Duffy

A close-up photograph of the Shamrock Helicopters' Westland Widgeon helicopter, G-APTE, based at the Iona ramp

Photograph courtesy Paul Duffy

Pearse, in overalls, stands beside a former Silver City DC3 in November 1960

Photograph courtesy Paul Duffy

A selection of Piper aircraft on display, for demonstration purposes, in front of the Iona hangar in June 1961. The caravan in the background, served as a clubhouse. Company name now on hangar doors.

Photograph courtesy Paul Duffy

For two and a half months during the winter of 1960-61, Iona were hosts to three Douglas DC3s (EI-ACG, EI-ACI (*IX) and EI-ACT) in the colours of Silver City Airways and bearing their original Aer Lingus registrations. Silver City Airways required them for an oil support contract in Libya. On completion of the contract work in October and November 1960 the three aircraft were returned to Dublin and parked on the Iona ramp pending their disposal. On 2 January 1961 they were registered to Benedar Air Limited as EI-ALR (EI-ACG), EI-ALS (EI-ACI) and EI-ALT (EI-ACT) to facilitate ferry flights to France following sale to Aeronavale (French Navy).

At the same time as this maintenance work was carried out by Iona, for Aircraft Associates Limited

While based at the Iona ramp, Arthur Wignall performed many roles for Iona. He is photographed above in later years in his popular role as one of Ireland's leading aerobatic pilots.

Photograph courtesy Paul Duffy

and Irish Air Charters Limited, another charter company was providing important maintenance revenue for Iona. On 4 November 1958 a new company called Skycraft Services Limited was formed by Jocelyn (Josh) Yates whose main purpose was as an aircraft operator, performing a variety of aviation functions. They were a subsidiary of a British operator, Air Condor. Its first aircraft was an Auster 5, purchased in France as F-BIAU. It was delivered to Dublin airport 9 December 1958 and was placed on the Irish Register, 2 January 1959, as EI-AKN. In March 1959, Arthur Wignall joined the company as a pilot. Roles performed by Arthur included banner-towing, pleasure flights, bog surveys, aerial photography, press photographers missions, and food drops by parachute to stranded islanders. Business was flourishing and on 8 April 1959, Arthur Wignall collected a Rapide 6, G-AKSE from Eastleigh. It was registered EI-AKH on 14 May 1959. The company then employed another pilot, Bill Howarth. Both these pilots stayed at the local *Boot Inn* and their office was a caravan adjacent to the pub. While EI-AKN went for a lengthy maintenance check, the lease of another Auster, G-AKXP, was necessary. This was required for a few weeks.

On 11 November 1959, Skycraft acquired, on a three-month lease, the prototype of a Bristol Freighter, G-AGPV. Part of the lease agreement

FOOTNOTE (*ix)
EI-ACI was involved in the D-Day landings in Normandy on 6 June 1944. It was attached to the USAAF`s 313rd Troop Carrier Group as a C-47 and was based at Folkingham, Lincolnshire. After crossing the French coast they came under intense ground fire sustaining numerous hits, resulting in several casualties aboard. The paratroops baled out over the designated Drop Zone and the aircraft limped back to base. On 14 December 1945 Aer Lingus acquired the war surplus C-47, along with 8 others, and it served with the airline until it was leased to Silver City Airways from 11 March 1959 until 3 November 1960. Cancelled by Aer Lingus 2 December 1960 and registered to Benedar Air Limited as EI-ALS on 2 January 1961. Further details in *Irish Air Letter*, issue 354, June 2004.

included the provision of Brian Dicker as pilot. During this period Skycraft earned a lucrative contract from the Wild Fowl Trust to conduct a wildfowl survey throughout Scotland and the west of Ireland. This survey necessitated the lease of yet another aircraft, a J5L Aiglet, G-AOFS, on 24 November 1959. Four days later it was damaged at Rosses Point, County Sligo and brought to Rearsby, Leicestershire for repairs. In January 1960 the Rapide, EI-AKH, required substantial overhaul at the Iona facility, necessitating it being out of service for several months. Its temporary replacement was another Rapide, G-AHLF that proved to be in poor condition and was hurriedly replaced by Rapide G-ALBA for one month. On 27 April 1960, G-AOFS was returned to Dublin and registered to Skycraft Services as EI-ALN. Skycraft were losing business in early 1960; the freight business was not

Auster Aiglet, EI-ALN, operated by Skycraft Services during the summer 1960. The pilots included Bill Howarth and Arthur Wignall

Photograph courtesy Paul Duffy

materialising as planned and some aircraft, particularly Rapide EI-AKH were out of service for particularly lengthy periods. On 9 September 1960, Auster EI-AKN was sold to J. Lanigan-Ryan and Jimmy Chadwick in Borrisoleigh, County Tipperary. The following day Arthur Wignall finished flying for Skycraft to take up employment with Aer Lingus. Shortly afterwards Bill Howarth joined him. The Rapide, EI-AKH was sold to England and restored to its original marks, G-AKSE. The remaining Aiglet, EI-ALN, was also sold to England and restored to its previous registration, G-AOFS, in March 1961. Thus ended the term of another operator at Dublin airport. Iona's involvement with this company was

extensive, providing the ongoing maintenance as it did simultaneously with Irish Air Charters. Iona proved they could handle maintenance for a wide variety of aircraft types.

A number of years lapsed before Pearse Cahill made his next purchase of an aircraft since his venture with the Chipmunks. On 14 March 1961 an Avro 643 Cadet, G-ACIH, was registered to Pearse

Avro 643 Cadet, G-ACIH, (later EI-ALU) photographed at Newtownards, Co. Down, prior to acquisition by Pearse in March 1961. This was his first aircraft purchased following his venture with Chipmunks

Photograph via Pearse Cahill collection

The remains of Percival Proctor, G-AHWO, languished for many years on the roof of the Crofton Airport (now Regency) Hotel. The aircraft was bought by Pearse and registered to him on 28 June 1961 as EI-ALY. It never flew in the marks

Photograph courtesy Liam Byrne via Ronny Vogt collection

as EI-ALU (see Table 11). This aircraft was delivered by truck from Newtownards, County Down. It never carried the marks EI-ALU. Another vintage aircraft purchased by Pearse in 1961 was a Percival Proctor 5. It was formerly G-AHWO registered on 31 July 1946. On 5 May 1959 it made a heavy landing in Northern Ireland, breaking its main wing spar. It never flew again. Though registered to Pearse as EI-ALY on 28 June 1961, it never took up its Irish marks (see Table 12). The fuselage was mounted on the roof of the Crofton Airport (now Regency) Hotel, Whitehall, Dublin and the engine was used by the Institute for Industrial Research and Standards to power a wind tunnel.

Pearse maintained his contacts with the Piper organisation. He purchased a Piper PA22 Tripacer 160, with United States marks N9239D. He registered it in the name of Iona Garage & Engineering Works Limited as EI-AMJ on 7 June 1962 (see Table 13). The aircraft was intended to get Iona back into the air taxi and charter business, and at the same time do some instruction work. However, Iona sold the aircraft two months later to Carlisle Trust Ltd.

Iona replaced EI-AMJ with another PA22 Tripacer 160, also imported from the United States, N8931D. It was air freighted by Pan American DC-7F to Heathrow and onwards to Shannon on 22 August 1962 and registered to Iona Garage & Engineering

Iona replaced Piper PA-22 Tripacer, EI-AMJ with similar PA160 Tripacer, EI-AMS, that joined Iona in September 1962 for pilot training, before moving on two years later to Coonagh, Limerick

Photograph courtesy George Flood

Works Limited, as EI-AMS on 31 August 1962 (see Table 14). On 22 May 1963, Pearse brought EI-AMS to Rotterdam to take part in the *'Rotterdam Rally.'* EI-AMS was to be the only aircraft working directly for Iona for some time, as it was to be two years before a further aircraft was added to Iona's books. Pearse enjoyed the Rally so much he decided to enter the following year, flying over on 6 May 1964. On one of Pearse's visits to Rotterdam, he stopped off at Arnhem, Holland, en route to celebrate the founding of the Dutch Aero Club. They were the only foreign registered aircraft to stop at Arnhem. For the occasion, Pearse brought with him Arthur Wignall and Tom Farrington. Following a dinner reception they sampled some of the local night club life. Pearse returned home to Dublin with some broken ribs. His version of events is that he fell in the bath. Paint your own picture!

On 22 June 1962, the newly formed company, Aer Turas Teoranta, took delivery of its first aircraft. It was a deHavilland dH89A Rapide, and arrived at Dublin airport in its UK marks, G-AKPA. On 15 June 1962 it had been registered to F. J. Connolly as EI-AML and on 11 September 1962

The first Piper aircraft purchased by Iona was Tripacer, EI-AMJ. It remained with Iona for two months during summer 1962

Photograph courtesy Paul Cunniffe

it was registered to Aer Turas Teoranta. This particular aircraft remained with Aer Turas for two years and was cancelled on 19 June 1964 to become F-BLHZ, later to go to USA as N89DH. The initial Aer Turas fleet were located at the Iona ramp and were maintained by Iona engineers, thus adding another fledgling airline to its portfolio of maintenance contracts. Aer Turas purchased Douglas C-47, EI-ANK, in March 1964 and this aircraft was also parked at the Iona ramp. In 1965 attempts were made to lease Viscounts, but these fell through and a DC-4, EI-AOR, was acquired from Air France instead. This aircraft was unfortunately shot down by rebel gunfire over Mozambique on 26 November 1977, many years after leaving Dublin airport. In 1966 Aer Turas acquired two Bristol 170s, EI-APC and EI-APM.

The first aircraft registered to Aer Turas was Rapide EI-AML. This aircraft was hangared at Iona and maintained by Iona engineers.
Photographed 25 May 1963.

Photograph courtesy George Flood

On Monday evening, 12 June 1967, EI-APM was returning empty from Prestwick, Scotland. On board was the pilot, a Canadian, Gordon Willis and co-pilot Percy Maynard, from Templeogue, Dublin. The evening rush hour was over at Collinstown and the Bristol Freighter was attempting an overshoot on runway 17 when they suffered an engine failure, sending the aircraft crashing into the Shell administration building at the southeast corner of the airfield. It burst into flames immediately making an attempt to rescue the crew impossible. Both perished in the crash. Sadly, this accident brought the airport's 27-year-old record of no fatal accidents to an end. (Tragically, ten days

after this accident, Aer Lingus Viscount, EI-AOF, *St. Cathal,* on a training detail from Dublin airport crashed near Ashbourne, County Meath killing the instructor pilot and both student pilots).

Iona was to change to a different type of aircraft for flying instruction. An Auster J/1 Autocrat was based at Cork. As a consequence of repair work, following damage during a storm in Cork, it was later acquired by Iona and registered EI-AMK to Iona Garage & Engineering Works Limited on 9 October 1964 (see Table 15). As this aircraft was to be used for flight training, for administration purposes, it was transferred to the Irish Aero Club on 11 October 1966.

Irish Air Charters Limited was Irish agent for Piper until their relocation to England in January 1960. It was three years before Pegasus Aviation Limited commenced operations in September 1963, as an air-taxi operator, when they took delivery of the Apache G-APCL. It was registered to them as EI-ANI on 12 December 1963. They retained the aircraft for over a year and it was returned to the British register on 14 December 1964 using its original marks G-APCL. Pegasus took up residency in the Iona hangar. On 13 October 1964 a new Cessna 172F was registered to them as EI-ANS, and delivered on 21 October 1964. Pegasus then acquired the Cessna agency for Ireland. EI-ANS was retained for almost two years until its cancellation on 16 June 1966 on sale to the United Kingdom as G-ATWJ. On 16 October 1965 they took possession of a Cessna 310B, G-ARIG, placed on the Irish register on 1 November 1965 in their name as EI-AOS. The 310B was cancelled from the register on 1 November 1966 on sale to UK following the demise of Pegasus. Could Iona survive where previous operators at the Iona ramp had failed in the ten years since the Cahills had relocated to Collinstown from Cross Guns Bridge?

The Cahill family received a blow in 1961 with the murder of Henry Cahill, (brother of Hugh Cahill) which prompted a review among a series of articles titled 'Unsolved Murders.' The *Evening Herald,* Monday, 18 January 1971 bore a heading '*An old man is clubbed to death – and the killer walks away with*

£10.' The Head of the Technical Bureau and Murder Investigation Squad, Detective Supt. Patrick McLoughlin referred to the case when he spoke at a symposium in 1967 on unexplained deaths. (Detective Supt. McLoughlin later became Commissioner of An Garda Siochana). The following is a synopsis of his talk:

The three aircraft operated by Pegasus Aviation Limited that were based at Iona between September 1963 and November 1966 were: (top) Piper PA-23 Apache 150, EI-ANI; (middle) Cessna F.172F, EI-ANS and (bottom) Cessna 310B, EI-AOS

Photographs courtesy Paul Duffy

'At 3 o'clock on the morning of 9 April 1961 a motorist called for petrol at the Iona garage in Glasnevin and was supplied by the attendant and night watchman, Henry Cahill, who was aged 68. A customer called to the garage the following morning and found Mr. Cahill lying in a pool of blood. Mr. Cahill walked to the ambulance, but later collapsed into a coma and died the following day. A post mortem by Professor Maurice Hickey established he had been severely beaten. Later, it was discovered £10 had been stolen. Many witnesses referred to a white Volkswagen car. This lead was checked out but to no avail. It appears Gardai were led astray by the mother of one of the suspects rounded up who said he had been in England for several weeks. It transpired some time later that he departed hurriedly on the morning of the slaying. Subsequently, a prisoner in Pentonville Prison confessed to a fellow prisoner that he had murdered Mr. Cahill, but vehemently denied this to detectives who interviewed him. Evidence pointed to him, unfortunately too great a period had elapsed between the murder and the examination of his clothing to establish if the blood was of the same type as Mr. Cahill's. Another killer escaped. In summing up at the symposium, Detective Supt. McLoughlin admitted *attention to detail, to the unguarded remark, and the minor slip were the basic essentials of good investigation because it was the small things that really solve cases.'*

Hugh Cahill died following a heart attack, in his 84th year, on 13 March 1966 – five days after Nelson's pillar was blown up in O'Connell Street, Dublin. His wife continued to reside at Prospect Villa until she vacated the house following the sale of the engineering works in 1974. The engineering works premises were later acquired by Hedigans, the proprietors of the *Brian Boru* public house, who demolished the vacant building to extend the car park. The family home, at the rear of the car park, where Pearse and his siblings were born and reared, still stands in ruin in 2004. Since 1928, the Cahill family had been frequent visitors to the seaside town of Skerries. In 1944 they purchased a new house on the Rush Road. The Cahills used the house for many years as a summer holiday house. In 1974, following sale of the engineering works at Cross Guns Bridge, Caroline moved to the Skerries house. In 1980, having reared their family, Pearse and Constance moved in with Caroline, to care for her in her twilight years. Caroline Cahill died in her 91st year on 16 May 1985. She is buried in Glasnevin Cemetery along with her husband, Hugh, and his brother, Henry, who predeceased him on 8 April 1961. Ironically, Hugh Cahill's death occurred six months following that of Colonel James C. Fitzmaurice, on 26 September 1965, and their graves are only a few yards apart. It was

Fitzmaurice's epic flight in the *Bremen* in 1928 that inspired Hugh Cahill to pusue his aspirations for commercial aviation in Ireland.

Pearse and Constance remained in the 'White House,' on the Rush Road in Skerries. Sadly, Constance died in St. Francis Hospice, Raheny, Dublin, on 27 January 1998, aged 78 years.

TABLE 6

Registration	EI-AJC
Aircraft Type	de Havilland DHC-1 Chipmunk Mk 22
Constructors Serial Number	C1 - 0061
Place & Year of Manufacture	Broughton, 1950
Previous Registrations	Royal Air Force, WB620
Registered to	Matthew P. Cahill, 21 July 1956
Delivery date	28 August 1956
Remarks	WB620 was delivered to 11 R.F.S. Perth on 3 April 1950. At time of purchase by Pearse Cahill this aircraft was lying at 10 Maintenance Unit, Hullavington, Chippenham, Wiltshire.

It was exchanged with EI-AJA to Desmond Hogan, Stoneyhurst, Sutton, Co. Dublin on 23 May 1957. Later cancelled on 25 September 1961 by Hogan and sold as G-ARTP. Delivered to England 21 October 1961, wearing both Irish and English registrations with the name *Alvin* inscribed on it. Later re-sold to Ireland as EI-AMH and registered on 19 April 1962 to J. H. F. Kenny. On 12 November 1964, it returned to the UK register as G-ARTP. It again returned to Ireland as Irish Air Corps serial number 200, registered to them 26 February 1965. On 24 April 1980 it crashed during a training flight at Gormanstown, Co. Meath, killing both crew. This was the first fatal crash of an Air Corps Chipmunk in twenty-five years of service.

TABLE 7

Registration	EI-AJD
Aircraft Type	de Havilland DHC-1 Chipmunk (Mk T10) Series 22
Constructors Serial Number	C1- 0072
Place & Year of Manufacture	Hatfield, 1950
Previous Registrations	Royal Air Force, WB630
Registered to	Matthew P. Cahill, 21 July 1956
Delivery date	28 August 1956
Remarks	WB630 was delivered to 18 Reserve Flying Services (R.F.S.) Fairoaks on 22 May 1950. At time of purchase by Pearse Cahill this aircraft was lying at 10 Maintenance Unit, Hullavington, Chippenham, Wiltshire, about twelve miles south east of Chalford.

On 31 January 1958 EI-AJD was registered to Robert Magill, 'The Moorings', Castlepark Road, Sandycove, Dublin and based at Weston. On 7 October 1958 it was flown to Liverpool and cancelled from the Irish register on 21 October 1958. It was not registered in the UK, but was resold to Australia in January 1959 as VH-BWD, subsequently as VH-BWE. On 9 January 1960 it struck a pole and overturned at Parafield, South Australia.

TABLE 8

Registration	EI-AJE
Aircraft Type	de Havilland DHC-1 Chipmunk, (Mk T10) Series 22
Constructors Serial Number	C1 - 0214
Place & Year of Manufacture	Broughton, 1950
Previous Registrations	Royal Air Force, WB764
Registered to	Matthew P. Cahill, 21 July 1956
Delivery date	21 September 1956
Remarks	WB764 was delivered to 24 R.F.S. Rochester on 12 December 1950 and withdrawn from active service 24 August 1953. At time of purchase by Pearse Cahill this aircraft was lying at No. 22 Maintenance Unit, Silloth, Carlisle, Cumberland.
	EI-AJE was cancelled from the Irish register on 29 September 1958 and registered as G-APPK on 8 October 1958 to Saxon (Welders and Machinists) Limited, Rhoose (south of Cardiff, Wales) and based at a strip near Bridgend. Delivered 27 August 1959 to Squires Gate and cancelled 28 September 1959. Restored to G-APPK 10 February 1960 to Air Navigation & Trading Co. Limited; on 14 February 1962 to Surrey and Kent Flying Club Limited, Biggin Hill; on 13 July 1972 to P. R. Spencer, Stapleford. Following sale to the USA as N4998T, it was purchased by Jo Brewer, Green Valley Aviation Inc., Everett, north of Seattle, Washington. It was dismantled at Stapleford on 10 May 1977 and shipped from Tilbury to Seattle on board the *California Star* on 7 June 1977. Cancelled from the UK register on 12 September 1977. It transferred ownership several times in USA. It was current early 2004 under the ownership of Faith Kent, Tulsa, Oklahoma.

TABLE 9

Registration	EI-AJF
Aircraft Type	de Havilland DHC-1 Chipmunk Mk T10
Constructors Serial Number	C1- 0277
Place & Year of Manufacture	Broughton, 1951
Previous Registrations	Royal Air Force, WD336
Registered to	Matthew P. Cahill, 16 July 1956
Delivery date	28 August 1956
Remarks	WD336 was delivered to 23 R.F.S. Usworth on 15 February 1951. At time of purchase by Pearse Cahill this aircraft was lying at No. 20 Maintenance Unit, Aston Down, Chalford, Stroud, Glostershire, near the mouth of the River Severn, separating Wales from England.
	EI-AJF was delivered Dublin-Prestwick-Perth on 7 July 1960 and was cancelled from the Irish register on 18 July 1960 when sold and registered as G-ARCR to Airwork Services Limited, Perth, Scotland on 26 August 1960 - the same destination as EI-AJA two years previously. It was written-off 2 September 1973 following a crash at Windlesham, Surrey.

TABLE 10

Registration	EI-AJA
Aircraft Type	de Havilland DHC-1 Chipmunk Series 22
Constructors Serial Number	C1 - 0078
Place & Year of Manufacture	Broughton, 1950
Previous Registrations	Royal Air Force, WB632
Registered to	Matthew P. Cahill, 8 March 1958
Delivery date	22 June 1956
Remarks	Delivered 30 May 1950 to 18 R.F.S., Fairoaks. It was struck off RAF charge 26 June 1956 on sale to Aero Club of Ireland Ltd. Registered 31 May 1956 to Desmond Hogan, Aero Club of Ireland, Weston Aerodrome, and delivered to him 22 June 1956. Certificate of Airworthiness completed by Pearse Cahill and transferred to Pearse 8 March 1958.
	One month later, on 15 April 1958, it was ferried via Nutts Corner, Belfast, to Perth, Scotland. It was cancelled from the Irish register on 17 April 1958 and sold in Scotland as G-APMW, being registered to Airwork Services Limited, Perth on 12 May 1958. On 27 June 1962 it struck a tree and crashed at Bishopshall Farm, Stanley, Perthshire, killing both occupants while on a training flight. UK registration cancelled 6 August 1962.

TABLE 11

Registration	EI-ALU
Aircraft Type	Avro 643 Cadet
Constructors Serial Number	657
Place & Year of Manufacture	Newtown Heath,
Previous Registrations	G-ACIH
Registered to	Matthew P. Cahill, 14 March 1961
Remarks	It was originally registered as G-ACIH to Midland and Scottish Air Ferries Limited, Renfrew near Glasgow on 9 March 1934. In November 1938 it was registered to Northern Ireland Aero Club, Newtownards, Co. Down. During the War it was immobilised by filling its fuel tanks with sand. Pearse acquired it in Monaghan and it was transported by road to the engineering works at the rear of the *Brian Boru* public house, Cross Guns Bridge. It later was moved to Dublin airport where some restoration work was carried out. Though some work was done in that regard it was not completed and was moved to Newcastle, County Wicklow for storage. In 1999 it moved to the United Kingdom for further restoration work by Avro Trust, Barton.

TABLE 12

Registration	EI-ALY
Aircraft Type	Percival P.44 Proctor 5
Constructors Serial Number	AE 72
Place & Year of Manufacture	Luton, 1946
Previous Registrations	G-AHWO
Registered to	Matthew P. Cahill, 28 June 1961
Remarks	G-AHWO was registered on 31 July 1946. On 5 May 1959 it made a heavy landing at Aldergrove airport, breaking its main wing spar. It never flew again. Though registered to Pearse as EI-ALY on 28 June 1961, it never took up its Irish marks. The fuselage was mounted on the roof of the Crofton Airport (now Regency) Hotel, Whitehall, Dublin and the engine was used by the Institute for Industrial Research and Standards to power a wind tunnel. It was cancelled from the register 15 February 1966. It is now in a museum at Dromad, Co. Leitrim where Philip Bedford hopes to restore it.

TABLE 13

Registration	EI-AMJ
Aircraft Type	Piper PA22 Tripacer 160
Constructors Serial Number	22-6299
Place & Year of Manufacture	Lock Haven, 1958
Previous Registrations	N9239D
Registered to	Iona Garage & Engineering Works Ltd 7 June 1962
Delivery date	9 June 1962
Remarks	On 9 June 1962 it was air freighted to Shannon airport in a crate from United States of America. Pearse assembled it at Shannon and it was flown to Dublin. Two months later, on 30 August 1962, it was registered to Carlisle Trust Limited-owned by John Byrne. Following an accident at Kilflynn near Tralee, County Kerry on 30 May 1964 it was destroyed and removed from the register on 23 June 1964.

TABLE 14

Registration	EI-AMS
Aircraft Type	Piper PA22-160 Tripacer
Constructors Serial Number	22-6089
Place & Year of Manufacture	Lock Haven, 1958
Previous Registrations	N8931D
Registered to	Iona Garage & Engineering Works Ltd 31 August 1962
Delivery date	3 September 1962

Remarks

It was air freighted by Pan American DC-7F to Heathrow and onwards to Shannon on 22 August 1962. It was assembled at Shannon and there it was test flown by Pearse at 18.00 hours on 3 September 1962. 40 minutes later he ferried it to Dublin in a flight time of one hour thirty minutes.

On 13 November 1964 Iona sold the Tripacer EI-AMS to Shannon Flying Services Limited, Coonagh, Limerick. EI-AMS returned to Dublin where it was registered to Setanta Flying Group, Weston on 23 November 1973. It was transferred to Commander Aircraft Sales (Ireland) Limited on 24 June 1974 and was back again in the Shannon area. It was 'written-off' following a fatal crash at Dundalk, Co. Louth on 9 March 1975 and removed from the register 16 May 1979.

TABLE 15

Registration	EI-AMK
Aircraft Type	Auster 5 Series J/1 Autocrat
Constructors Serial Number	1838
Place & Year of Manufacture	Taylorcraft Aeroplanes, Rearsby, 1945
Previous Registrations	G-AGTV on 2 October 1945
Registered to	Iona Garage and Engineering Works Ltd, 9 October 1964
Registered to	Irish Aero Club Ltd, 11 October 1966
Remarks	On 5 February 1962 it arrived at Cork, where it suffered damage during a storm in April 1962. Following repair by Iona, this all-white aircraft was placed on the Irish register to Ronald F. Rohu, Cork, on 19 September 1962 as EI-AMK. It was subsequently acquired by Iona.

EI-AMK suffered engine failure and force landed near Birr, Co. Offaly on 1 June 1979. Never flew again and stored in Iona hangar. It was listed for sale by the Liquidator but not sold at auction. Pearse later donated it to the Irish Air Corps for use in their museum. On 17 September 2002, the 57-year-old aircraft was registered to John J. Sullivan, Gorey, Co. Wexford, as a possible restoration project.

Chapter

5

THE CESSNA–IONA MARRIAGE

*The creation of a relationship with Cessna
leading to the development of commercial aviation
services and activities*

Chapter Five

THE CESSNA–
IONA MARRIAGE

Early in 1964 Pearse Cahill travelled to the United States of America on a working holiday. Johnny Maher, a long time friend of Pearse and then Out-Station Manager with Aer Lingus, contacted the New York office of Aer Lingus advising them of Pearse's impending visit across the Atlantic. The New York office made arrangements for Pearse to be brought to many of the airfields in the area to see how they operated. Among the places he was shown were Long Island, New Jersey and Teterboro. It was at the latter location he met with representatives of Teterboro Aviation, that were the main Cessna dealers in New York. He was very impressed with the way Cessna operated; so impressed that he purchased a Cessna 150E, N2125J, which was to be delivered to Ireland the following year. In 1964 Cessna offered the high wing, two seater 150E in three classes; (i) standard at US$7,825; (ii) trainer at US$8,925; and (iii) inter-city commuter at US$9,425. While enjoying a swim at Jone's Beach, Pearse was caught unawares by a freak hurricane and was thrown from the water onto the beach, the fall resulting in Pearse coming home a week early with a broken shoulder and a long tale to tell the folks at home!

The Cessna 150E was shipped to Shannon in a crate and was road transported by Coras Iompair Eireann (C.I.E.) to the Iona hangar at Dublin airport, where it was assembled. On 30 April 1965 it was placed on the register to Iona Garage & Engineering Works Limited as EI-AOO and made its first flight on 20 May 1965 (see Table 16). EI-AOO holds the distinction of being the first of a long line of the Cessna 150 family to grace the Irish register for many years to come.

The first Cessna 150 came off the production line in September 1957. Ironically, also on the day of the test flight of EI-AOO at Dublin airport, the European representatives of the Cessna Aircraft Corporation, based in Brussels, visited the Iona hangar to meet Pegasus Aviation. They were surprised to find EI-AOO in the hangar and equally astonished to learn that Pegasus Aviation had not supplied the aircraft to Pearse. The representatives were even more impressed with Pearse when he placed an order on the spot with them for delivery of two Cessna aircraft. Pegasus ceased operations in October 1966 and Pearse was offered the Cessna agency for Ireland. So, after a whirlwind romance and short courtship, a marriage took place that was to last for almost three decades. With Thompson Boyes acting as Iona's first Chief Flying Instructor, EI-AOO became a regular feature of the Dublin circuit. The instructional flying rate was the princely sum of £5.10.0 per hour.

The first Cessna 150 on the Irish register, EI-AOO, arrived in Ireland in crates. It is shown above in Iona hangar prior to assembly in May 1965

Photograph courtesy Paul Duffy

EI-AOO, was to have a long life in Ireland, used as a basic trainer aircraft for 25 years following its acquisition by Iona in May 1965

Photograph courtesy George Flood

Clyde Cessna flying his second airplane, 'Silver Wings' in early spring 1912

Photograph courtesy Cessna Corporation

CESSNA AIRCRAFT COMPANY

Clyde Cessna was born in Iowa in 1880 and moved to Kansas with his family when he was one year old. Clyde showed an aptitude for mechanics from an early age and by 16 years of age he was repairing local farm machinery. Through this he progressed to motor repairs. On 11 February 1911 an air circus took place at Oklahoma City, so Clyde decided to see at first hand what these bird-like devices looked like. He was attracted to a Bleroit monoplane. Thereafter he set about building his first airplane. The wings were of spruce and the covering was made from the finest Irish linen – the first connection between Cessna and Ireland! The first test flight of this aircraft took place in May 1911. Firstly, Clyde had to learn to fly. On his first attempt the aircraft ground-looped, yet it was to be his 13th attempt before the wheels left the ground. His second aircraft was called 'Silver Wings.' Each year an improved model was produced and in the fall of 1916 Cessna moved to Wichita to commence aircraft production. From the end of World War One to 1925, Clyde Cessna returned to farming.

Early in 1925 Walter Beech and Lloyd Sterman, who had both just left the Swallow Airplane Company, approached Clyde with an offer to head up a new aircraft manufacturing company they were forming, to be called Travel Air Manufacturing Company. Clyde stayed with this company until he sold his share to Beech in April 1927. By now Cessna was determined to design

and build a new cabin monoplane – along the lines of a model built by a Dutchman he read about called Fokker. He obtained financial backing from a Mr. Roos and the Cessna-Roos Aircraft Company was formed on 8 September 1927. Roos sold his share to Clyde and the company name was changed to Cessna Aircraft Company on 31 December 1927. The cantilever wing developed by Cessna could support the weight of 17 men. Certification eventually followed and in February 1929 he entered a contract to supply the Curtis Flying Services with all the aircraft he could manufacture.

Clyde Cessna arranged for 17 men to stand on the wing to emphasize to the public the strength of the new cantilever wing

Photograph courtesy Cessna Corporation

New factory premises with assembly lines were constructed and production had increased to 18 per month. The 'Wall Street Crash' occurred on 29 October 1929 and Curtis went bankrupt. Cessna's own Board of Directors voted to close the Cessna plant. Clyde was heartbroken. Aircraft racing was popularized in the 1920's and 1930's and Clyde soon earned a reputation for building fast and efficient aircraft, including retractable undercarriage for the first time in 1932. In Chicago in 1933, Johnny Livingston created a new World Speed Record for aircraft under 500 cubic inch displacement when he reached a speed of 242.35 miles per hour in Clyde's latest model.

Walter Beech formed the Beech Aircraft Corporation in 1932 and hired a portion of the Cessna plant to start his business. In 1934 Cessna returned to aircraft manufacturing and within a year he produced his first aircraft to incorporate wing flaps. Clyde Cessna resigned from the company on 8 October 1936, age 55 years, to return to farming. In 1954 Clyde died at the age of 74, active and alert almost to the last minute.

During the summer of 1938 the Cessna Company examined twin-engine aircraft and their first production, the Cessna T-50, had its maiden flight on 26 March 1939. The US Army expressed interest and ordered 33 models. Likewise, the Canadian Government placed an order for 180 military versions of the T-50. In May 1940 a 25,000 square foot assembly building was added. Employment increased from 200 persons in July 1940 to 1,900 in May 1941. Buildings totalled 360,000 square feet. Between 1940 and 1943, 5,402 versions of the T-50, mostly military, were manufactured. In April 1942 Cessna received an order from the US Government for 750 troop-carrying gliders destined for Europe. At the peak of the War effort, Cessna employed 6,074 persons. By war end it dropped to 450 persons.

As war drew to a close, Cessna returned to civilian aircraft production. A *'Family Car of the Air'* was the next project, resulting in the 4-seater Model 190, with the prototype making its maiden flight on 7 December 1944. Based on the T-50, it had all metal wings and tail surfaces and was Cessna's first use of the spring steel landing gear. Cessna realized the rapidly developing market for 2-seater deluxe aircraft and the prototype of the Model 140 made its first flight on 28 June 1945. A 'stripped down' version for pilot training was the Model 120. Both models were an immediate success and production spiralled upward by autumn 1946. Employment later dropped back to 1,873. At the same time a 5-seater version went into production in July 1947 as

the Model 195. The market for 2-seater aircraft soon filled up and Cessna turned their attention to the business market and designed the 4-seat Model 170 in 1948, with a top speed of 140 mph. 729 such aircraft were built that year.

Cessna diversified into non-aircraft business, mostly for farm machinery. They received a contract from the US Air Force in 1947 to produce aluminium and wood furniture for use in overseas Air Force Bases. From 1945 to 1950 many companies tried and failed in the commercial aircraft production business. Cessna was one of the few to survive. During the following five years to 1955 Cessna re-entered the military production. The USAF required an aircraft to do Artic rescue work in Alaska. The Cessna Model 195 was selected to perform the task and 20 units were ordered and re-configured for military use as the LC-126 series. In the Spring of 1952, 63 similar machines were ordered. A 2-seater Model 305 entered production and its maiden flight was in December 1949. The USAF for combat use in Korea also took these by January 1951 as Model L-19. This was later modified to become the world's first turbo-prop light plane, setting an altitude record of 37,063 feet for aircraft in this category on 16 July 1953. Another of its features was its large wing flaps. The commercial version with the improved wing flaps was the 1952 Model 170B. Also in 1952, Cessna produced an aircraft to meet the demand of an enhanced 4-seater single aircraft, which, for the first time since 1927, featured the square-tail. This new aircraft had its maiden flight in January 1952 as the Model 180.

In the summer of 1953, Cessna produced a Model A195, incorporating a spinner, enlarged wing flaps and altered elevators. This enhanced model was to replace the Model 190. 1954 to 1960 produced the years of greatest expansion for Cessna. Still working closely with the US military they designed a light twin-engine airplane, the Model 310, prototype of which first flew 3 January 1953; 200 of which were produced in each year 1955 and 1956. In December 1953 Cessna were successful in a competition by the USAF to design a jet trainer. The Model 318 (military version XT-37) was the chosen project. On the commercial side the Model 170B continued to be Cessna's leading seller from 1952 to 1956, however customers were clamouring for a tricycle landing gear. To satisfy this need the Model 172, featuring the square tail, was developed in 1955 and placed into production in 1956 with sales of 1,178 that year. In 1958 this was supplemented with a higher horsepower Continental engine version called the Model 175, and adding an exterior baggage door, filled the gap between the 170 and 180 series. Following the success of the tricycle gear on the Model 172, Cessna modified the 180 series to incorporate this tricycle landing gear and called it the Model 182. A deluxe version called the 'Skylane' was offered in 1958.

The Cessna 172 started production as a 1956 model. It was the same as the model 170B except for the tricycle landing gear and new square tail.

Photograph courtesy Cessna Corporation

Since 1950, when the Model 140A was dropped from production, Cessna had not manufactured a two-seat airplane. By 1959, dealers were relying heavily on aging 140's for training. Cessna responded with a two-seat trainer, with tricycle landing gear, 100hp engine and high lift wing flaps. The Cessna 150 was developed and 719 models were delivered in 1959, its first year of production.

Cessna did not ignore corporate customers and in 1953 they designed an aircraft featuring the following qualities: all weather capabilities; pressurized and air-conditioned cabin; multi-engine safety; reasonable price, and 8 to 10 seater. After 3 years of development the four-engine

propeller driven, low wing Model 620 first flew on 11 August 1956. While indications were this was the aircraft Cessna expected, early price estimates of the new aircraft were not encouraging against a backdrop of new generation jet aircraft for the corporate market. The final cost analysis indicated the Model would be too expensive and with sad resignation, management cancelled the 620 programme in October 1957.

The Cessna 620 never went into production. It was powered with four 350 h.p. supercharged engines and had a top speed of 282 mph.

Photograph courtesy Cessna Corporation

Cessna ushered in the 1960's with a major exterior change – the swept tail on its range of 172A, 175A, 182 and 310 models. Cessna's first aircraft since the racing planes of 1933 to incorporate a retractable landing gear was produced in 1960 as the Model 210. This was novel to the industry for 4-seater single-engine aircraft. In August 1961, Cessna improved the Model 310 by supercharging it to produce the Model 320, 'Skynight', a twin-engine aircraft capable of reaching an altitude of 27,200 feet and with a top speed of 265 mph. Simultaneously the Model 185, 'Skywagon', capable of carrying 6 persons was produced in March 1961.

To diversify from fixed wing manufacturing Cessna spent nine years developing the 'Skyhook' two-seat helicopter that was certified in 1955. The US Army purchased ten such helicopters, one of which made history by climbing to 30,000 feet over Wichita. Further acquisitions and mergers saw Cessna become agents for Aircraft Radio

Corporation (ARC) on 1 February 1959, thus entering the military and commercial aviation electronics market. On 15 February 1960 they acquired a 49% stake in the Avions Max Holste plant in Reims, France for future aircraft production in Europe. In 1962 this company was renamed Reims Aviation. 1 August 1960 saw Cessna acquire McCauley Industrial Corporation, one of the leading manufacturers of light aircraft propellers. 1962 saw development of a novel design in that the engines are mounted in tandem; one in front and one at the rear of the fuselage. This was the Model 336 'Skymaster.' The Models 182E, 'Skylane' and 210B featured wider cabin, new rear windshield, electric wing flaps and new interior and exterior styling. The revamped 1962 Model 310G incorporated new canted wing-tip fuel tanks.

The first Iona Cessna 182 was an 'A' type, ferried from the USA and registered as EI-ANC to Iona in September 1965. Pearse had a client in UK for the aircraft and it only remained at Iona for a few weeks

Photograph courtesy Paul Duffy

Later in 1965, Pearse acquired a second-hand Cessna 182A from United States of America. On 25 September 1965 it was ferried across the Atlantic to Dublin bearing the United States registration, N6078B. In anticipation of its arrival it had been placed on the Irish register on 9 September 1965 as EI-ANC to Iona Garage and Engineering Works Limited (see Table 17).

The first of the two new Cessnas ordered from the Brussels representatives was a Cessna 172G. On 16 March 1966, (the day Pearse's father, Hugh, was laid to rest in Glasnevin cemetery), Arthur Wignall flew to Reims, France to facilitate its collection and Thompson Boyes ferried it to Dublin(*x). Arthur performed many ferry flights for Iona. The 172 was placed on the Irish register as EI-AOK in the name of Iona Garage and Engineering Works Limited on 14 March 1966 in anticipation of its arrival (see Table 18). On 29 March 1966 the Iona Cessna 172 was transferred to Irish Aero Club Limited for use

FOOTNOTE (*x)
The following extract was taken from *Break Out!*, published in 2004 and used here with kind permission of the author Paddy Hayes:-

Some years after Thompson Boyes left Iona he achieved uninvited international prominence. On 31 October 1973 he was in his second week of employment with Irish Helicopters and was pilot of their Alouette helicopter that was chartered to fly a client to County Laois for some aerial photography. On the ground at Stradbally a masked man placed a gun against his head. Boyes, a Protestant, had grown up in Newtownards, County Down and knew immediately that this was an IRA operation. The armed volunteer ordered him to follow the Royal canal into Dublin. Scared out of his wits, he obeyed. Approaching Dublin, Boyes was informed about the mission to lift three men from Mountjoy jail. He explained the extreme risks of taking off from the enclosed yard. They also had a full tank of fuel and he had not planned on four passengers. Dusk was falling as the helicopter approached the city centre jail. The eight prison officers on duty in the yard were overpowered as part of the escape plan and as the helicopter landed in the yard, amid dust and debris, senior Provisional IRA prisoners Kevin Mallon, J. B.(Joe) O'Hagan and ex-Chief of Staff Seamus Twomey, clambered aboard and with Twomey still half in and half out of the helicopter it rose slowly from the yard, rocking from side to side as Boyes tried to counteract the turbulence rebounding from the surrounding walls. Once free of the jail they headed for Baldoyle racecourse in north county Dublin where they landed six minutes later to be met by more IRA volunteers that had hi-jacked a taxi. They sped away leaving Thompson Boyes ashen faced and grateful to be alive. The *'Helicopter Song'* released by the Wolfe Tones was a number one chart hit for several weeks and the jail break grabbed headlines throughout the world. The escape was featured in a television programme broadcast on TG4 in April 2004 in conjunction with Paddy Haye's book.

Iona's first Chief Flying Instructor at Dublin Airport was Thompson Boyes. He later received international acclaim as the helicopter pilot hijacked by an armed volunteer to spring three leading IRA men from Mountjoy Prison on 31 October 1973

Photograph courtesy
Ronan Lee/RTE Archives

in training student pilots. See elsewhere in this publication for activities of the Irish Aero Club Limited. The second aircraft was Cessna 150F, EI-APF. (see Table 36). See also the section dealing with the Irish Aero Club.

January 1960 to Airwork Services Limited, Blackbushe. This was the first of its type in the UK and the only example in Ireland. Part of the sale of EI-AOD involved Iona acquiring EI-AND. On 19 February 1975 it was registered to Pearse Cahill (see Table 19). Subsequent owners were Alan and Mary Cooke. Alan Cooke and Michael Gray were both tragically killed when the aircraft crashed into the Irish Sea between north Wales and the Isle of Man, on 30 October 1994. It was routing Guernsey to Isle of Man following some maintenance work. The wreckage was located two miles north of

The first Cessna 175A to grace the Irish register was EI-AND. Originally registered to Dr. Colm Killeen and Terry Rowan. On 19 February 1975 it was transferred to Pearse Cahill. Photographed at Iona, 3 May 1974

Photograph courtesy Paul Cunniffe

The first new aircraft sold directly to a client was a Cessna 182J. It was built in Wichita and flown to New York. There the wings were removed and it was brought across the Atlantic on 8 June 1966 in the hold of a Pan American cargo airliner to Shannon. Pearse obtained the use of a lorry in Dublin and drove to Shannon, from there he returned with the aircraft to Dublin airport where he reassembled it. The radios and navigational equipment were installed by Colm Killeen in the few spares hours he had from his busy medical practice. It was registered to Terry Rowan and Dr. T. Colm Killeen on 13 June 1966 as EI-AOD. This was not the first Cessna owned by these two aviators. On 1 July 1963 a Cessna 175A, bearing registration G-APYA, was delivered to Dublin, and registered in both names on 29 August 1963 as EI-AND. It first entered the UK register on 25

Anglesey when it fouled the nets of a fishing trawler on 3 January 1995.

Sunday afternoon, 24 March 1968, marked the most tragic occasion in the history of Aer Lingus. The Viscount EI-AOM, *St. Felim*, on a scheduled flight from Cork to London, crashed into the sea near Tuskar Rock off the coast of County Wexford; fifty seven passengers and four crew members died in the tragedy. An array of shipping and aircraft took part in the search and rescue operation. Among them were Iona aircraft.

Iona's air taxi and charter work was somewhat hampered due to a rule that forbade single-engine over-water charter flights, which confined activities of this nature to within Ireland. A twin-engine aircraft was required. The first Cessna twin

Aer Lingus Viscount EI-AOM that crashed near Tuskar Rock on 24 March 1968. Iona aircraft were involved in the search and rescue operation.

Photograph courtesy Paul Duffy

to appear at Iona was owned by Paramount film director, James Clavell. During Summer 1968 he was in Ireland filming *Hijack*. He brought with him Cessna 337, N5384S and based it at the Iona Ramp. Terry Rowan, among others, flew it on missions for Mr. Clavell.

Iona were introduced to a twin-engine Cessna aircraft when Cessna 337, N5384S was based at Iona during Summer 1968

Photograph courtesy Paul Duffy

On 3 August 1968, a Cessna 310G, registration G-ARWF, suffered an undercarriage collapse on runway 17 at Dublin airport. The damaged aircraft was removed to the Iona hangar for investigation and subsequent repair. The aircraft was only six-

years-old, having been first registered on 9 March 1962. The Cessna 310s had first gone into production with Cessna in 1954. Its owners did a deal with Pearse, whereby Iona supplied the owners of G-ARWF with a new Cessna 310N. It was placed on the Irish register 2 September 1968 as EI-ATB to the Irish Aero Club and ferried from the United States on 9 September 1968 as N4154Q (see Table 20). It was only to be on the Irish register for a few weeks, as it was registered G-AWTA to Lowland Aero Services Ltd., Turnhouse on 8 November 1968. The above deal involved Iona retaining G-ARWF following completion of repair work. The repair work, involving both engines being overhauled and substantial work to the undercarriage, took considerable time to complete, due in the main to Iona opting to leave the work until engineers were available from regular maintenance duties. It was over a year after its accident, that the 310G was placed on the Irish register on 8 October 1969 as EI-ATC (see Table 21). This enhanced Iona's range and capabilities as this now moved them into the twin-engine type aircraft.

The fortieth anniversary of the establishment of Hugh Cahill's aviation business was celebrated in true Cahill style. The Iona hangar was transformed

The starboard undercarriage of Cessna 310G, G-ARWF, collapsed when landing on runway 17 at Dublin airport on 3 August 1968. The aircraft was removed to the Iona hangar for repair. It was to become Iona's as EI-ATC and remain with the company for a quarter of a century. In the background of above photograph is Cessna 337, N5384S

Photograph courtesy Paul Duffy

Cessna 310N, EI-ATB, was only with Iona for a few weeks in September 1968. It was a replacement for Cessna 310G, G-ARWF, that was damaged on runway 17 at Dublin airport on 3 August 1968

Photograph courtesy Paul Duffy

The acquisition of twin-engine Cessna 310G, EI-ATC, allowed Iona to operate charter flights over water. This aircraft was to remain with Iona for 25 years. Photographed at Iona 20 Febuary 1971

Photograph courtesy Paul Cunniffe

for the occasion on Friday, 25 September 1970. The *Evening Herald* was one of the newspapers represented and published an account of the evening that included the following:

> 'Managing Director Pearse Cahill, his mother Caroline and his wife Constance welcomed over 200 guests to a party which went into the small hours. Pride of place went to a 40-year-old flag bearing the words 'Kildonan Aerodrome.' Around the wall old photographs took up the story of one man's vision and business enterprise.'

Pearse Cahill's eldest son, Hugh, managed the commercial operations for many years at Iona

Photograph courtesy Pearse Cahill

The article continued with a profile of the company's early operations. In 1972, a clubhouse was added to the existing hangar at Dublin airport.

Originally Pearse's father, Hugh, registered the name Iona National Airways Limited, when he set up operations in February 1931. When the company ceased trading and no returns were being filed, the name was struck off by the Companies Office. Pearse decided to reinstate the name that had been used as a trade name in the interim by Iona Garage and Engineering Works Limited. Iona National Airways Limited was registered again on 7 April 1972, receiving Certificate of Incorporation number 36987. Its first Directors in April 1972 were Pearse and Constance Cahill, 1 Prospect Road, Glasnevin, Dublin. Both were listed as Directors of

Iona Garage and Engineering Works Limited and the Irish Aero Club Limited. On 1 November 1975, Hugh and Peter Cahill, sons of Pearse and Constance, were appointed as Directors of Iona National Airways Limited. By 1 April 1974, the garage business had been totally separated from the aviation activities. The engineering works at Cross Guns Bridge was sold. By this time Pearse was now totally committed to the aviation industry. At this stage Catherine Greene had departed Iona.

In 1965, as a young school-leaver, Catherine Greene joined the Iona garage in Glasnevin in a clerical / secretarial capacity. By 1970, when Iona became established at Dublin airport, Catherine Greene moved to the office there. Between 1972 and 1974 she left after taking up employment with a car-hire company and later a pharmaceutical company. Obviously she couldn't stay away for too long and the lure of the expanding aviation business witnessed her return to the Iona operations at Dublin airport. She was to remain with the company from 1974 to 1983. Following the demise of Iona in 1994, Catherine returned to the organisation, where she remains to the present day, performing administration tasks on behalf of Iona Aero Engineering Limited. On 5 October 2002 Catherine was honoured by the *Aviation Trailblazers of Ireland* and presented with the Tissander Trophy for her contribution and services to Irish aviation.

Iona's confidence received a major boost in 1972 with an order placed by the Irish Department of Defence to supply the Irish Air Corps with eight brand new Cessna FR. 172Hs. In their book *Irish Air Corps - A View from the Tower*, Capt. Kevin Byrne and Comdt. Peter Tormey, describe the military's decision to purchase the aircraft:

> 'The Cessna 172 (or Reims Rocket as the French call it) is sometimes a maligned aircraft in Irish Air Corps service; the slowest of the fixed wing fleet, it is also outpaced by the Gazelle and Dauphin helicopters; however, this high-wing four-seater has proven to be one of the most versatile and economical of all Irish military aircraft in recent years.

> 'Its arrival came about because of the increased requirement for army co-operation duties, and as

none of the existing fleet was considered suitable, an obvious choice was the Cessna 172, a civil light aircraft which was universally popular, and already in widespread military service. In 1972 eight aircraft were purchased, the first four delivered on 4 October. The version chosen was extremely similar to the civil model. Because of its short field take-off and landing capabilities, the Cessna 172 has been seen at every licensed airfield in the country, in addition to the landing strip at the Curragh and at Finner Camp, County Donegal, which was opened in 1978.

'The new squadron did not remain at Baldonnel for long and were despatched to Gormanstown, County Meath, to replace the Chipmunk training aircraft. Initially, the squadron was involved operationally on reconnaissance and escort duties, and it was soon obvious that the aircraft's duties could be extended to include VIP transport, search and rescue, Garda co-op, target towing (army and naval), photography, parachute training, display flying, air ambulance and Air Traffic Control co-operation (civil and military). Several hundred men have jumped from the Cessnas, at least five times each, to earn their Parachutist's Wings. The Cessnas have featured at many air shows over the past 30 years.'

On 21 September 1978 Air Corps Cessna, number 204, was conducting a bird counting mission on behalf of the Forestry and Wildlife Services in the Shannon Estuary, when it suffered a bird strike. Fortunately the pilot made a skilful landing in the water and both crew safely swam ashore, suffering only minor injuries. The aircraft was 'written-off' and Iona supplied the Department of Defence with a replacement Cessna FR.172K Rocket, serial number 243 on 7 April 1981.

Tragically No. 243 was involved in the first fatal crash of an Air Corps Cessna in almost 32 years of service, when Second Lieutenant Raymond Heery (22) died when the aircraft crashed at Clonbullogue, Co. Offaly on 6 May 2004.

Iona continued its relationship with the Department of Defence and the Air Corps, mostly performing specialised maintenance work, and provision of Cessna spare parts. Even in February

The sunlight is reflected from the wings of a formation comprising seven of the eight Cessna aircraft supplied by Iona to the Irish Air Corps in October 1972

Photograph courtesy Paul Duffy

1990 it was performing repairs to the wings of serial 209 following its forced landing near Gormanstown, County Meath on 10 November 1989.

At 9.30am on Wednesday, 29 August 1973, 35-year-old Roger Mallison and 28-year-old Roger Chapman were near the surface of the Atlantic, 93 miles south west of Mizen Head, County Cork. The men were in a mini submarine, *Pisces III*, contracted by the British Post Office to lay a £30 million underwater trans-Atlantic telecommunications cable. Near the surface one of the hatches flooded and the vessel immediately sank to the sea bed, 1,375 feet below the mother ship. A rescue operation involving United States Navy, Royal Air Force and rescue teams from Canada, Scotland and England was immediately mounted. At 4.10am on Friday morning the rescue submarine, *Pisces II*, having been flown to Cork from Teeside aboard a Hercules aircraft for the rescue, developed a fault and had to surface. The trapped men were in constant radio communication with their rescuers and had oxygen and food to last until 10am on Saturday morning. A replacement rescue submarine, *Pisces V*, was flown from Canada to Cork. It was shipped to the scene and descended to the sea bed. The rescue proceeded and the mini submarine was brought to the surface on Saturday. Both men were flown to hospital for observation. *Irish Times* photographer, Tom Lawlor, who had chartered an Iona aircraft to fly to the scene, exclusively captured the dramatic photograph of the stricken vessel breaking the surface of the Atlantic. This was amongst the first of many occasions the media were to use Iona aircraft for such dramatic public interest stories.

The *Pisces* rescue robot being unloaded at Cork airport from a USAF C-130 flown from Canada to assist in the rescue of the stricken submarine from the sea bed off Mizen Head, Co. Cork in August 1973. Iona aircraft were chartered to photograph the rescue

Photograph courtesy Ronny Vogt collection

Cessna 310G, EI-ATC, went for a major overhaul at the end of 1974 and Iona decided to fill the void with the purchase of a Cessna 337F. This aircraft was originally purchased new by Iona, though temporarily carried an American registration, N4757, for its ferry from United States of America to Brussels for demonstration in Ireland. On 8 July 1971, Pearse did some trial flights in the 337 routing from Dublin to Baldonnel and back to Dublin. Iona sold it to Henry Bell Limited, a company operated

by John Maher, and registered to them as EI-AVC on 26 August 1971. On 17 April 1972 it was registered to Bellaire International Limited and to Iona National Airways Limited on 22 May 1975 (see Table 22). Almost immediately Pearse was making use of the aircraft when he flew non-stop in two hours 50 minutes to Beauvais to attend the Paris Air Show on 30 May 1975. Random samples of its charter flights over a three-day period show the following:

- 2 November 1976, Dublin – Liverpool – Oxford – Gatwick – Zurich.

- 3 November 1976, Zurich – Luton – Oxford.

- 4 November 1976, Oxford – Leeds – Manchester – Dublin.

The western confines of Dublin airport and in particular the area in close proximity to Iona, were to play host to one of the largest gathering to date of light aircraft at the airport. The inaugural Shamrock International Air Rally occurred on the weekend of 15 June 1974. The competition was essentially a timed arrival contest as per flight plan. The weekend was generally for socialising by visitors with a meal arranged at one of the city venues, including the Great Hall at Trinity College on one occasion. The event was inspired by the Rotterdam Rally attended by Pearse and Tom Farrington several years previous. For the second such event the entry was increased to 38 aircraft and it took place on 6, 7 and 8 June 1975 in weather conditions far beyond the hopes of the Rally officials. 13 British registered aircraft along with 12 bearing German registrations and a further 5 representing Belgium, Finland and Denmark joined eight from Ireland. Iona had two entries; Cessna 182P, EI-AYJ, flown from Dundalk by P. Donegan won the award in the category *'Best Irish PPL – without ratings.'* The other Iona entry was the Cessna 172M, EI-BAS, arriving from the Isle of Man. All aircraft were parked on the grass between the Iona ramp and runway 17 / 35.

In 1976, the Shamrock International Air Rally attracted a reduced number of competitors for the

Cessna 337 'push-pull', EI-AVC, on ramp at Iona. Note additional under-belly baggage storage.
On the left is Cessna 310G, EI-ATC.

Photograph via Pearse Cahill collection

weekend 11 to 13 June 1976. Weather conditions were poor. Several entrants did not arrive at Dublin or reached an intermediate destination. The following year the event occurred over the period 10 to 12 June 1977. Numbers were again down, with only 11 taking part in the competition. The fifth Rally was scheduled for Dublin airport for the 26 to 28 May 1978. This international competition, in which Iona aircraft and members were deeply involved, including Tom Farrington who was one of the principle organisers, was to be the final such event to be hosted at Dublin airport by Iona.

The *Irish Air Letter* in its July 1978 issue reported:

> 'Bad weather again dogged the fifth Shamrock International Air Rally held at Dublin airport between May 26 and 28 last. There were sixteen entrants from Germany, Finland and England as well as Ireland. It was the third Shamrock Rally for the overall winner, the Finnish entrant, J. Saksa (Cherokee Arrow OH-PCX) who took the Shamrock International Trophy and prize for the longest distance flown – Helsinki to Dublin via Southend. Runner-up and also best German entry was R. Bainka (Rallye Commodore, D-ECYZ) while the other German entrant, G. Bainlinch (Cessna 172, D-EGTH)

was winner of the concours d'elegance. Oldest original aircraft was won by W. Rafter (Auster Autocrat, EI-AGJ) and the arrival time competition was won by Dr. William Phelan (Rallye Commodore, EI-AWJ), with Anthony Leonard and Paddy Donegan (Cessna 182, EI-AOD) as runner up and also best Irish entrant. Nationally, the Shamrock National Trophy and best elapsed time was won by David Abrahamson (Cherokee 140, EI-AOB) with runner-up Ken Walters (AA-5 Traveller, EI-AYD). Best Irish pilot with no rating was Eamon Shiel (Rallye EI-AUN) and the prize for flight planning was won by Kieran O'Connor (Cessna 182, EI-BCL) and Mick Rogers (Cessna 310, EI-ATC) was runner-up. Other aircraft taking part were Beech Baron, G-BAAG, Sportavia-Fournier RF-5, G-AZJC, Auster J/1 Autocrat, EI-AUM and Cessna 337, EI-BET.'

Staff at the Iona offices were somewhat taken aback on Sunday, 14 September 1975, when a little old lady walked into the clubhouse. She quietly mentioned to a few present that she had just flown the Atlantic. This would not have sounded unusual except for the fact the lady was 83 years of age and she had just completed such a remarkable flight alone. The *Chicago Sun Times*, Tuesday, 16 September 1975, carried a picture of Marion Hart

View of participants at the inaugural Shamrock International Air Rally occupying ground adjacent to Iona ramp 15 June 1974

Photograph courtesy George Flood

View of participants at the 2nd Shamrock International Air Rally occupying ground between runway 17/35 and Iona ramp 7 June 1975

Photograph courtesy George Flood

standing with Peter Cahill beside her aircraft. The caption stated:

> 'Miss Hart, believed the oldest woman to fly the Atlantic alone, said she did it 'for fun'. En route to the Mid East, she was grounded in Dublin by a bad cold.'

It was not her first time to attempt this adventure. On 27 August 1953, when she was a mere 61 years of age, she landed at Shannon in her Beech Bonanza, N507C. Her co-pilot and navigator on that occasion was Wayne Veterlein (a Pan American pilot). That time the journey took her 13 hours 23 minutes from St. John's, Newfoundland to Shannon, to achieve the first non-stop crossing from Newfoundland to Ireland since the pioneer days of aviation in a non-airliner type aircraft. Shannon airport was crowded with spectators to welcome her after her epic flight. She learned to fly nine years previously. She was also the first woman to qualify as a chemical engineer. Marion Hart spent a week in Ireland, mostly due to a bad cold and weather delays, before continuing to France and other destinations in Europe, through to Libya, Sudan, Ethiopia, Burma and Malaya.

83-year-old Marion Hart at Iona with Peter Cahill on 14 September 1975, following her successful solo crossing of the Atlantic

Copy Newspaper via Pearse Cahill collection

Cold grounds ocean flier, 83

Marian Hart, 83, of Washington, who flew solo across the Atlantic on Sunday, stands by plane at Dublin airport with flying instructor Peter Cahill. Miss Hart, believed the oldest woman to fly the Atlantic alone, said she did it "for fun." En route to the Mideast, she was grounded Monday in Dublin by a bad cold. (AP)

Throughout Pearse's life in aviation he was to receive many accolades, most coming from organisations within Ireland. On 22 September 1975, he accepted the Paul Tissander Diploma presented by the Federation Aeronautique Internationale from the Head Office in Paris.

Sad news reached the Iona hangar in June 1976. Seamus Kelly had been employed in the hangar as an engineer for several years until he took up an appointment with Aer Arann in 1975. On 6 June 1976 he was piloting Stampe SV-4C, EI-AVT, with his wife as passenger, when it crashed near Castlebridge, County Wexford. Seamus was killed and his wife sustained serious injury. He was an accomplished aerobatic pilot and was overall winner of the Wexford Aerobatic Trophy in 1975.

In mid-April 1977 Cessna 310G EI-ATC returned to service, following a two and a half year overhaul, and the company's air-taxi work began to grow steadily. In addition to points in the UK, these charters took Iona aircraft to places such as Lourdes, Zurich, Cologne and Cherbourg. Iona also performed various forms of aerial work such as photography and banner towing, the latter using Cessna 172, EI-BAS. Dealerships were at that stage held for Lycoming and Continental engines, Hartzell and McAuley propellers, NARCO and ARC radios and instruments, and for Goodyear tyres. Iona was responsible for maintaining some fifty aircraft in all.

For the summer of 1977, Iona undertook to provide an 'on-demand' service to Lambay Island for the local residents as the normal sea service was withdrawn. Around the same time and throughout the winter months of 1977 / 1978 construction commenced on an additional hangar beside the main hangar at Iona; when complete it would measure 60m x 10m and accommodate eight aircraft.

Continuing expansion in the air-taxi business led to the acquisition of a second Cessna 310. This was a considerably newer model than the existing EI-ATC in the fleet. This latest acquisition was a 1971 model and bore previous registrations N7733Q and D-ICEQ. It was purchased in Germany and ferried via Amsterdam on 3 April 1978. It joined the Irish register on 13 April 1978 as EI-BEO to Iona National Airways Limited (see Table 23). It was most fortunate Iona purchased the Cessna 310Q for the other 310, EI-ATC, suffered substantial damage to its undercarriage following an incident when a wheel contacted a rabbit hole on the grass runway at Carrickfin, County Donegal, on 10 January 1979. There were no injuries but the aircraft was extensively damaged. It was transported to Dublin for a lengthy period of repairs – six years in fact.

Cessna 310Q, EI-BEO, was added to the Iona fleet in April 1978. Photographed above on 29 April 1978 - 3 weeks after delivery

Photograph courtesy Paul Cunniffe

Cessna 310G, EI-ATC, lay for six years undergoing repairs in the Iona hangar following its incident at Carrickfin, Co. Donegal on 10 January 1979

Photograph courtesy Paul Duffy

In June 1978, the monthly publication *Irish Air Letter,* conducted a review of the fast expanding Air Taxi Operations in Ireland. The following is an extract from the article:

'At the time of the review there are five such operators in Ireland. In Dublin, Executive Air Services have two 5-seat Aztecs, whilst

Iona National Airways operate two Cessna 310s and one Cessna 337 (both 5-seat types) plus some single-engine aircraft. Shannon Executive also uses two Aztecs from Shannon plus a single-engine Cessna 206 and is in the process of adding a Navajo Chieftain to the fleet. Aer Arann also offer charter work on their fleet of Islanders, which are based at Galway / Carnmore, but they normally have one of these 9-seat aircraft stationed at Dublin. From Cork, Joyce Aviation operates a Cessna 310 on such work.

'For a day return operation from Dublin to Luton, a nine seat Islander will cost around £525, or £58.33 per seat, or 10.84p per seat mile. This compares with the basic airfare of £63.00 or 11.29p per seat mile for Dublin – London (Heathrow).

'For internal flights in Ireland, a Cessna 310 / 337 works out at about £160.00 for Dublin – Shannon, £32.00 per seat or 13.11p per seat mile, whilst a single engine Cessna 172 or 182 with 3 seats costs about half that, giving a seat price of £26.67 and a seat mile rate of 10.93p.

'It was noted that most companies concentrate on the five-seat piston twin for air taxi work.'

One of the worst maritime disasters to strike Ireland in recent years occurred on 8 January 1979. The French oil tanker *Betelgeuse* exploded off Whiddy Island, Bantry Bay, County Cork, killing 50 people. Tom Lawlor, a photographer with *The Irish Times* contacted Iona to fly to the area. With Ray Di Mascio at the controls of the Cessna 310, EI-BEO, the Iona aircraft was at the stricken tanker about 4am ahead of any of the rescue service aircraft, and was in a position to give them exact directional details as they raced to the scene from Wales and other UK bases. This resulted in a question raised in the Dáil (Irish Parliament) regarding the response time of the rescue services. At that time the only Air Corps helicopters were the Alouettes and we were largely dependent on Royal Air Force and Royal Navy helicopter support. Shortly after this tragedy the Air Corps were approved for a Gazelle.(*xi)

Aerial photograph of the *'Betelgeuse'* the morning after the disaster at Whiddy Island, Co. Cork, during which 50 people died in the inferno on 8 January 1979. The first photographs of the disaster were taken by *Irish Times* photographer Tom Lawlor at 04.15am from Iona's Cessna 310, EI-BEO piloted by Ray Di Mascio

Photograph courtesy *Irish Times*

matching this competition. To keep up the pace, management at Iona made the brave decision to invest in a pressurised cabin-class twin-engine eight-seat aircraft. The model selected was a 1978 Wichita built Cessna 414A Chancellor II. The 414A had only commenced production in 1978. On 28 March 1979, EI-BGP was registered to Iona National Airways Limited (see Table 24). The 414A was quite a departure from the original 414, which made its debut in 1970. At that time the 414 was being offered as a cheaper alternative to the top-of-the-line Cessna 421. The 414A Chancellor had a bigger wing, in performance its single engine ceiling shoots from 11,350 feet to 19,850 feet. Its cruising speed was 224 knots and it had a range capability of 1,099 nautical miles. Its useful load was 2,388 lb. With the new fuselage, its interior was the same as the 421C, but it had slightly better fuel economy. The new acquisition gave Iona an interesting competitive edge; at the time it kept the company well in the forefront of the rapidly growing executive charter business and offered a lower cost alternative to the sophisticated turboprops then active in the Irish marketplace. Compare this with the first air-taxi service operated by the Desoutter, EI-AAD, at one shilling per mile, 50 years previously.

On Friday 18 May 1979, a Cessna Conquest was demonstrated to members of the media. On Saturday and Sunday, members of the public were invited to attend the demonstration.

By early 1979 the air-taxi and executive charter business was developing quite rapidly. Competition for the business in this category was coming from Avair with KingAir 200s and Flightline with a Turbo Commander 690. It was evident Iona could not keep up and the Cessna 310, when returned to service, was far from capable of

While 1970 saw Iona as probably the only company seriously involved in air-taxi and executive charter work, using a Cessna 310 and a Cessna 172, the decade finished somewhat differently. By the end of 1979, six companies were competing in the Irish market. The main operator remained Iona, using a Cessna 310 (EI-BEO), a Cessna 337 (EI-AVC) and a Cessna Chancellor 414A (EI-BGP) plus a variety of single engine aircraft at their disposal. Shannon Executive Aviation had 2 Aztecs and a Cessna 206; Aer Arann with 4 BN2 Islanders; Flightline with a Rockwell Commander 690B and Avair with 2 Beech

FOOTNOTE (*xi)

The first Gazelle, number 237, arrived at Baldonnel on 30 December 1979, and early in 1980 it came into use for pilot conversion courses, and subsequently for basic helicopter flying training. The first twin-engine helicopter to enter Air Corps service was Aerospatiale SA330L Puma, number 242, which arrived in July 1981. It was July 1986 before Dauphins 244 & 245 were added to the Air Corps fleet.

King Air 200s. Executive Air Services with one Aztec were not active towards the end of 1979.

In 1980, Iona was awarded the Irish agency for Bendix-King avionics equipment. Towards the end of 1980, Iona took out an advertisement in *Aero Ireland* for the sale of 14 aircraft. For comparison purposes, the following prices were quoted for the four new aircraft on the list:

• Cessna FA152 Aerobat, fitted with NAV/COM, VOR. Full panel and long-range tanks - £18,500

• Cessna F152 II, fitted with King NAV/COM, KX175b, full panel and long-range tanks - £15,500

• Cessna F172 Skyhawk (1980 model), fitted with twin NAV/COM, 300ADF, 400 Transponder, 400 Marker beacon, blind encoding altimeter and 200A NAV-O-Matic, long-range tanks and numerous additional equipment - £25,000

• Cessna F172 Skyhawk II (1981 model), fitted with full IFR equipment: dual 300 NAV/COM RT385A, 300 ADF, 300 Transponder, 400 Glidescope, Antenna and Coupler, long-range tanks - £26,500.

Dublin witnessed one of its worst fire disasters when a Valentine's night disco, on Friday night 13 February 1981, went horribly wrong and forty nine young people, whose average age was 19, perished in an inferno in the Stardust ballroom, Artane.

The first aerial photographs taken by *Irish Times* photographer Tom Lawlor, from Iona Cessna 172, EI-BAS, piloted by Peter Cahill, of the *'Stardust'* disaster at Artane, Dublin on Valentine's night 1981. The fire resulted in the deaths of 49 teenagers

Photograph courtesy Tom Lawlor / *Irish Times*

To maintain competitiveness for charter work, Iona purchased its first pressurized cabin-class twin-engine aircraft Cessna 414A Chancellor, EI-BGP. Aircraft is photographed at Iona on 22 March 1980.

Photograph courtesy Paul Cunniffe

The first aerial photographs of the tragic scene were taken by *Irish Times* photographer Tom Lawlor from an aircraft chartered from Iona. Peter Cahill flew Tom on four sorties that tragic morning in Cessna 172, EI-BAS, commencing at 7.50am.

Pearse returned to the clubhouse on the evening of Monday, 27 April 1981 following a holiday to the United States. Expecting to turn up for a few drinks and the typical recollection of his holiday experiences, Pearse was greeted by well wishers, and more to his surprise, Terry Rowan, President, Irish Aviation Council. The I.A.C. was honouring Pearse by presenting him with the Col. James Fitzmaurice Award for his outstanding services to Irish aviation. At the reception, Pearse was not hesitant in his speech to remind those present '*that while Iona was a smaller airline than Aer Lingus it is, nevertheless, an older one.*' Pearse was only the third person to be so honoured by the I.A.C. The first recipient was Captain 'Darby' Kennedy, and the previous year Captain J. C. Kelly-Rogers.

On 27 April 1981, Terry Rowan presented Pearse with the Col. James C. Fitzmaurice trophy in recognition of his services to aviation. Pearse was only the third person to be honored with this award. In the background is Cessna F152, EI-BIN, delivered four weeks previously.

Photograph courtesy Paul Duffy

Plans were in place to establish a base at Waterford. For this purpose a company called Iona National Airways (Waterford) Limited was incorporated on 25 May 1981. It was allocated Certificate of Incorporation number 082803. The plans included the erection of a hangar at the airport. Nothing of significance emerged from the plans. By the end of the summer of 1981, work in Dublin had commenced on the construction of a storage building at the Iona ramp. A recent extension of the parking area had just been completed. The new building was sited between the two existing hangars and was to be used, among other things, to store the many aircraft components that then took up quite an amount of badly needed space at the rear of the main hangar.

On the weekend of 12 and 13 September 1981, the population of Dublin witnessed something that had not been seen in the sky over the city for quite a number of years – banner towing. Iona Cessna 172, EI-BCK, undertook several sorties towing a banner advertising Opel cars. This was the first banner-towing operation in Dublin since the period from the latter part of the 1950s to the early years of the 1960s, when Skycraft regularly undertook banner towing using Austers EI-AKN and EI-ALN. In early 1982, the Cessna 172, EI-BCK, again performed further banner towing sorties advertising Budget Travel. One such banner-towing mission was not so fortunate. Cessna 172, EI-BAS, was operating to the west of Dublin airport on 4 September 1983, in the vicinity of Dunsoghly Castle, when it encountered control difficulties while towing a banner in winds gusting 35 knots. The Cessna was undamaged and was flown back to Dublin immediately.

Cessna 182P, EI-BCL picking up a banner at Iona in April 1985

Photograph courtesy Paul Duffy

The Cessna 310, EI-ATC, was still undergoing repairs three years following its incident at Carrickfin. Iona decided to acquire another similar aircraft and on 1 March 1982 they added their third Cessna 310 to the Irish register. It was a 1973 Wichita built 310Q model. The 310 was registered to Iona National Airways Limited as EI-BMK and was ferried by Peter Cahill to Dublin via Liverpool on 5 March 1982 (see Table 25). Iona had the distinction of operating two 'Mike-Kilos,' with EI-AMK languishing at the rear of the Iona hangar since its accident at Birr on 1 June 1979.

On 5 July 1982, the Cessna 414A Chancellor, EI-BGP, had the nose-wheel jam in the intermediate position after take-off from Dublin airport for Coventry. Two fly-bys of the control tower were made with the gear extended, and following activation of the CO_2 bottle a normal landing was affected.

At approximately 9.30pm on Sunday, 21 August 1983, the Coras Iompair Eireann train from Tralee to Dublin broke down at Cherryville junction near Kildare. The Galway to Dublin train travelling on the same tracks, in the same direction, ploughed into the rear of the stationary Tralee train. The crash resulted in the deaths of seven people with 27 seriously injured. This was one of the worst rail tragedies in recent years. At 11am the following morning Iona's Cessna 182, EI-BCL, took off from Dublin airport, piloted by Peter Cahill and with *Irish Times* photographer Peter Thursfield on board, to capture images of the scene of carnage at Cherryville junction.

Towards the end of summer 1983 work commenced on an extension to the clubhouse offices and bar and, on Friday, 2 December 1983 former Taoiseach, Charles J. Haughey, TD, officially opened the extension.

Cessna 310Q, EI-BMK, was the third of this type of aircraft to be operated by Iona for charter and air taxi work when it joined the fleet 5 March 1982

Photograph courtesy Liam Byrne via Ronny Vogt collection

Locating a successful flying organisation at an international airport comes, however, with a hefty price tag. At the end of 1983, Iona received a bill from Aer Rianta for passenger handling charges of about £17,000 retrospectively covering the years up to 1978. In addition they were levied £2,000 contribution towards the new security fence being erected.

With the fleet increasing it was time to take a look at the marketplace and explore where other business opportunities lay.

Official opening of Iona clubhouse on 2 December 1983. Ceremony performed by former Taoiseach, Charles J. Haughey, T.D., seen here holding the wooden propeller from an Avro Cadet. Newspaper photo includes Pearse and Peter Cahill

Copy newspaper article courtesy Pearse Cahill

The aftermath of the Cherryville train crash photographed by *Irish Times* photographer, Peter Thursfield, from Iona's Cessna 182, EI-BCL on 22 August 1983

Photograph courtesy Peter Thursfield / *Irish Times*

The brochure content (rotated) reads:

AIR CHARTER

Iona National Airways operates a fleet of Cessna aircraft. You can choose one to suit your personal needs from our four seat single engine Cessna to our eight seat twin-engine pressured executive Cessna aircraft.

Our service is ideal for the business executive offering total flexibility in relation to times and destinations.

Iona's flexibility allows you to drive straight to the steps of the aircraft. You can be airborne literally in minutes if your aerial it our present terminal. Your schedule is our schedule. Your destination is our destination.

AIR FREIGHT

Iona operates a comprehensive air freight service with aircraft on 24 hour stand-by. Our service is invaluable for transporting emergency spares for a variety of equipment, notably computer and medical equipment.

AIRCRAFT MAINTENANCE

Iona National Airways is the main Cessna dealer in Ireland and has the largest maintenance facility for light aircraft. We are experienced and highly-trained engineers backed up by a full complement of service staff.

AIRCRAFT ADVERTISING

Iona introduced aircraft banner advertising to Ireland and are the leading exponents of the service in this country. We can have your very own slogan flying where you want it when you want it at very short notice. This is the most impressive form of advertising and promotion available today. Your message becomes the centre of attraction for thousands of people. No other form of advertising makes such an impact.

AMBULANCE SERVICE

Iona offers a complete air ambulance service capable of transporting patients, medics and/or vital organs at a moment's notice. As with all our other services one can bring the patient or organ with accompanying medics or attendants straight to the aircraft and has them met in a similar fashion upon landing.

AERIAL PHOTOGRAPHY

We have aircraft available for a variety of photographic purposes from aerial surveys to film unit shoots. We will provide photographers if required.

Opel Senator
courtesy of General Motors in Ltd.

Centre page of promotional brochure distributed by Iona in 1982 outlining services offered

Brochure courtesy Pearse Cahill

Table 16

Registration	EI-AOO
Aircraft Type	Cessna 150E
Constructors Serial Number	150-61225
Place & Year of Manufacture	Wichita, 1965
Previous Registrations	N2125J
Registered to	Iona Garage & Engineering Works Ltd, 30 April 1965
Delivery date	18 May 1965
Registered to	Irish Aero Club Ltd, 18 February 1966
Remarks	Aircraft was intended for use by Galway Flying Club Limited, but was not formally transferred to them until 14 November 1967. As a result of a heavy landing at Galway in September 1969, the aircraft was taken to Iona for repair. Following completion of the repairs it was re-registered to Irish Aero Club Limited on 16 April 1970. The newly incorporated Limerick Flying Club Limited acquired the aircraft and it was ferried to Coonagh airfield on 6 February 1971, piloted by Pearse and arriving at 5.20pm. It was registered to the Limerick club on 14 April 1971. Registered on 3 August 1976 to Richard Hassett and remained at Coonagh until its sale to John James Woodhouse, Crumlin, Dublin on 27 November 1992. It was transferred to the United Kingdom register as G-BURH on 2 December 1992 and removed from the Irish register 10 June 1993. On 12 February 1999 ownership transferred to Trustees of BURH Flying Group with an address at Twickenham. At 31 December 2002 total flying hours were recorded at 5,375.

Table 17

Registration	EI-ANC
Aircraft Type	Cessna 182A Skylane
Constructors Serial Number	182-34078
Place & Year of Manufacture	Wichita, 1957
Previous Registrations	N6078B
Registered to	Iona Garage & Engineering Works Ltd, 9 September 1965
Delivery date	25 September 1965
Remarks	These marks were previously reserved for a Nord 1002 by J. E. Hutchison. The registration was not taken up by him and was reallocated to the Iona Cessna. Pearse already had a potential client for the Cessna 182 and it was promptly sold by Iona and cancelled from the Irish register on 15 November 1965. It was registered to R. Sullivan as G-ATNU on 27 January 1966 following sale to England. Its marks changed to G-OLSC on 19 August 1987, when it became a possession of the London Skydiving Centre Limited, Cranfield - incorporating their initials in its registration. It's final owner on the UK register was Factultra Limited, Coton, Cambridge until it was de-registered 3 April 1997.

Table 18

Registration	EI-AOK
Aircraft Type	Cessna F.172G
Constructors Serial Number	172-0208
Place & Year of Manufacture	Reims, France, 1966
Previous Registrations	New aircraft
Registered to	Iona Garage & Engineering Works Ltd, 14 March 1966
Delivery date	16 March 1966
Registered to	Irish Aero Club Ltd, 29 March 1966

Remarks

This registration was reserved by Aer Lingus for the ex-KLM Vickers Viscount 803, PH-VIC. Due to possible radio call-sign confusion with EI-AKO, the marks EI-APD were instead allocated to the Viscount. This Viscount was a sister aircraft of EI-AOM that crashed off Tuskar Rock on 24 March 1968.

EI-AOK remained part of the Iona fleet until its sale to Kerry Airways Limited on 24 February 1971, bearing the name *Rose of Tralee*. It remained with several Irish owners, viz. Seamus Ryle, 4 June 1976; R. J. Cloughley & N. J. Simpson, 4 November 1977; Oliver Bruton, 9 May 1996 and David Bruton 27 November 1998. In recent years it has been at Abbeyshrule in a partly dismantled condition. On 22 April 2002 it was formally cancelled from the Irish register. It was reported to have been roaded into Water Leisure Park, Skegness, Linconshire, to be used as spares in the rebuild of Reims Cessna 172G, G-AVPI.

Table 19

Registration	EI-AND
Aircraft Type	Cessna 175A Skylark
Constructors Serial Number	175-56444
Place & Year of Manufacture	Wichita, 1960
Previous Registrations	G-APYA; N6944E
Registered to	Pearse Cahill, 19 February 1975
Remarks	This was the first Cessna 175 on the UK register. Registered G-APYA, 25 January 1960 to Airwork Services Ltd, Blackbushe and delivered crated on 12 March 1960. Cancelled from UK register 28 August 1963 and placed on Irish register the following day as EI-AND to D. T. Rowan and Dr. C. Killeen. Subsequent owners included Tom Farrington, 25 May 1966; D. McDermott Bradshaw, 26 February 1970; Pearse Cahill, 19 February 1975; Jack Braithwaite (Ireland) Ltd, 9 May 1975; Mary and Alan Cooke, 9 March 1988. Alan Cooke and Michael Gray were both tragically killed when the aircraft crashed into the Irish Sea between north Wales and the Isle of Man, on 30 October 1994. It was routing Guernsey to Isle of Man following some maintenance work. The wreckage was located two miles north of Anglesey when it fouled the nets of a fishing trawler on 3 January 1995. Cancelled from the Irish register 26 June 1995.

Table 20

Registration	EI-ATB
Aircraft Type	Cessna 310N
Constructors Serial Number	310N-0054
Place & Year of Manufacture	Wichita, 1968
Previous Registrations	N4154Q
Registered to	Irish Aero Club Ltd, 2 September 1968
Delivery date	9 September 1968
Remarks	This new aircraft was obtained by Iona as a replacement for the Cessna 310G, G-ARWF, that suffered an undercarriage collapse at Dublin airport on 3 August 1968. It was only to be on the Irish register for a few weeks, until 6 November 1968, as it was registered G-AWTA to Lowland Aero Services Ltd., Turnhouse on 8 November 1968. It was cancelled from the United Kingdom register 13 November 1996 and placed on the American register as N510PS. Its current owner is Aircraft Guaranty Trust, Houston, Texas to whom it was registered 28 October 2002.

Table 21

Registration   EI-ATC

Aircraft Type   Cessna 310G

Constructors Serial Number   310G-0050

Place & Year of Manufacture   Wichita, 1960

Previous Registrations   G-ARWF, 9 March 1962

Registered to   Iona National Airways Ltd,
                                    8 October 1969

Remarks   On 3 August 1968, G-ARWF suffered undercarriage collapse
                                    at Dublin airport. The aircraft was removed to Iona for repair.
                                    The owners purchased a new Cessna 310Q from Iona,
                                    EI-ATB, and G-ARWF became the property of Iona.
                                    Following repair it became part of the Iona fleet as EI-ATC.
                                    On 22 January 1985 its ownership transferred to M. P. Cahill.
                                    It remained with Iona for 24 years. In July 1993 EI-ATC, along
                                    with EI-BMK, was sold to Preferred Aircraft Parts,
                                    Cleveland, Ohio for spares. They were dismantled in the Iona
                                    hangar and loaded into two containers. The containers
                                    departed Dublin airport on 28 July 1993 for shipment to the
                                    United States. It was cancelled from the Irish register 4 August
                                    1993.

Table 22

Registration	EI-AVC
Aircraft Type	Cessna F.337F Skymaster
Constructors Serial Number	337-0032
Place & Year of Manufacture	Reims, France, 1970
Previous Registrations	N4757
Registered to	Iona National Airways Ltd, 22 May 1975
Remarks	Iona took delivery of this aircraft and sold it to Henry Bell Limited, Waterford, to whom it was registered 26 August 1971. Ownership transferred to Bellair International Limited on 17 April 1972. Iona acquired it 22 May 1975 and operated the Cessna 337 for ten years until they sold it on to the 337 Flying Group, Dublin on 7 May 1985. On 26 January 1994 its ownership changed to Christy Keane (Saggart) Limited. It later moved to Abbeyshrule for use as spares. In 1999 one wing was used for G-RORO and the engines went to the UK. On 5 October 2001 it was noted at Castlerock, Northern Ireland for use as spares for Cessna 337, RA-04147 (later G-BOYR). It was removed from the Irish register on 26 June 2003. In early 2004 the owner of G-BOYR was reported as Tri-Star Farms Limited, Mount Rule, Douglas, Isle of Man and Certificate of Airworthiness valid until 27 August 2006.

Table 23

Registration	EI-BEO
Aircraft Type	Cessna 310Q
Constructors Serial Number	310Q-0233
Place & Year of Manufacture	Wichita, 1971
Previous Registrations	N7733Q, D-ICEQ
Registered to	Iona National Airways Ltd, 13 April 1978
Delivery date	3 April 1978
Remarks	On 27 August 1985 EI-BEO suffered an undercarriage collapse at Farranfore, Co. Kerry, and was ferried back to Dublin after temporary repair. Ex-Taoiseach, Charles J. Haughey was a passenger at the time of the incident. The aircraft was repaired at Iona and air-tested, four years later, on 6 November 1989. On 28 June 1994, it suffered a propeller blade failure - with the number one propeller detaching on take-off at Carrickfin, Co. Donegal. It remained there with the port engine and propeller missing. Following liquidation of Iona it was sold at auction to Christopher Keane, Saggart, Co. Dublin. It was cancelled from the Irish register on 16 November 1995, and registered to the new owner on 19 January 1996. It was cancelled by him on 27 November 2000 and removed to the United States as N7733Q for possible restoration to flying status. It was registered to Mid Atlantic Aircraft Inc on 9 February 2001 and on 8 July 2003 ownership transferred to Deutsch American Trading, Wilmington, Delaware. Recorded as current early 2004.

Table 24

Registration	EI-BGP
Aircraft Type	Cessna 414A Chancellor III
Constructors Serial Number	414A-0016
Place & Year of Manufacture	Wichita, 1978
Previous Registrations	N6574C (For ferry to Brussels as demo)
Registered to	Iona National Airways Ltd, 28 March 1979
Delivery date	2 May 1979
Remarks	EI-BGP operated as a demonstration aircraft in United States of America bearing the marks N6574C. It was ferried across the Atlantic on 3 March 1978 to Leeds and then to Brussels. It arrived in Dublin on 2 May 1979.
	As a result of the general scale-down in business, EI-BGP was ferried to Staverton on 12 May 1992 for disposal. The Chancellor was subsequently returned to United States of America as N414AS and delivered Cranfield to Glasgow 19 November 1992 and to Reykjavik, Iceland, on 20 November 1992. It was cancelled from the Irish register on 25 November 1992. It later acquired the marks N43MR. On 14 June 1995 it was registered to Hemmeter George Mead, 1900 Myrtle Island Dr., Las Vegas, Nevada. Recorded as current early 2004.

Table 25

Registration	EI-BMK
Aircraft Type	Cessna 310Q-II
Constructors Serial Number	310Q-0919
Place & Year of Manufacture	Wichita, 1973
Previous Registrations	G-BBNS, N69685
Registered to	Iona National Airways Ltd, 1 March 1982
Delivery date	5 March 1982
Remarks	Originally registered N69685 it went to the UK register on 22 October 1973 as G-BBNS and delivered in these marks via Shannon to Brussels on 3 November 1973. On 1 March 1982 it was cancelled from the UK register on its sale to Ireland and placed on the Irish register the same day.

In July 1993, the two Cessna 310s EI-ATC and EI-BMK were sold to Preferred Aircraft Parts, Cleveland, Ohio for spares. They were dismantled in the Iona hangar and loaded into two containers. The containers departed Dublin airport on 28 July 1993 for shipment to the United States. Cancelled from the Irish register 4 August 1993.

Chapter

6

TAKING UP THE CHALLENGE

*New business from scheduled services, air-taxi,
and small parcel contracts resulting in the
acquisition of larger commercial aircraft*

Chapter Six

TAKING UP THE CHALLENGE

In March 1984 Iona commenced a scheduled service on the Sligo – Dublin route. The reason for this departure was the collapse of Avair Limited at the end of February 1984, leaving a major gap in the air services market. The operation commenced on 12 March 1984, just over two weeks after the Avair collapse, with a Monday to Friday operation departing from Sligo at 8am and Dublin at 7.30pm with the aircraft usually overnighting in Sligo. On the first occasion, Peter Cahill departed Dublin at 7.10am in Cessna 414 Chancellor, EI-BGP, arriving Sligo at 7.45am. The schedule commenced, following some formalities, when Peter was airborne from Sligo 25 minutes later and arrived in Dublin after a flight time of 40 minutes. EI-BGP, was the aircraft normally used on the service, but when it was unavailable, a Cessna 310, either EI-BEO or EI-BMK, was substituted. The initial trial period of the scheduled service was for one month, with a round trip fare of £66.00 per person. Shortly after the introduction of the service, Pearse, in an interview with *Business and Finance*, 1 November 1984, titled *'The curious case of Iona Airways,'* was quoted as saying:

> 'Avair was spending money like water. It had 12-seater King Air 200s operating with a pilot, a co-pilot and a hostess. And there were often more crew members than passengers. That was just madness. It was like Aer Lingus – employ plenty of people and lose all the money you can.'

One of Avair's better-known pilots, Arthur Wignall (54), was tragically killed in an aerobatic manoeuvre at Strandhill, County Sligo on 1 April 1984 - a few weeks after the collapse of Avair. His large funeral service was arranged by his friend for over 25 years, Paul Duffy, and took place in St. Patricks Cathedral, Dublin on 8 April 1984, with burial afterwards in the newly opened cemetary on the Hill of Howth. A more detailed account of Arthur's aviation career is recounted in Madeline O' Rourke's book: *Air Spectaculars-Air Displays in*

One of Avair's pilots, Arthur Wignall, undertook many roles for Iona and more in keeping with his character of later years he is photographed performing some aerobatic maneuvers in his Pitts S-2A, EI-BKA. Arthur had requested the registration EI-CAW, containing his initials. Out of sequence registrations were not encouraged by the Department of Transport when Arthur's Pitts arrived in October 1980, however, the best they would do is allocate him EI-BKA, for *'King Arthur'*

Photograph courtesy Paul Duffy

Ireland. For many years Arthur performed regular flying duties for Iona and his aircraft was based at the Iona ramp.

In conjunction with the commencement of the scheduled passenger air services, Iona decided on a new corporate image. An orange and white paint scheme, with 'IONA' on the tail, was initiated. Cessna 310, EI-BEO, was the first Iona aircraft to be repainted by Aer Lingus. In order to assist with additional capacity Iona leased Tom Farrington's Cessna 414, EI-AWW, which gained small Iona titles. In later months, Cessna 310s and Cessna 337, EI-AVC were used, reflecting the low load levels. Unfortunately, the loads on the Sligo route failed to reach economic levels, and Iona's first venture into the schedule service business was terminated, nine months later, in December 1984. The Dublin – Sligo route was the only one of the Avair schedules to be continued following its demise. Iona operated the Cessna 337, EI-AVC, for ten years until they sold it to the 337 Flying Group, Dublin on 7 May 1985.

Cessna 310Q, EI-BEO, at Iona ramp with the new corporate image and logo on 12 May 1984

Photograph courtesy Paul Cunniffe

Cessna 310G, EI-ATC, returned to service after a six year lay off following its incident at Carrickfin, Co. Donegal. It is seen on the Iona ramp with the new corporate image and logo 26 July 1986

Photograph courtesy Paul Cunniffe

During Summer 1977 Iona were approached by the Parish Priest of the Parish incorporating Fairyhouse racecouse. He sought their assistance in organising an air show at the racecourse. The show featured many Iona aircraft along with guest aircraft. The following year the first of the Air Spectaculars took place at the County Meath racecourse. The organising secretary and show co-ordinator, for what was to become Ireland's biggest one-day event, was Madeline O'Rourke, who acted in that capacity for ten years from 1978 to 1987. The first seven Air Spectaculars were hosted at Fairyhouse with the 1985 event scheduled for Cork - and later cancelled due to a 200 foot cloudbase.

1986 and 1987 were held at Baldonnel. Iona Airways played its part in these displays. The first scheduled appearance of an Iona aircraft was on Sunday, 17 August 1980. Their involvement was a flypast of Cessna 172N, EI-BCK; Cessna F337F, EI-AVC; Cessna 310Q, EI-BEO and Cessna 414A Chancellor, EI-BGP. Their next appearance was on Sunday, 22 August 1982. A banner pick-up and tow was demonstrated to the estimated 40,000 spectators that packed the stands. The flypast was facilitated by three of the Iona aircraft - EI-BMK; EI-BEO and EI-BGP. Iona participated in the 1986 Air Spectacular at Baldonnel on Sunday, 17 August with a triple banner tow.

Peter Cahill at the controls of Cessna 414A, EI-BGP, performs a low high-speed pass in front of the crowded stands at Fairyhouse Air Spectacular on Sunday, 17 August 1980

Photograph courtesy Paul Duffy

Three of the Iona fleet perform a low flypast in front of the 40,000 spectators gathered at Fairyhouse racecourse on Sunday, 22 August 1982. The aircraft involved were, left to right: Cessna 310Q, EI-BEO; Cessna 414A Chancellor, EI-BGP and Cessna 310Q, EI-BMK

Photograph courtesy Paul Duffy

During the Air Spectacular at Fairyhouse on Sunday, 22 August 1982, using Cessna F172N, EI-BCK, Iona demonstrated a banner pick-up and tow. The banner read: *'IONA No. 1 business airline'*.

Photograph courtesy Paul Duffy

The cycle of damage and repair was an unavoidable part of the aviation business. On 5 November 1984, EI-ATC was test-flown at Dublin airport by Peter Cahill and, on 22 January 1985 it returned to active status after a marathon six-year rebuild following its undercarriage damage at Carrickfin, County Donegal on 10 January 1979. On its return it was re-registered in the name of M. P. (Pearse) Cahill. At this stage most of the twins were painted in the Iona house colours, including EI-ATC. However, the active Cessna 310 fleet only remained at three units for a short period as EI-BEO was to suffer a similar unfortunate fate seven months later. On 27 August 1985 the aircraft suffered an undercarriage collapse, this time at the other end of the country, at Farranfore, County Kerry, and was ferried back to Dublin after temporary repair. Ex-Taoiseach, Charles J. Haughey was a passenger at the time of the incident. The aircraft was repaired at Iona and air-tested, four years later, on 6 November 1989. This incident did not deter the Fianna Fail leader from flying with Iona. Knock airport was officially opened on 30 May 1986. With Peter Cahill at the controls, Charles J. Haughey and Pearse Cahill were flown from Dublin airport to Knock to perform the official ceremony, in the presence of Monsignor James Horan. Owing to the inclement weather on the day, the Iona aircraft was the only aircraft to land at Knock to mark the occasion.

As aerial photography became an important part of media coverage, newspaper photographers increasingly used Iona aircraft. Terrorism came to the skies off the coast of County Kerry on the morning of Sunday, 23 June 1985. An Air India Boeing 747, VT-EFO, with 329 passengers and crew on board was en route from Montreal, Canada to Bombay, India and was cruising at 31,000 feet when it vanished from the radar screens of Shannon Air Traffic Controllers at 8.13am, at a position about 80

miles west of Valentia Island. Wreckage and bodies were reported to be scattered over an area of $4_{1/2}$ miles. A massive air and sea rescue operation involving Irish, British and American personnel was launched almost immediately, but only bodies and uninflated life rafts were found. Experts immediately suspected a bomb to have caused the

Iona's Cessna 310, EI-BMK, assisted in the search for bodies and wreckage from the Air India disaster off Co. Kerry, 23 June 1985. Photograph shows ships in the search area

Photograph courtesy *Irish Times*

disintegration of the aircraft. Cessna 310, EI-BMK, flown by Peter Cahill, left Dublin several hours later for Cork, arriving there at 1.30pm. Throughout the day they assisted in the search operation and took aerial photographs of the scene. At 6.50pm they returned to Dublin and within 30 minutes Peter was again airborne in EI-BMK along with an RTE camera crew to record the scenes. Sorties were flown between Shannon and Cork and along the County Kerry coast until the aircraft arrived back at Dublin at 1.55am the following morning.

The south west coast of Ireland bore witness to yet another tragedy, this time an ecological rather than human disaster. The 85,000 tonne iron ore carrier *Kowloon Bridge*, with 900 tons of fuel, left Bantry Bay, County Cork on Saturday morning, 22 November 1986, in forecast storm conditions. It began drifting with damaged steering off Sherkin Island, County Cork. Sea King helicopters from RAF Brawdy, Wales, winched the 25 crew to safety in difficult conditions. The tanker ran aground at 3am on Monday morning on the Stags Rocks, 10 miles east of Baltimore. Later that morning, 24 November 1986, Iona received a request from Tom Lawlor, photographer with *The Irish Times*, to fly him to the area of the stricken vessel to take some aerial photographs. Peter Cahill was again tasked to fly the Cessna 310, EI-ATC, along with Tom, and captured on camera the scene of devastation that appeared the following morning on the front page of *The Irish Times*.

Within months Peter Cahill was again involved in a rescue mission off the County Kerry coast. An Italian pilot, Mr. Marino Salon, 34, was ferrying a new Cessna 182 across the Atlantic when his fuel lines became blocked about 120 miles south west of Valentia Island. He broadcast a May-Day distress call and was forced to ditch into the freezing Atlantic waters on Tuesday evening, 10 March 1987. Yet again, Iona accepted a request to fly to the area for some aerial photographs. Peter Cahill flew Cessna 310, EI-BMK to Shannon and onwards out into the Atlantic in a detail that lasted over four hours. The pilot was trapped by his legs for a while as water filled the cockpit. An RAF helicopter later rescued him. The following day he was able to continue to his home near Pisa, Italy. These instances reflect the versatility and ability of Iona to respond to calls for use of their aircraft at relatively short notice, and the high regard in which the media held them.

In May 1986, Aer Lingus celebrated its 50th anniversary. To commemorate the occasion they re-

The *Kowloon Bridge* aground on the Stags Rocks, 24 November 1986, with the ocean-going tug, *Smit Rotterdam*, standing by. Photograph taken by *Irish Times* photographer, Tom Lawlor, from Iona's Cessna 310, EI-ATC

Photograph courtesy Tom Lawlor / *Irish Times*

As part of the celebrations to mark Aer Lingus's 50th anniversary, Pearse Cahill was a guest of the airline, when he was taken for a flight to Bristol in the replica of their first aircraft, EI-ABI, *Iolar*.

Photograph courtesy Paul Duffy

enacted the inaugural flight from Baldonnel to Bristol as flown by Captain Oliver Armstrong in the de Havilland Dragon, EI-ABI, on 27 May 1936. By way of recognising the fact that Aer Lingus's first pilot, Captain Armstrong, was previously with Iona, they invited Pearse to travel to Bristol as their VIP guest in another Dragon that had been painstakingly restored by Aer Lingus engineers. It was re-registered EI-ABI.

The year 1987 was to be a watershed for Iona, seeing the start of diversification from their core business of air-taxi, charter, and flying club operations. The first development commenced on 14 December 1986 when Iona were awarded a United Parcel Service (UPS) / Walsh Western small package contract. The contract involved flying Shannon – Dublin – Stansted to connect with a Talair Shorts 330 that flew to UPS's European hub at Cologne in Germany. However, almost immediately, Iona were flying to Cologne from Shannon and following an overnight in Cologne would return to Shannon and finish in Dublin. It was usually the Cessna 414 Chancellor, EI-BGP, that was deployed for this task.

United Parcel Service (UPS) was founded in 1909. It was described as a company run on a business philosophy, which was half Marine Corps and half Quaker. At the time of Iona becoming involved with the company they employed approximately 250,000 people worldwide. Its fleet comprised 6 Boeing 747–100s, 30 Boeing 757PFs, 36 Boeing 727-100, 42 DC-8-71F/73Fs, 11 Metro III/ Expeditors. In addition it relied heavily on a large back-up fleet from other US operators as an insurance against problems with its own operation. The hub at Standiford Field, Louisville, Kentucky occupied 87 acres of ramp space and over one million square feet of interior space. The facility at the time was processing 120,000 packages an hour and their air operation was then handling 650,000 packages daily. The West Coast base was at Ontario, California.

UPS's aircraft first appeared in Ireland in 1985 after the new Federal Aviation Authority (FAA) noise rules grounded Aer Turas's own DC-8-63F from US operations. Aer Turas came to an agreement with UPS to fly the weekend Aer Lingus transatlantic freighter schedules. A complex arrangement, involving Aer Lingus, Aer Turas, UPS and the actual operator (Evergreen, Interstate and Orion), was agreed.

Shannon Executive Aviation held the contract for the Shannon – Dublin – Luton service. Ryanair using Bandeirante EI-BPI also operated it, but poor loads meant the operation was uneconomic and was sub-chartered on occasion to Iona, generally using one of the Cessna 310s. On 9 November 1987 routing was changed to Southend instead of Stansted. Occasionally Iona would operate direct and non-stop from Dublin to Cologne. Iona normally used Cessna 414, EI-BGP, on the run, but other aircraft were substituted from time to time. The majority of the sectors, totalling eight hours flying time per day approximately, were flown by the 414 for the first five months of the contract – clocking up almost 1,000 hours with this contract alone. However, it was obvious that the plush, executive interior of EI-BGP was not really appropriate to the rigours of cargo haulage, and so Iona arranged to acquire a pair of more rugged Cessna 404 Titans. The first Titan ordered by Iona was a 1980 Wichita built Titan Ambassador II, with convertible passenger / cargo interior. It was registered to Iona National Airways Limited as EI-BUM on 15 May 1987 (see Table 26). On learning of this registration, Pearse contacted the Department of Transport and firmly registered his comments!! The prototype of the 404 first flew in February 1975, with deliveries commencing the following year. It was a very flexible, capable aircraft, ideal for air taxi / charter operations. It could carry a full complement of nine passengers over a range of 900 miles. With small payloads, like small packages, its range could extend to 1,500 miles and, with double doors, the aircraft was well suited to cargo operations. The last Titan came off the assembly line in 1982, carrying a sales tag of US$500,000.

Iona's only involvement in scheduled passenger services to date had been the nine month operation of the Sligo – Dublin service in 1984. This was to change in the late 1980s. In 1987 Iona were awarded the contract to ferry Cyprus Airways crew from

With the increase in small package and light cargo business Iona purchased the more rugged Cessna Titan Ambassador 11, EI-BUM, in May 1987. It is shown on the Iona ramp 6 May 1989

Photograph courtesy Paul Duffy

On 3 May 1987 the Irish Government awarded Iona the licence for a twice-daily Dublin – Derry scheduled service linking Dublin – Derry (Eglinton airport). This was awarded the day prior to the arrival at Iona of Titan, EI-BUM. Initially Iona used the Cessna 310s, however as demand altered they placed the Cessna 414A, EI-BGP, or the Titan, EI-BUM on the route. This was not the first occasion the Irish Government had experience of the Titan. In early April 1977, Iona acting as Irish Cessna dealer for the new type of aircraft took the opportunity to present the aircraft as a possible candidate for the fishery protection role. Military personnel flew the aircraft on their, by now, regular mission profile for such evaluations, Baldonnel – Killiney – Tuskar Rock and return.

Dublin to Belfast, previously held by Shannon Executive Aviation. Iona commenced duty on 11 April using the Cessna 414A, EI-BGP, and two Cessna 310s, EI-BMK and EI-ATC. EI-BEO was still unavailable following the undercarriage collapse at Farranfore in August 1985.

The Derry – Dublin service was operated by Avair prior to its collapse in February 1984. On 1 May 1985 Aer Arann commenced servicing this route on a twice daily basis using a nine-seat Piper Navajo Chieftan, G-WSSC, later registered EI-BRC. Aer Arann received the subsidy previously paid to Avair. The inaugural flight carried many dignatories including An Taoiseach, Dr. Garret Fitzgerald. Payloads remained poor despite an excellent record of reliability, and the subsidy proved essential to keep the route viable. The Chieftan suffered an in-flight engine failure in April 1986 and was substituted by one of the Galway based Islanders until the Navajo resumed service a month later. However, on 9 May 1986 the Department of Transport and Tourism announced that Aer Arann had lost the licence for the route and awarded it to Shannon Executive Aviation Limited at a lower rate of subsidy.

The Dublin – Derry timetable allowed for two flights each direction on each day Monday to Friday. The first departed Dublin at 7.50am arriving Derry 8.35am and departing Derry at 8.55am, arriving Dublin 9.40am. In the evening the departure from Dublin was at 5pm, arriving Derry 5.45pm and departing Derry 6.05pm arriving Dublin 6.50pm. The quoted fares were £50.00 one-way; £95.00 return; a three - day return ticket cost a patron £85.00. This service received an Irish Government subsidy of £100,000. The service was handled by Iona at the main airport terminal using the former Aer Arann desk in the main concourse. Iona's previous Sligo – Dublin service had been handled at the Iona facilities on the west side of the airport.

Iona was granted the licence to again operate the Sligo – Dublin route in June 1987. The operation was Monday to Friday, commencing in Sligo at 8.00am and arriving Dublin 8.45am. It departed Dublin at 7pm arriving Sligo 7.45pm and departing Sligo at 8pm arriving Dublin 8.45pm. The service commenced 22 June 1987 for an initial trial period terminating 31 July 1987. The fares advertised were the same as for the Dublin – Derry service. By the end of 1987 it was decided once again to terminate the Sligo – Dublin service. The route was taken over by Aer Lingus Commuter. By this time, Iona were operating frequent night Manchester – Dublin newspaper charters, carrying overflow from the regular Aer Lingus 737 freighter service. These flights were normally operated by one of the Cessna 404 Titans. The second Titan acquired by Iona was registered to Iona National Airways Limited on 29 July 1987 three days following delivery. It was a 1978 Wichita built Titan II Courier. It entered the Irish register as EI-BVA (see Table 27). It had an 11-seat configuration and was to be operated on passenger schedules. The other Titan, EI-BUM, was retained mostly for cargo / air freight work.

Iona were so impressed with the capabilities of EI-BUM, they purchased another version of the Titan. This Cessna 404 was registered EI-BVA on 29 July 1987 and served the company for six years. Above photograph taken at Iona in September 1987

Photograph courtesy Paul Cunniffe

The Cessna 310 fleet was now ageing, with EI-ATC now almost 19 years with Iona. The next acquisition for the growing fleet of aircraft to be used for air-taxi work and small charters was a new Cessna T.303 Crusader. This was to be the second pressurised aircraft in the Iona fleet, the first such aircraft being the 414 Chancellor, EI-BGP. The Crusader was only built in 1984 and had the previous registration N5087V. It was also Wichita

constructed and was flown across the Atlantic on 16 April 1988. Four days previously it was allocated the marks EI-BVP (see Table 28). This six-seater cabin class twin-engine aircraft had a cruise speed of 196 knots and a range of over 1,000 nautical miles. Its useful load was 1,811 pounds. It was used as a supplement for the Cessna 310s in the air taxi and charter work and proved popular with the customers who had up to now been using the much older Cessna 310s. The Crusader proved effective for the tasks assigned it and remained at Iona for five years.

In February 1988, the Department of Tourism and Transport granted Iona licences to operate Dublin – Shannon, Dublin – Carrickfin and Dublin – Belfast. A special inaugural flight on the Dublin – Belfast (Aldergrove) route was flown on 19 May 1988 with a Cessna 404 carrying a party of senior business, airline and travel trade executives. Another special inaugural flight on the Dublin – Shannon route took place the following day. Scheduled passenger services on both routes commenced on Monday, 23 May 1988, initially operated by the Cessna 404 Titans, to be replaced by the 19-seat Embraer Bandeirante on order at the time, though this aircraft was also used for the small package contracts.

The timetable showed two flights daily on Dublin – Belfast, Monday to Friday, departing Dublin at 9.30am and arriving Belfast 10.05am; departing Belfast 10.20am and back in Dublin 10.55am. In the afternoon the service departed Dublin 4.40pm, arriving Belfast 5.15pm, departed Belfast at 5.30pm and arrived back in Dublin 6.05pm. The schedule was timed to coincide with transatlantic flights, east and westbound, operated by Aer Lingus, with whom a joint commercial agreement had been formalised.

The second pressurized aircraft to join the Iona fleet, to assist with air taxi and charter work, was Cessna T.303 Crusader, EI-BVP. The aircraft is photographed on the apron at Dublin airport 16 April 1988 following its ferry flight across the Atlantic that day

Photograph courtesy Paul Cunniffe

On the Shannon route, the service departed Shannon at 6.45am Monday to Friday, arriving Dublin 7.30am. The return flight left Dublin at 7.35pm arriving Shannon 8.20pm. On a Friday only, a flight departed Shannon at 8.35pm arriving back in Dublin 9.20pm. Iona continued with the Dublin – Derry schedules at the same time. Unfortunately, passenger loads on the Dublin – Shannon route were uneconomical and the service was suspended after a couple of months. By this time Iona had not exercised their options on the Dublin – Carrickfin route.

In March 1988, three new British registered Piper Warriors arrived at the Iona ramp. They were G-BNOT, G-BNOV and G-BNOW. They had completed a 13 1/2 hour leg of a ferry flight from Gander. Iona was given the task of de-tanking the aircraft in preparation for their delivery to the British Aerospace Flying College at Perth, Scotland. In early 2004 all three aircraft were in Spain on pilot training duties.

One of the last great air adventures of the Atlantic prior to the outbreak of War in 1939 was the tale of the 31-year-old Californian carpenter, of Irish heritage, who departed Long Beach, California on 8 July 1938 with the intention of flying to New York and back to California. On 17 July he departed Floyd Bennett Field, New York and 26 hours later his Curtis Robin touched down at Baldonnel. On realising where he was he declared: *'Gosh! I must have turned the wrong way.'* Douglas Corrigan had thus immortally earned himself the nickname *'Wrong Way Corrigan.'* Paul Duffy, Vice-Chairman of the Royal Aeronautical Society (Dublin Branch), arranged a presentation to Douglas and he returned to Ireland. On 17 July 1988, to coincide with the 50th anniversary of his epic flight he visited Baldonnel and later delivered a talk to members of the Society at Trinity College, Dublin. He later visited Clery's Department store, O'Connell Street, Dublin where he had gone in 1938 to acquire a new outfit. There he was introduced to a number of guests, including Pearse Cahill and Catherine Greene.

On 20 March 1988 three Piper PA-28-161 Warriors arrived at Iona to be de-tanked following their marathon 13 1/2 hour ferry flight across the Atlantic

Photograph courtesy Paul Duffy

EST. 1930

Head Office:
**CLOGHRAN,
CO. DUBLIN,
IRELAND.**
Ph: 424400, 424182,
424346, 424580
Fax: 378323
Telex: 32296 IONA EI

* EXECUTIVE CHARTER inc. HELICOPTER
* FREIGHT CHARTER
* AIRCRAFT BANNER ADVERTISING
* AERIAL PHOTOGRAPHY
* FLIGHT TRAINING

DETAILS PERTAINING TO THE ABOVE MAY BE HAD UPON
REQUEST TO OPERATIONS DEPARTMENT — CHARTER SECTION.

★ EXECUTIVE CHARTER ★

Iona National Airways operates a fleet of Cessna and Bandeirante Aircraft and you can choose one to suit your personal needs from our 3 Passenger Seat Single-Engine Cessna to our 19 Seat Twin-Engine Turbo Prop Bandeirante.

Our service is ideal for the Business Executive offering total flexibility in relation to times and destinations:

* *Your Schedule is our Schedule* •
* *Your Destination is our Destination* •

★ AIRCRAFT ADVERTISING ★

Iona introduced aircraft banner advertising to Ireland and are the leading exponents of the service in this country. We can have your very own slogan flying where you want it, when you want it at very short notice. This is the most impressive form of advertising and promotion available today. Your message becomes the centre of attraction for thousands of people. No other form of advertising makes such an impact.

★ AERIAL PHOTOGRAPHY ★

We have aircraft available for a variety of photographic purposes from aerial surveys to film unit shoots. We will provide photographers if required.

Est. 1930

SUMMER TIMETABLE
1988

Effective 27 March - 22 October

*The First Commercial Aviation Company
in Ireland*

1930   1988

DERRY
BELFAST
SHANNON
DUBLIN
CORK

Times and Prices are subject to change without notice
Belfast and Shannon Effective 23 May - 22 October

Summer timetable 1988, indicating details of the scheduled flights to/from Belfast, Derry, Cork and Shannon to be operated by Iona

Brochure courtesy Simon Nolan

EST. 1930

DUBLIN - DERRY (LDY) ** - DUBLIN

Days	Flt No	Dep	Time	Arr	Time	Class	Baggage Allowance
12345..	YJ022	Dublin	09.15	Derry	10.00	Y	20 kgs.
12345..	YJ023	Derry	10.15	Dublin	11.00	Y	20 kgs.
12345..	YJ024	Dublin	17.25	Derry	18.10	Y	20 kgs.
12345..	YJ025	Derry	18.25	Dublin	19.10	Y	20 kgs.

DUBLIN - BELFAST ALDERGROVE (BFS) - DUBLIN

Days	Flt No	Dep	Time	Arr	Time	Class	Baggage Allowance
12345..	YJ031	Dublin	09.30	Belfast	10.05	Y	20 kgs.
12345..	YJ032	Belfast	10.20	Dublin	10.55	Y	20 kgs.
12345..	YJ033	Dublin	16.40	Belfast	17.15	Y	20 kgs.
12345..	YJ034	Belfast	17.30	Dublin	18.05	Y	20 kgs.

SHANNON (SNN) - DUBLIN - SHANNON

Days	Flt No	Dep	Time	Arr	Time	Class	Baggage Allowance
12345..	YJ028	Shannon	06.45	Dublin	07.30	Y	20 kgs.
12345.7	YJ029	Dublin	19.35	Shannon	20.20	Y	20 kgs.
....5.	YJ030	Shannon	20.35	Dublin	21.20	Y	20 kgs.

Flight times subject to change without notice. Please confirm 24 Hours before departure.

CORK - BELFAST/DERRY - CORK

Day Return Flights available in conjunction with Aer Lingus from Cork to Dublin, connecting with Iona National Airways (YJ) service

SHANNON - BELFAST/DERRY - SHANNON

Day Return Flights available with Iona National Airways (YJ) via Dublin, or Aer Lingus connecting with YJ services at Dublin.

Reservations:
IONA - DUBLIN: 01-425466 / 01-379900 Ext. 4254
IONA - DERRY: 0504-811140 / 0504-810123
IONA - BELFAST: Aer Lingus 0232-245151
IONA - SHANNON: 061-61444. Ext. 267. - 360555 Direct
Local Travel Agent or Airline

**Eglinton · Public Holidays Subject to Confirmation

Est. 1930

FARES

IONA NATIONAL AIRWAYS FLIGHTS ONLY

	One-Way	Return	3-Day *	
Dublin - Derry	45	85	75	IR£
	40	77	68	UK£
Dublin - Belfast	43	81	71	IR£
	39	73	64	UK£
Shannon - Dublin	45	85	75	IR£
	-Nil-	-Nil-	-Nil-	UK£
Shannon - Belfast	88	150	140	IR£
	79	136	126	UK£
Shannon - Derry	90	150	140	IR£
	80	136	126	UK£

Cork - Derry	Fares available upon request to Iona National
Cork - Belfast	Airways or Aer Lingus.

Infants: 0-2 yrs: 10% of Appropriate Adult Fare
Children: 2-12 yrs: 50% of Appropriate Adult Fare
There is no 3-day fare available to Infants & Children

★ IONA PREFERRED HOTELS ★

everglades hotel   EUROPA HOTEL BELFAST

(A MEMBER OF THE EMERALD GROUP OF COMPANIES)

In Derry or Belfast for quality accommodation to suit all price ranges Iona recommend you stay at the Everglades Hotel, Derry and the Europa Hotel, Belfast.
For reservation, phone: Derry: 0504-46722 Belfast: 0232-327000

AVIS   ★ CAR HIRE ★   AVIS

This facility is available through our preferred rental company — **AVIS** with whom very competitive rates have been agreed for your benefit. Further information may be obtained from any Iona representative.

* Minimum Stay: 2 NIGHTS

Douglas *'Wrong-way'* Corrigan with a group representing the Royal Aeronautical Society (Dublin Branch) at Clery's store, Dublin on 17 July 1988. Front row, Douglas is flanked by Marguerite Molloy (RAeS) and Catherine Greene (Iona) on left. Back row, left to right: Brendan Downey (Aer Lingus), Michael Keating, Col. John Moore (Air Corps and Chairman RAeS), Jarlath Conerney (RAeS) and Pearse Cahill (Iona)

Photograph via Pearse Cahill collection

In an article in *Business and Finance*, 14 July 1988, titled *'Ireland's Oldest Airline,'* the following was quoted: -

'Now Iona has a fleet of nineteen Cessna and Bandeirante planes, employs 50 people, carries over 5,000 passengers a year and has an annual turnover of £2m. The charter and scheduled flights account for nearly 40% of Iona's total business. The other main source of income is from a parcel and freight service that accounts for a further 40% of business. The remainder comes from a flight training school, an aerial photography service, an aircraft advertising service as well as a maintenance service for the 35 privately owned planes at its base in Cloghran.'

Iona's first involvement with Federal Express came in early 1988 when they were awarded the contract for a small package feeder service from Shannon to Dublin and onto a Federal Express

F-27 Friendship, which was operated by Channel Express. Federal Express had commenced its transatlantic small package operation on 15 June 1985, serving Stansted and Brussels. It had been hoped that Shannon would become one of the hubs. The service originates in Federal Express' hub in Memphis, Tennessee, using Boeing 727-200s to Stansted and on to Brussels, refuelling at Shannon on the return leg, and operating five nights, Tuesday to Saturday. Iona's involvement was delayed by licensing restrictions. From 11 April 1988, Iona reached agreement with the company to operate the Dublin – Birmingham sector of their European network, with the Cessna 404 Titan assigned to this role five nights per week. There was not deemed, by any party, to be a conflict of interest with the UPS operations. During July 1988, Iona secured a contract to ferry Air Canada 747 crews from Belfast to Shannon on a weekly basis. This was in addition to the contract to ferry the Cyprus Airways crews from Dublin to Belfast.

Iona had entered discussions with the Department of Tourism and Transport to permit the company to operate two or three Cessna 208 Caravan Ones for Federal Express on feeder routes, such as Shannon – Dublin and Sligo – Dublin on a night Instrument

A further increase of growth in the small package business required Iona to purchase Embraer EMB.110P1 Bandeirante, EI-BVX. The aircraft was delivered 2 June 1988

Photograph courtesy Patrick J. Cummins

Embraer EMB.110P1 Bandeirante, EI-BVX, with father
and son, Pearse and Peter, at the controls

Photograph via Pearse Cahill collection

To assist Iona with the growth in the small package business, in the main as a consequence of the increased UPS contract and the Federal Express deal, an aircraft bigger than the Cessna Titan was required. The aircraft selected was an Embraer EMB.110P1 Bandeirante. On 30 May 1988 the Bandeirante was registered to Iona National Airways Limited and delivered via Reykjavik, Iceland to Dublin on 2 June 1988 as EI-BVX (see Table 29). Crew training duties commenced the following day.

The Cessna 414, EI-BGP, was out of service for a major overhaul and in June 1988 was replaced by leasing a Reims Cessna 406 Caravan II from Aero Lease, Holland. The aircraft was registered PH-LAS and it remained on the Dutch register throughout the term of the lease, which terminated 1 February 1989, following the return to service of EI-BGP. During its lease term with Iona it operated a number of passenger and cargo charters and was available as a back-up for the Cessna 404s on the nightly small package operations.

Developments with Federal Express were initially rapid. The company were placing Cessna 208 Caravan Ones with contract operators in Europe to act as feeders from the smaller traffic points, and it was decided to start a Shannon – Dublin feeder

Flight Rules (IFR) basis. Night IFR in Irish airspace was only permitted to suitably equipped multi - engine aircraft, although recent legislation changes had allowed turboprop powered Caravan Ones to operate in this role in countries such as United States of America, Canada, France and Scandinavia.

Iona leased Cessna 406, PH-LAS from June 1988 to February 1989 from Aero Lease, Holland while Cessna 414, EI-BGP was out of service for major overhaul

Photograph courtesy Paul Duffy

When Iona received approval to operate flights at night, or IFR, it made Ireland only the second European nation to grant such approval. As a result Federal Express placed a Cessna 208A Caravan I with Iona from 25 August 1988. This was F-GEOH that later became EI-FDX

Photograph courtesy Paul Duffy

Cessna 208A Caravan I, EI-FDX, in Federal Express colours and Iona logo on tail was the first aircraft operated by Iona for Federal Express from September 1988

Photograph courtesy Patrick J. Cummins

frequently received awards from Cessna *'in recognition for excellence in the development of dealership personnel.'* When Federal Express was establishing a base in Norway they requested Iona to supply maintenance personnel and pilots to assist with the commencement of the Norwegian operation. Federal Express prefers to deal with well established but smaller operators who will be able to accord the FedEx operation the priority and flexibility needed to achieve the desired levels of reliability. At the time Iona were well established as a FedEx contractor with their nightly Dublin – Birmingham Cessna Titan operation. The introduction of the Caravan marked a new phase in the development of Iona's specialised contract cargo operations.

The Cessna Caravan I came from Cessna's desire to find a successor to the Cessna 206 piston single but with increased cabin volume and payload, and greater engine power, possibly a turboprop power plant. The Cessna 208 emerged as the largest of the Cessna singles. The prototype made its first flight 9 December 1982, with the first production model flying in July 1984. Certification followed a few months later. A typical price tag was over US$750,000. By the early 1980s Federal Express had become a household name, with their slogan *'absolutely positively overnight.'* They operated a variety of aircraft with varying degrees of reliability, mostly with twin-engine aircraft.

They set about rectifying this situation by purchasing a fleet of standardised aircraft that would be contracted out to their qualified operators. Their studies showed that the Cessna Caravan was easily the winner in terms of operating cost and projected reliability, particularly with the Pratt and Whitney PT6 engine. In early 1985, Federal Express placed an order with Cessna for 30 Caravans with an option for 70 more. Within

using the type. This required Irish regulatory approval for single-engine night / Instrument Flight Rules (IFR) commercial operations. Ireland was to become the second country in Europe, after France, to authorise night IFR operations in single engine aircraft. So, Iona was very much to the forefront of progress in this area and was the first operator in Europe to fly the Cessna 208 in IFR conditions. The approval granted did not extend to over water flights at night or in IFR conditions. As soon as the approval was received, Cessna 208A Caravan I, F-GEOH was delivered Reims – Lille – Dublin on 25 August 1988. This aircraft had only been manufactured at Wichita in 1986 and initially carried the marks N9525F. On 7 September 1988 it was jointly registered in the names of Iona National Airways Limited and Federal Express as EI-FDX (see Table 30).

Federal Express's choice of Iona as the contract operator for its Irish services was a prestigious endorsement of the company's organisation and operational standards. Iona sent the appropriate maintenance staff and pilots to the Cessna establishment at Wichita, Kansas, for training on the Cessna 208. From the outset of Iona's relationship with Cessna it became a policy to maintain a high standard of qualified personnel. For many years Iona sent staff to Cessna and

four years their fleet of Caravans totalled 110 and had accumulated over 110,000 flying hours without an engine failure, and dispatch reliability of 99.81%. Their fleet had full de-ice, weather radar, King avionics, flight control and autopilot, as standard. The 208A had a payload of 2,800 pounds and cargo volumes of 335 cubic feet. Cruising speed was 183 knots at 8,000 feet. Federal Express bought over 300 Cessna 208A's and 208B's.

The scheduled passenger services that were launched on 23 May 1988 between Dublin – Shannon and Dublin – Belfast were dropped by the beginning of September 1988. First to go was the Shannon service. The company had briefly operated the Belfast service as a combined Dublin – Belfast – Derry route, but shortly afterwards decided to drop Belfast altogether. Iona announced their intention to terminate the Dublin – Derry scheduled service on 25 November 1988, unless a greater level of financial support was forthcoming. The company stated the level of subsidy was insufficient to maintain viability. At this stage Dublin – Derry was the only scheduled service being operated by Iona. The operation proved not to be viable, despite the availability of an initial Irish Government subsidy and was terminated on 25 November 1988. Avair, Aer Arann and Shannon Executive Aviation had previously operated the route.

By way of extending their operations and offering the facilities of Iona to visiting General Aviation traffic, a proposal was submitted to Mr. John Wilson, Minister for Tourism and Transport on 20 December 1988. The intention was to become a Fixed Base Operator (FBO). The services would include Customs facilities, a larger hangar and additional parking place for light aircraft. This followed on the growth in staff levels from 25 to 60 as a consequence of obtaining the contracts with Federal Express and UPS.

The Iona directors felt they were not getting the full support of the Minister's Department and detailed these grievances in their submission. The issues included:

* The special training of staff in USA for a month to work in a propeller overhaul shop that had to be discontinued due to the failure of the Department to grant approval for the workshop - £30,000 spent on equipment and four jobs lost

* Commercial Pilot Licence (CPL) examination results were taking a long time to be advised to students – one student went to the UK to sit a similar exam and got his results in two days

* The impression that air traffic control was hindering flying training at Dublin airport – due to staff shortages in the control tower

* If they had the use of Gormanstown or Baldonnel for specific training functions they could train Aer Lingus cadet pilots, thus saving the airline up to £1,000,000 per annum

* The submission included the comment *'regarding Aer Rianta, we are treated as the poor relation on the other side of the airport and we now get the impression that they would like us out of the way'*

* For mechanics it was taking 12 months between applying for their licences and sitting the exams – staff trained by Iona were now going to other operators and abroad

* Any previous planning submissions were *'granted with awkward conditions'*

The submission also included a summary of the points regarding the Outline Permission for *'Light Aircraft Building, Aviation School and Residence at Huntstown, Cloghran'* (this application referred to lands across the road, west of the present location of Iona). The application progressed as follows:

* 1980 – Application submitted

* 1981 – Additional information supplied

* 1981– Outline permission granted 7 May 1981, conditions included restrictions on height (36 feet) and use of metallic cladding

* 1983 – Airport authority required 'set-back line,' due navigational aids, inside which no

building could be erected. Application for approval submitted 29 July

* 1983 – Decision to grant approval was made 7 October 1983

* 1984 – Resubmission for Bye-Law approval made 23 January 1984

* 1988 – Meeting with Aer Rianta to discuss metallic cladding, security etc held 4 February

* 1988 – Planning permission due to expire 7 October 1988 - project proceeded with

* 1988 – Despite reminders from P. Cahill no further meetings took place. Details of the structure submitted to Dublin County Council 25 May 1988 – no response until 17 October 1988, ten days after the expiry of the Planning Permission.

It was pointed out that Aer Rianta had, meantime, constructed a control building and hangars inside the 'set-back line' and these had contained metallic cladding similar to that proposed by Iona. Iona offered the conclusion that the objections to Iona's plans could now be removed. History showed that Iona's detailed submission proved relatively fruitless. In fact, throughout the following years much correspondence was exchanged between Pearse, the Department of Tourism and Transport, and various Government Ministers, highlighting his frustration with certain persons in authority and perceived attempts to frustrate his efforts at developing and progressing his company and facilities.

Despite these frustrations, the small package contract business continued to expand. During April 1989, one year after commencing the Dublin – Birmingham feeder service for Federal Express, the contract was reviewed so that Iona would now do the feeder service Dublin – Brussels non-stop direct to FedEx's European hub. The Shannon – Dublin Cessna Caravan I feeder service continued to operate. Approval was not yet granted to permit the Caravan operate cross-channel at night. The expansion continued into 1989; Iona also arranged to take over two contracts from Ryanair with effect

from 26 June 1989. A Cork – Dublin feeder for DHL and a Dublin – Stansted mail contract for the Post Office. Included in the deal was Ryanair's Bandeirante, EI-BPI (see Table 31).

In 1989, Iona became involved with DHL, a company with an interesting story behind its creation. In 1969, a young man arrived at a shipping office in San Francisco to take the ship-owner's daughter out on a date. Realising one of the owner's ships had sailed without its cargo's documents; the young man abandoned his date and caught a flight to Honolulu to deliver the papers for the shipping company. Needless to say the owner was impressed and gave the man further consignments to deliver. Soon he was clearing cargos through Customs. As the workload grew he obtained the assistance of two friends. Soon they were delivering important documents and small packages all over the world. Other industries sought their services as their reputation spread. The documents became more urgent, the parcels got heavier and the customers became more numerous. The names of the three entrepreneurs were Adrian Dalsey, Larry Hillblom and Robert Lynn – and the company became DHL; a household name with one million customers around the world(*xii).

Flying Post Office mail is almost as old as aviation itself, and Iona was to play a part in this illustrious tradition. The first time an airmail service was attempted on a large scale in Ireland was 1946 when Railway Air Services provided the service

---

FOOTNOTE (*xii)
Scope of DHL in 1989:
<u>Worldwide</u>
175 countries
99 aircraft
19,000 employees
7,500 collection / delivery vans
1,153 service centres / freight depots
<u>Ireland</u>
1 aircraft (a Merchantman operated by Air Bridge)
148 employees
35 collection / delivery vans
3 service centres / freight depots (Dublin, Cork and Shannon)

between Liverpool and Collinstown until 1953. From then, it was carried on using an Aer Lingus DC-3 between Dublin and Manchester until 1964. Between 1964 and 1978 it was carried by Aer Lingus on scheduled freighter services until it became no longer viable. In September 1978 the contract was awarded to Clyden Airways using DC-3s EI-BDT and EI-BDU. Clyden ceased trading in January 1981. The contract then went to Air Ecosse until May 1985.

In June 1984 the Irish Post Office joined The Express Mail Service (EMS). UNIPOST, comprising 21 member states was formed and forged links with over 100 of the world's postal administrations. The International EMS provides express mail delivery of documents and packages to over 100 countries worldwide. Delivery is guaranteed within specified times. A hub was established at Brussels for overnight transport throughout Europe and to and from North America. Each individual national postal authority makes its own arrangements. In Ireland's case the Air Ecosse Bandeirante transported the mails between Dublin and Luton, for onward transmission to Brussels. Air Ecosse ceased this contract in May 1985 and Shannon Executive Aviation (SEA) took over, operating their Skyvan and Metro, until February 1987, when Southend based National Airways continued, operating Beech KingAirs and Piper PA31 Navajos on these routes. This continued until November 1987 when the contract was awarded to Ryanair. The Bandeirante, EI-BPI, was used for the service, operating Dublin – Luton – Manchester – Dublin as flight 'Ryanair 970.' Ryanair operated the service from 2 November 1987 to 25 June 1989. The contract was then awarded to Iona National Airways, who also obtained the Bandeirante from Ryanair to operate the route. The flight number remained as 'Iona 970.' The Cork – Dublin feeder for DHL was to link in with the Air

Bridge / Elan Merchantman operating Shannon – Dublin – East Midlands. On 19 May 1989, Iona leased another Bandeirante, G-BNOC, from National Airways, Southend, England. The day after delivery an unmanned Aer Rianta fire tender damaged it at Cork airport while it was operating a flight for DHL. Pending completion of repairs at Southend another Bandeirante replaced it.

The Bandeirante acquired from Ryanair, EI-BPI, was older than EI-BVX having been constructed in 1980. It was the first of its type to appear on the Irish register. It was later leased to Ryanair becoming their first aircraft when delivered to Dublin 3 May 1985, using the callsign 'Ryanair 1', and officially registered to them on 10 May 1985. Ryanair used it on their inaugural flight from Waterford to Gatwick on 8 July 1985. After withdrawal from Ryanair service, it was leased to Business Flight Centre and subleased to Euroair on 31 May 1987. However, it returned to Dublin in July 1987 pending clarification of UK CAA requirements for UK marks. Leased again to Business Flight Centre on 19 July 1987 and sub leased to La Stampa at Rome / Ciampino from 19 July to 30 September 1987. Leased to Euroair

Bandeirante, EI-BPI, was the first aircraft operated by Ryanair when they commenced commercial operations from Waterford to Gatwick, London on 8 July 1985. It was acquired from Ryanair by Iona in June 1989

Photograph courtesy Paul Duffy

Transport from 1 October 1987 to January 1988. To coincide with taking over the Ryanair contracts the aircraft was registered to Iona National Airways Limited on 25 June 1989.

The leased Bandeirante, G-BNOC, supplemented Iona's EI-BVX, and the two were engaged on the company's expanding night cargo operation. The Bandeirante had now taken over these operations from the two Cessna 404 Titans that had operated the service up to then, and were used to support the Bandeirantes, when extra capacity was required, and for 'ad hoc' charter work.

By the end of the summer of 1989 Iona had an impressive nightly operation. For UPS, 'IONA 1911' left Cork each weekday and Sunday evening and routed Cork – Shannon – Dublin – Cologne, returning Dublin – Shannon – Cork as 'IONA 1912'. For Federal Express, the Cessna Caravan, EI-FDX, left Shannon each weekday evening as the 'IONA 056Y' routing to Dublin and transferring the load of small packages to the Bandeirante that continued to Brussels as 'IONA 015Y', returning in the early hours Brussels – Birmingham – Dublin as the 'IONA 055Y'. The Shannon bound cargo was then transferred to the Caravan, which returned to Shannon as the 'IONA 016Y', where the Caravan spent the day, flying back to Dublin that evening as the 'IONA 056Y'. For DHL there was a daily Dublin – Cork – Dublin service, bringing cargo from Cork to join the Elan Merchantman, when it arrived from Shannon, and then the Merchantman continued to

Cologne. Iona also took over the Post Office night mail contract operating Dublin – Luton – Manchester – Dublin as 'IONA 970'. The Bandeirante, EI-BPI, acquired from Ryanair at the time of taking over the Post Office contract, was painted in the house colours of Iona in early August 1989, and retaining the *'Express Mail Service'* logo. In addition to previous crew positioning contracts for Cyprus Airways and Air Canada, Iona secured similar contracts for Air Malta for a Dublin – Manchester flight and a weekly flight carrying Aer Turas crews from Shannon to Dublin. Iona had successfully adapted to the changing needs of the world of aviation, emerging as a significant company with an imposing schedule.

Pearse's contribution to aviation had been recognised by the Royal Aeronautical Society in June 1987, when the Dublin branch honoured him and presented him with an engraving and plaque in recognition of his service to the Irish aviation industry. In October of the following year, Pearse visited Tasmania, Australia. There he paid a nostalgic visit to Launceston airport where the Desoutter, EI-AAD was on prominent display in the terminal building. This was the first commercial aircraft purchased by Pearse's father, Hugh, in 1930 to initiate commercial air services in the State. Standing in front of that aircraft and thinking of the activity on the Iona ramp at the other end of the globe must surely have brought a lump to his throat.

Table 26

Registration	EI-BUM
Aircraft Type	Cessna 404 Titan Ambassador II
Constructors Serial Number	404-0650
Place & Year of Manufacture	Wichita, USA, 1980
Previous Registrations	N5313J
Registered to	Iona National Airways Ltd, 15 May 1987
Delivery date	4 May 1987

Remarks

It was originally registered in USA to Wolverine Air Charter, Downtown Detroit (City) airport. Its Export C of A was completed at Grand Rapids, from where it departed 2 May 1987, carrying the registration N5313J. Its routing was Grand Rapids - Bangor, Maine where it overnighted. It continued to Goose Bay and Reykjavik, Iceland on 3 May. The following afternoon it arrived at Dublin.

On 7 October 1994 it was ferried from Dublin by an Iona crew as 'IND404' for pre-sale overhaul by SCA at Dinard, France. It was cancelled from the Irish register 29 November 1994. On 2 December 1994 it was registered TL-ACB to Minair of Bangui, Central African Republic.

It was later leased to Air Affair Aifric based at Douala airport in west Cameroon. On 16 August 1998 it was taking off from Douala airport with a consignment of cargo when it suffered an engine failure. About 20 seconds later while attempting to return to the airfield the second engine failed. Both crew survived the crash though seriously injured. The aircraft never flew again and lies derelict at Douala airport.

Table 27

Registration	EI-BVA
Aircraft Type	Cessna 404 Titan II Courier
Constructors Serial Number	404-0237
Place & Year of Manufacture	Wichita, USA, 1978
Previous Registrations	SE-GYN; LN-LML; SE-GYN; N88723
Registered to	Iona National Airways Ltd, 29 July 1987
Delivery date	26 July 1987

Remarks

It was registered as LN-LML in September 1978. Restored to SE-GYN on 15 July 1985 to Avia AB, Visby, Sweden. Iona operated it from July 1987 until June 1993. EI-BVA was sold to Business Air of Bennington, Vermont as N404BA and was cancelled from the Irish register on 16 September 1993. It was ferried from Dublin across the Atlantic via Reykjavik, Iceland in its US marks on 18 September 1993.

On 13 May 2001 it was on an evening internal flight on the Caribbean Island of Puerto Rico with a landing scheduled for the capital San Juan. It crashed in the Caribbean National Forest colliding into a 3,524 foot mountain at an altitude of 2,700 feet. The sole occupant was a commercially rated pilot who was fatally injured.

It was cancelled from the US register on 21 May 2002 with the annotation *'destroyed'*. At time of de-registration it was owned by Air Cargo Sytems International Inc, Aguadilla, Puerto Rico and operated by City Wings Inc.

Table 28

Registration	EI-BVP
Aircraft Type	Cessna T.303 Crusader
Constructors Serial Number	303-00286
Place & Year of Manufacture	Wichita, USA, 1984
Previous Registrations	N5087V
Registered to	Iona National Airways Ltd, 12 April 1988
Delivery date	16 April 1988
Remarks	The Crusader was built in 1984 and had the previous registration N5087V. It was flown across the Atlantic on 16 April 1988. Its routing for the ferry flight was Wichita - Bangor - Goose Bay- Reykjavik- Dublin. Offered for sale in *Aeromart*, 1992 by Iona National Airways with 1486 hours TT, with a price tag of £125,000. As a consequence of the reduction of the Iona fleet, it was removed from the Irish register on 27 August 1993 following sale to Casper Air Services, Wyoming, USA and delivered Dublin to Jersey on 18 August 1993 as N7079U. Two days later it routed Jersey- Glasgow - Reykjavik. On 28 April 1995 it was registered to McClure Engineering Co., Fort Dodge, Webster, Iowa and recorded as current early 2004.

Table 29

Registration	EI-BVX
Aircraft Type	Embraer EMB.110P1 Bandeirante
Constructors Serial Number	110419
Place & Year of Manufacture	Sao Jose dos Campos, Brazil, 1983
Previous Registrations	N870AC; PT-SGL
Registered to	Iona National Airways Ltd. 30 May 1988
Delivery date	2 June 1988

Remarks

It acquired the initial registration N870AC to the Embraer Aircraft Corp on 27 August 1983. It was delivered to American Central Airlines in February 1984 and leased in December 1986 to Gulf Air. In November 1987 sale took place to Duncan Aviation Inc. and US marks were cancelled May 1988. Delivered via Reykjavik to Dublin on 2 June 1988 as EI-BVX.

Owing to Iona's financial circumstances, on 29 December 1994 it was registered to Cathal O'Sullivan and Declan Fitzpatrick c/o PARC Aviation Limited. On 6 March 1995 it was ferried Dublin - Exeter for overhaul by Jersey European Airways prior to sale. It was cancelled from the Irish register on 19 May 1995 and was sold to Air Fiji, Suva, Fiji Islands and registered to them on 20 July 1995 as DQ-AFO. On 9 August 1995 it departed Exeter on the first leg of its marathon delivery flight.

In early 2004 it was still in operation by Air Fiji in the southern Pacific Ocean and had a total time of approximately 17,000 hours and 23,000 landings.

Table 30

Registration	EI-FDX
Aircraft Type	Cessna 208A Caravan I
Constructors Serial Number	208-0084
Place & Year of Manufacture	Wichita, USA, 1986
Previous Registrations	F-GEOH, N833FE, N9525F
Registered to	Iona National Airways Ltd, 7 September 1988
Delivery date	25 August 1988
Remarks	It was registered as N833FE to Federal Express and was one of 13 Caravans operated by Mountain Air Cargo of Denver, North Carolina. On 25 June 1987 it was registered F-GEOH to Federal Express SARL, Nice, France for operation by Aviasud Aerotaxi. It was exhibited at the Paris Air Show in June 1987. The French registration was cancelled 2 August 1988 prior to its transfer to the Irish register.
	Following the withdrawal of Federal Express from Europe, the aircraft was to be returned to FedEx. At 3pm on Saturday, 25 April 1992, along with EI-FEX, the two aircraft taxied out from the Iona ramp, for the last time and together they took off for Prestwick, Scotland, on the first leg of their three-day return journey to Wichita, Kansas. It was cancelled from the Irish register on 23 April 1992.
	The following day, 24 April 1992, the aircraft was placed on the US register becoming N833FE in the name of Federal Express Corporation, Memphis, Tennessee and is recorded as current to them early 2004.

Table 31

Registration	EI-BPI
Aircraft Type	Embraer EMB110P1 Bandeirante
Constructors Serial Number	110308
Place & Year of Manufacture	Sao Jose dos Campos, Brazil, 1980
Previous Registrations	OY-ASY
Registered to	Iona National Airways Ltd, 23 June 1989

Remarks

Original registration was OY-ASY to Alkair V/Per Alkaersig, Skodsborg, Denmark on 22 December 1980. It was leased several times until it was cancelled from the Danish register on 22 December 1984 and placed on the Irish register to Air Tara on 4 January 1985. It was the first of its type to appear on the Irish register. It was later leased to Ryanair becoming their first aircraft when delivered to Dublin 3 May 1985, using the call sign 'Ryanair 1', and registered to them on 10 May 1985. After withdrawal from Ryanair service, it was leased to Business Flight Centre and subleased to Euroair on 31 May 1987; sub leased to La Stampa at Rome / Ciampino from 19 July to 30 September 1987. Leased to Euroair Transport from 1 October 1987 to January 1988. To coincide with taking over the Ryanair contracts the aircraft was registered to Iona National Airways Limited on 23 June 1989. Later operated by Muk Air, Denmark as OY-ASY.

In 2000 the aircraft was transferred from Muk Air to ScanCon Airways and is based at Thisted airport, northern Denmark (about 800nm south of the Arctic Circle). In early 2004 it was still active carrying passengers and cargo between Thisted and Copenhagen with occasional flights to Norway.

AIR NAVIGATION AND TRANSPORT ACT, 1965

Class C

Name ...... Iona National Airways Ltd., ...

Address ..Cloghran.,.Co...Dublin. ....

hereinafter referred to as the holder is hereby authorised by the Minister for Communications in Ireland to operate in both directions the non-scheduled air service(s) described below subject to the terms and conditions set forth herein.

Nature of Service(s):— for the carriage of passengers, cargo and mails.

Period of Validity:— This Authorisation shall come into effect on........11.May,.1990......and shall continue in force up to and including........10 May, 1991

AUTHORISATION

Nationality and Registration Marks	Name and Type	Added	Deleted
EI-BGP	Cessna 414		
EI-ATC	" 310		
EI-BEO	" 310		
EI-BCL	" 182		
EI-BGH	" 172		
EI-BRM	" 172		
EI-BMM	" 152		
EI-BMN	" 152		
EI-BNC	" 152		
EI-BRO	" 152		
EI-BVW	" 152		
EI-BVU	" 152		
EI-BUM	" 404		
EI-BVA	" 404		
EI-BVP	" 303		
EI-BVX	Bandeirante EMB110 PL		
EI-FDX	Cessna 208 Caravan 1		
G-ASVO	Handley Page Herald		
EI-BPI	Embraer Bandeirante		
F-GCLQ	Fairchild FH227B (valid for cargo operations only)		
G-ASVO	Handley Page Herald		

FOR COMMUNICATIONS READ TOURISM AND TRANSPORT

DEPARTMENT OF COMMUNICATIONS AND TRANSPORT
Expiration AND
11 July 1990

DEPARTMENT OF TOURISM AND TRANSPORT
Expires the 31 May 1990
CIVIL AVIATION

The Authorisation issued by the Department of Tourism and Transport, permitting 20 Iona aircraft to carry passengers, cargo and mails. Effective date is 11 May 1990.

Hugh Cahill 1883 - 1966

From a family portrait painted by G. Collie, A.R.H.A., 1943

Courtesy Pearse Cahill collection

Cessna 310G, EI-ATC, photographed on the Iona ramp following its return to service in January 1985. It was painted in the new Iona fleet colours.

Photograph courtesy Paul Duffy

Cessna 337, EI-AVC, at Iona 23 September 1971

Photograph courtesy Paul Cunniffe

Cessna 310Q, EI-BEO, photographed 18 May 1985

Photograph courtesy Paul Duffy

Cessna 414A Chancellor, EI-BGP photographed 18 May 1985

Photograph courtesy Paul Duffy

Cessna 310Q, EI-BMK photographed 18 May 1985

Photograph courtesy Paul Duffy

Cessna 404 Titan Ambassador, EI-BUM photographed 15 June 1987 - 4 weeks after delivery to Iona

Photograph courtesy Paul Duffy

Seven of the eight Cessna 172's supplied to the Irish Air Corps by Iona in a formation flight from their base at Gormanstown on 7 April 1988

Photograph courtesy Paul Duffy

Commandant Ralph James (now Brigadier General, Officer Commanding Air Corps) flying a Chipmunk, leads a formation of six of the eight Cessna 172's supplied to the Air Corps by Iona

Photograph courtesy Lt. Col. Kevin Byrne / Irish Air Corps

In 1997, the Irish Air Corps Co-op Squadron celebrated 25 years of service using the Iona supplied Cessnas. To mark the occasion they painted the tail of 203 with a special colour scheme. The inscription reads: 'Cessna FR 172H, 1972 - 1997, Reims Rocket'

Photograph courtesy
Lt. Col. Kevin Byrne / Irish Air Corps

Cessna 404 Titan II, EI-BVA at Iona 15 October 1988

Photograph courtesy Paul Cunniffe

Cessna T.303 Crusader, EI-BVP photographed over Powerscourt Demense, Co. Wicklow,
on 7 May 1988- 4 weeks after delivery to Iona

Photograph courtesy Paul Duffy

Aerial view of Iona ramp in 1975, following extension of clubhouse and prior to erection of second hangar

Photograph courtesy Paul Duffy

Embraer EMB. 110P1 Bandeirante, EI-BVX, photographed 5 July 1988

Photograph courtesy Paul Duffy

Cessna 208A Caravan I, EI-FDX, bearing the Federal Express logo, coasts in toward Dublin over Dun Laoghaire, on 12 September 1988 - 3 weeks after delivery.

Photograph courtesy Paul Duffy

Chapter

7

ONWARD AND UPWARD

By the early 1990's, Iona was established as the leading company in the small-package business and had a wide range of aircraft available

Chapter Seven

ONWARD AND UPWARD

The beginning of the 1990s saw the peak of Iona's fortunes as a commercial airline. The small package delivery business had multiplied worldwide, and Iona changed and adapted the fleet to keep apace of the expansion of the industry.

Iona maintained a very high level of schedule reliability on their night small package contracts for Federal Express, UPS and DHL. The company had won several awards from UPS for punctuality. Further confidence was placed in Iona's ability to provide an efficient service for the small package and feeder service. The workload increased to the extent that, by mid 1989, the Bandeirante proved inadequate for the requirements of UPS. Rather than purchase outright a larger aircraft, Iona prudently decided to wet-lease an aircraft from the Danish operator Star Air for seven months. Star Air is an all-cargo subsidiary of Danish carrier Maersk. The aircraft selected was a 1969 version Fokker F-27 Friendship, OY-SRR, and was introduced to the UPS Dublin – Cologne route on 4 September 1989. On 3 April 1990 the lease of the aircraft terminated; the final service being performed by PH-FKT. In subsequent weeks a Bandeirante or Cessna 404 Titan fulfilled the role, according to the load. Following from this, Iona opted to lease a stretched version Fairchild FH227B from the French carrier, TAT. This aircraft, F-GCLQ, did not enter service with Iona until 4 May 1990.

aircraft, the word 'Friendship' was dropped and it became the Fairchild F-27, with its inaugural flight on 12 April 1958. Delivery to its first customer, West Coast Airlines was on 22 June 1958 and services by them commenced 28 September 1958. On 21 September 1964 Fairchild merged with the helicopter manufacturer Hiller to become Fairchild-Hiller Corp. The F-27 was stretched by six feet and this version of the F-27 became the FH-227, launched in February 1965. This resulted in an early order of 18 FH-227s valued at US$24 million. The FH-227 was fitted with an auxiliary power unit in the starboard nacelle as standard, and its payload was increased to 11,500 pounds. The FH-227 entered service in July 1966. The FH-227B version (F-GCLQ) featured increased operating weights, larger diameter propellers, bigger wheels and brakes and higher operating speeds. The later version FH-227D (see EI-CAZ) was similar to the

To increase capacity for small cargo work, in May 1990, Iona leased an FH-227B, F-GCLQ, from TAT, France. It returned to France 12 September 1990

Photograph courtesy Patrick J. Cummins

The aircraft type had an interesting history, dating back to the 1950s. The Dutch aircraft manufacturer Fokker designed the F-27 Friendship, which resulted in an agreement materialising between them and the US manufacturer Fairchild on 26 April 1956. As part of the Americanisation of the

227B fitted with an improved anti-skid braking system and higher power Dart engines. In all 78 FH-227s of all variants were built, with 67 going to airlines and 11 to Governments and corporate bodies. By the end of 1981 TAT of Dinard, France held the largest number of FH-227, with sixteen in operation, having acquired their first in April 1979.

F-GCLQ was built at Hagerstown, Maryland in 1966. It was ferried to TAT on 4 May 1980 that included a stop at Cork. It returned to Cork 31 May 1980 in TAT livery. F-GCLQ's first visit to Dublin was on a charter for an Ireland v. France rugby international 21 March 1987. On Wednesday, 11 April 1990 it was delivered Dinard to Dublin on commencement of the 'damp' lease to Iona National Airways. It carried the TAT colours and incorporated the Iona fuselage and tail titles. Iona was to supply the crews. Initially these were Australian, supplied by PARC. Iona then supplied the pilots that had undergone conversion courses with Air UK in Norwich on the Fokker F-27 and TAT in Dinard on the FH-227. TAT provided maintenance and technical support with the

On 12 September 1990, the FH-227B, F-GCLQ, went to Dinard for overhaul and was replaced by a sister aircraft F-GCPZ, also bearing the Iona titles on the fuselage and tail

Photograph courtesy Leo Murray collection

aircraft returning to Dinard each weekend for such checks.

The FH-227 entered service on its first revenue flight on 4 May 1990 when it operated the Dublin – Cologne night freighter run for UPS. The flight could truly be called an international operation – Irish operated for an American company, with a French registered aircraft flown by Australian crews each evening to Germany, bringing packages for distribution all over the world. The Federal Express and UPS night contracts were then operated by the FH-227 and BAF Herald, with the Bandeirante covering the Express Mail Service contract. This left one of the Bandeirantes available for lease. On 12 September 1990, the FH-227B, F-GCLQ, went to Dinard for overhaul and was replaced by a sister aircraft F-GCPZ, also bearing the Iona titles on the fuselage and tail. On 24 December 1990, this aircraft was ferried by an Iona crew to Dinard. On 10 January 1991 FH-227, F-GCPX, was ferried to Dublin to continue the UPS contract. On 23 March 1991, F-GCPZ was severely damaged in a fire at Dinard.

Due to the loss of the Federal Express contract on the Dublin – Brussels route, Iona returned the leased Bandeirante, G-BNOC, to National Airways on 26 August 1989; three months after the lease had been acquired. The operation was running out of capacity for Federal Express but Iona was not in a position to help and British Air Ferries Heralds, took over the route. (*xiii)

FOOTNOTE(*xiii)
In the winter of 1960 Iona had played host to three Silver City Airways DC-3s (see Chapter 4). Silver City was formed in 1946 in connection with the South African and Australian mining industry. On 1 January 1963 this company merged with the car ferry operations of Channel Air Bridge to form British United Air Ferries (BUAF). On 1 October 1967 the company changed to British Air Ferries (BAF). While the Dublin based FedEx operation had used Heralds, BAF also operated a Fokker F-27 Friendship on behalf of FedEx in their colours, registered G-FEAD. The aircraft visited Dublin on 26 September 1990 on a sub charter for Iona. In March 1992 BAF phased out operating Heralds for FedEx and reverted to Viscounts. One of the Viscounts, G-AOYN, visited Dublin on 8 December 1992, operating for Iona. To reflect a new image being portrayed by BAF, the company again changed its name on 6 April 1993 to British World Airlines. Following the terrorist activities of 11 September 2001 and the resultant decline in the aviation business, the activities of British World ceased on 14 December 2001.

After a four-year overhaul, resulting from the undercarriage collapse at Farranfore in August 1985, Cessna 310 EI-BEO was air tested on 6 November 1989 prior to returning to service.

Express mail delivery could be an exciting business, with speed and efficiency of paramount importance. *Irish Air Letter* no. 183, March 1990, gives an excellent account of an Express Mail Service flight in the Bandeirante 'Papa India' on the night of 2 February 1990, with Peter Cahill and Paul Cullen at the controls. The article also gives a graphic insight into the activity at the Iona ramp and was indicative of the efficiency that Iona handled the small package and mail contract business. The Bandeirante arrived from Cork carrying small packages for the Air Bridge / Elan Merchantman as part of the DHL contract. It was then readied for the Express Mail Service to Luton on behalf of the Post Office. The two Cessna 404 Titans were on stand-by prepared to take over should a technical problem arise. The Cessna Caravan, EI-FDX, was en route from Shannon to fulfil the Federal Express contract to link up with the BAF Herald that would continue to Brussels. The Iona / Star Air F-27 was on the way from Shannon to pick up more freight at Dublin for the UPS service to Cologne.

All these flights radioed in their departure times and arrival estimates, along with load details using the Iona company frequency. Iona ground staff ensured the consignments were expeditiously handled, and despatched to their destinations. Timing was critical. The operations personnel remained on duty until after 11pm when all the outbound flights were well and truly on their way. They returned again at 4am in preparation for the return of the first of the incoming flights. Delays had to be avoided like the plague or they would have Pearse and his colourful language to deal with! A similar detailed article appeared in the *Irish Air Letter* issue 191, November 1990, covering the night flight to Cologne in the FH-227 with Australian pilots Brian Britton and Mike Kelly at the controls.

An indication of the aircraft on the books of Iona National Airways Limited (including Irish Aero Club) was incorporated in the authorisation issued by the Department of Tourism and Transport dated 10 May 1990 (*xiv). These 20 aircraft were:

*	Cessna 414	EI-BGP
*	Cessna 404	EI-BUM, EI-BVA
*	Cessna 310	EI-ATC, EI-BEO
*	Cessna 182	EI-BCL
*	Cessna 303	EI-BVP
*	Embraer Bandeirante	EI-BVX, EI-BPI
*	Fairchild FH-227	F-GCLQ
*	Handley Page Herald	G-ASVO
*	Cessna 208 Caravan 1	EI-FDX
*	Cessna 172	EI-BGH, EI-BRM
*	Cessna 150 / 152	EI-BMM, EI-BMN, EI-BNC, EI-BRO, EI-BVU, EI-BVW

In the heyday of its success, Iona entered a float in the 1990 St. Patrick's Day Parade in Dublin. Iona had been involved in formation flights during St. Patrick's Day parades over Dublin since 1971.

Although the courier services that the company offered formed the bulk of its commercial enterprise, Iona's activities were by no means confined to delivering packages. The company had been involved in an exciting episode on Monday, 4 December 1989. At 8am Ahmed Garamanli left Dublin airport for Zurich, Switzerland, as a stop for his apparent destination of Tripoli in Libya. With him were his two children and his mother. Swiss police intercepted him. Later that day his wife, Martina, from Bawnogue, Clondalkin, obtained a High Court order granting her exclusive custody of her children. The children, 11-month-old Jamal and four-year-old Sarah, had been taken from her without her consent. Iona was contacted to assist with the rescue of the children in Zurich. Peter Cahill flew Martina Garamanli, her solicitor, Robert Hennessy, and her mother Mary Corrigan in

FOOTNOTE(*xiv).
The authorisation concerned the following route approvals: Dublin – Belfast, Dublin – Shannon, Dublin – Southend, Dublin – Cork (cargo only), Dublin – Brussels (cargo only), Dublin – Cologne (cargo only).

Cessna 414, Chancellor, EI-BGP to Zurich late that Monday night. Considerable delicate international judicial and police processes and arguments took place throughout Tuesday, culminating in the successful return of the children to Dublin in the Chancellor. Following a four-hour flight, the aircraft touched down at Dublin airport at 11.50pm

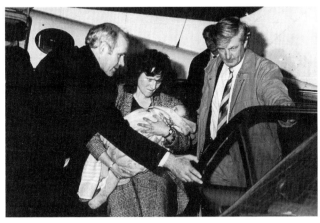

11 month old baby Jamal Garamanli, is carried from Iona's Cessna 414, EI-BGP, to a waiting car at Dublin airport on 5 December 1989. Mrs. Garamanli had obtained the safe return of her two children from their father at Zurich airport

Photograph courtesy *Irish Times*

Peter Cahill, with Sarah Garamanli in the cockpit of Cessna 414, EI-BGP, at Dublin airport following the rescue of two children at Zurich, Switzerland on 5 December 1989

Photograph via Pearse Cahill collection

that Tuesday night and a smiling Mrs. Garamanli was ushered into a waiting car by Aer Rianta officials. Accompanied by her children, mother and solicitor, she was driven from the airport compound at high speed, without speaking to waiting journalists.

Many of the operations of Iona, however, went unpublished and little was heard of them outside the confines of the Iona ramp. As a tribute to the efforts of the staff I feel it a gesture to reproduce an extract from the Iona newsletter, written by John Colvin, assistant flight operations manger, concerning an emotive human-interest incident that occurred in August 1990:

'Last August a call was received from Crumlin Children's Hospital at 21.30 on a Wednesday asking for a standby plane at 3/4 hours notice, this was to enable an 8-year-old girl in a critical condition to fly to Birmingham for a liver transplant as soon as her condition stabilized. The call to 'go' came at 08.45 on Saturday morning, and in the intervening three days the aircraft had been utilised elsewhere and required immediate servicing.

'The aircraft had to be re-configured to take a full stretcher, 2 full size oxygen tanks, a defibrillator, ECG monitor, 2 batteries and passengers, including a nurse, two doctors another specialist and the child's father. So serious was this child's condition that her heart stopped twice, once in the elevator of the hospital and in the ambulance en route to Iona. One may be forgiven for wondering how much such a condition was regarded as 'stabilised' but the doctors considered her situation was so serious that the risk of moving her was worth taking. Without exception, everyone who was contacted reacted immediately.

'Customs and ATC in Dublin and Birmingham cleared the necessary channels to facilitate rapid departure and arrival. Police in Birmingham closed one section of the airport and a road link direct to the motorway to expedite the escort and ambulance departure to hospital.

'The operation was a success. I am delighted to report that the girl is alive and well. That is the ultimate form of co-operation stemming from one call to an operations department.'

The girl in this emergency dash to Birmingham made a complete recovery and went on to lead a full and active life, recently celebrating her 21st birthday. One of the staff at Crumlin Children's Hospital, Jim Davenport, recalled the occasion vividly, being his first involvement on such a mercy mission, and complimented the Iona staff and crew for their professionalism throughout the incident. Iona performed many such emergency missions over their years of operations – consequently many patients owe a lot to the dedication of those at Iona involved in such flights.

1 October 1990 saw the reinstatement of the Federal Express Dublin – Birmingham route. The Dublin – Brussels route was a different matter. Because it was a Fifth Freedom operation, the contract only received limited approval, and from 2 January 1991, it adopted an Iona flight number to circumvent operating rights limitations. A Flanders Airlines Fokker F-27 took over the operation; this was an interim measure until Federal Express could put in an F-27 of its own into Iona. The schedule provided for a Brussels – Stansted – Dublin – Shannon run on a Sunday, followed by a Shannon – Dublin – Brussels – Dublin – Shannon rotation Monday to Friday. The aircraft finally acquired for the route was also a Fokker F-27-600 Friendship.

Trans Australia Airlines (TAA) were the first company to place an order for the Fokker F-27 Friendship, when they ordered six 100 series on 9 March 1956. The series 200 had higher power and higher weight capacity. The first F-27-600, which was the 200 series incorporating a large forward cargo door, was delivered to TAA in June 1967. Federal Express had chosen the F-27 as its turboprop feeder to its main trunk routes, and it planned to buy a fleet of good used F-27s and place them with selected specialist contract cargo operators, who would fly the aircraft for FedEx. Initially, they purchased all eight of SAS's F-27-600s, 11 Malaysian Airline Systems F-27-500s and

two Britair F-27-500s. The freighter conversion involved stripping out the passenger interior, blanking-out the windows, installation of sidewall liners, strengthening the floor and installing a smoke bulkhead at the forward end of the cabin. The opportunity was also taken to install a number of update modifications, including hush-kitting the engines.

Fokker F-27, OO-FEA, arrived at Dublin airport 15 February 1991 for operation by Iona National Airways on behalf of Federal Express. It remained in Belgian marks until 14 March 1991 when it was transferred to the Irish register as EI-FEA

Photograph courtesy Simon Nolan

Additional business generated by Federal Express saw the company enter a deal for a second aircraft with Iona. This was the Fokker F-27, EI-FEA

Photograph courtesy Paul Duffy

The Iona aircraft was manufactured at Schiphol, Holland in 1968. OO-FEA first appeared in Dublin on 16 May 1990 operating under a Servisair flight number but operating for Federal Express, supplementing the BAF Herald, which was also operated for FedEx under an Iona flight number. Servisair Belgium later became Flanders Airlines. The F-27 was delivered Brussels – Dublin on 15 February 1991 bearing the Belgian registration OO-FEA for operation by Iona National Airways Limited on a Federal Express contract. The marks OO-FEA were cancelled on 8 March 1991 and became Irish as EI-FEA on 14 March 1991 (see Table 32). Five days later it entered service, operating Shannon – Dublin – Brussels – Dublin – Shannon. The Iona F-27 was the first on the Irish register since the departure of the Aer Lingus F-27 aircraft in June 1966, nearly a quarter of a century previously.

The arrival of the Fokker F-27 in March 1991 coincided with an increase in demand with the DHL feeder service. It had been steadily growing since coming to Iona two years previously from Ryanair. The Bandeirante, once again, proved insufficient for the growing requirements. In an attempt to resolve this issue, Iona took advantage of a three-month wet-lease rate available from east European airlines. A LOT Antonov An-26, SP-LWB, flown by a LOT aircrew, arrived in Cork from Poland on Saturday, 23 March 1991. The Antonov mechanics accompanying it were also Polish. A notable feature of the aircraft is the rear door, forming the underside of the rear fuselage when closed; it can be slid forward under the fuselage to facilitate direct loading. This enables the forklift trucks to place their loads directly into the hold. It also allowed loads to be dropped, in the event of jettisoning. Inside the hold are 39 bench type tip-up seats: 20 along one side and 19 along the other. Along the roof there is an electrically powered mobile winch, which can hoist crates through the rear entrance and which runs on a rail in the cabin ceiling to position payloads in the cabin. There is also a conveyor, which is built-in flush with the cabin floor. Pallets of freight are placed on this conveyor through the rear door, and are then brought into the cabin by vigorous cranking of a handle. The cockpit seats the five flight crew. A flight engineer sits in a jump-seat between the captain and the first officer. Behind the captain is the navigator's station, the navigator having the use of a large blister window on the port side. Behind the first officer sits the radio operator, facing aft. The An-26 has a third engine located in the starboard nacelle. This is not used merely as an Auxiliary Power Unit (APU) for the self-contained starting of the main engines, but can also be used as required, at take-off, during climb and in level flight. It has its own throttle.

SP-LWB entered service on the Cork – Shannon – Dublin route on 25 March 1991, using Iona flight number 'IONA 109', feeding cargo to the DHL Merchantman, which by then was turning around at Dublin. The An-26 overnighted at Dublin, and then returned Dublin – Shannon – Cork as the 'IONA 110' the following morning, distributing cargo brought in by the Merchantman. Iona had relatively little involvement with this aspect of the operation. The wet-lease was extended for a further three-month term while Iona continued to search for a suitable replacement. The LOT-coloured An-26 was replaced in late June 1991 by SP-LWC. Both SP-LWB and SP-LWC were Polish Air Force aircraft, but by arrangement were available to LOT when required. On 20 June SP-LWC operated a Dublin – East Midlands –

Iona took advantage of a three-month wet-lease rate available from east European airlines. A LOT Antonov An-26, SP-LWB, flown by a LOT aircrew, arrived in Cork from Poland on Saturday, 23 March 1991

Photograph courtesy Patrick J. Cummins

The LOT An-26, SP-LWB, was replaced in late June 1991 by SP-LWC, a Polish Air Force machine still in grey overall colours

Photograph courtesy Patrick J. Cummins

Dublin rotation after the Air Bridge Merchantman went unserviceable. SP-LWC was still in Air Force grey colours. It operated its first Cork – Shannon – Dublin trip on the evening of 21 June 1991. On 27 / 28 June 1991, SP-LWC was used to operate the Post Office Express Mail charter Dublin – Luton – Manchester – Dublin, in lieu of the Bandeirante.

On 8 March 1991 a new company called Iona Aero Engineering Limited was formed, with Certificate of Incorporation number 171035. It was formed with the intention of segregating engineering works and supplies of spare parts to the aviation industry in Ireland. It was anticipated the planned building across the road from the Iona operation at Cloghran would operate under this name. This company remains in operation and Pearse Cahill is the Managing Director. It is primarily based at the home of the Irish Aero Club at Newcastle, County Wicklow, although some business is transacted from Pearse's home at Skerries.

The extent to which Iona dominated the small package courier business is best illustrated by a survey conducted by the *Irish Air Letter* on Thursday, 4 April 1991. The table on the following page shows the action at Dublin airport on the night selected by them for the survey, Thursday, 4 April 1991. Times quoted are Greenwich Mean Time (GMT) – local time minus one hour.

The *Irish Air Letter* commented:
'As can be seen, all the major players are represented, and Iona National Airways' large share of this market, on behalf of Federal Express, DHL, UPS and the Post Office is also apparent. Most of these flights form part of a larger network.

For DHL, the Antonov is based in Cork, and routes Cork – Shannon – Dublin – each evening as the 'IONA 109', feeding its consignment to the Air Bridge Merchantman, which then takes the cargo and the Dublin originating cargo to Castle Donington and then on to Cologne. On returning to Dublin, the Merchantman brings in cargo from these points, which is then distributed by the An-26 to Shannon and Cork as the 'IONA 110'.

'For Federal Express, the Cessna 208 Caravan spends the day at Waterford, routing Waterford – Cork – Dublin in the evening as the 'IONA 056Y', feeding traffic to the F-27 which then brings the freight to the FedEx hub at Brussels, and back to Dublin in the early morning. The Cessna 208 then flies Dublin – Shannon – Cork – Waterford as the 'IONA 016Y'. Also operated for FedEx is the '06Y' / 046Y', a Bandeirante on Dublin – Birmingham – Dublin. The F-27 is based at Shannon, and operates Shannon – Dublin – Brussels – Dublin – Shannon as the 'IONA 015Y / 055Y'.

'For UPS, a Cessna 404 feeder service is flown each evening as the 'IONA 1914, routing Cork – Dublin, feeding traffic to the FH-227, returning the following morning as the 'IONA 1913' Dublin – Shannon – Cork. The FH-227 spends its day at Shannon, routing Shannon – Dublin – Cologne each evening as the 'IONA 1911' and Cologne – Dublin – Shannon as the 'IONA 1912'. At Cologne, the freight is fed into huge UPS sorting sheds for distribution in Europe, or onwards to the United States.

'For An Post, the 'IONA 970 / 971' is flown with a Bandeirante, routing Dublin – Luton – Manchester – Dublin. From Luton, the Express Mail is taken on to the hub at Brussels.'

0017	G-BJRZ	Partenavia P68	f Castle Donington	Allied Irish Banks
0026	**EI-BPI**	**Bandeirante**	**f Manchester**	**Post Office (EMS)**
0030	G-OFLT	Bandeirante	f Southend	Newspapers
0048	G-BJRZ	Partenavia P68	t Castle Donington	Allied Irish Banks
0055	EI-ASE	Boeing 737	f Manchester	Newspapers
0214	G-OFLT	Bandeirante	t Southend	Newspapers
0221	EI-ASE	Boeing 737	t Frankfurt	General Cargo
0315	**EI- BVX**	**Bandeirante**	**f Birmingham**	**Federal Express**
0354	G-APEP	Merchantman	f Castle Donington	DHL
0400	**EI-FEA**	**Fokker F27**	**f Brussels**	**Federal Express**
0440	**F-GCPX**	**Fairchild FH227**	**f Cologne**	**UPS**
0455	G-TNTA	Bae 146	f Luton	TNT
0522	**F-GCPX**	**Fairchild FH227**	**t Shannon**	**UPS**
0524	**EI- FEA**	**Fokker F27**	**t Shannon**	**Federal Express**
0541	**EI- FDX**	**Cessna 208**	**t Shannon**	**Federal Express**
0650	**EI- BUM**	**Cessna 404**	**t Shannon**	**UPS**
0753	**SP- LWB**	**Antonov An26**	**t Shannon**	**DHL**
1821	**EI- FDX**	**Cessna 208**	**f Cork**	**Federal Express**
1827	**EI- BUM**	**Cessna 404**	**f Cork**	**UPS**
1838	**F-GCPX**	**Fairchild FH227**	**f Shannon**	**UPS**
1847	**EI- FEA**	**Fokker F27**	**f Shannon**	**Federal Express**
1904	**SP- LWB**	**Antonov An26**	**f Shannon**	**DHL**
1941	**F- GCPX**	**Fairchild FH227**	**t Cologne**	**UPS**
2003	**EI- FEA**	**Fokker F27**	**t Brussels**	**Federal Express**
2004	G-APEP	Merchantman	t Castle Donington	DHL
2007	G-TNTA	Bae 146	t Luton	TNT
2010	**EI-BPI**	**Bandeirante**	**t Birmingham**	**Federal Express**
2043	**EI-BVX**	**Bandeirante**	**t Luton**	**Post Office (EMS)**

On 2 July 1991 the TAT, FH-227B, F-GCPT took over the Iona lease, in an all white scheme with Iona titles, operating the nightly UPS Shannon – Dublin – Cologne return rotation

Photograph courtesy Patrick J. Cummins

On 2 July 1991 the TAT, FH-227B, F-GCPT took over the Iona lease, in an all white scheme with Iona titles, operating the nightly UPS Shannon – Dublin – Cologne return rotation. Iona worked on a replacement for the An-26 and came up with a second Fairchild FH-227D. The experience gained with this type of aircraft while operating the UPS contract convinced them to purchase a similar machine. The machine selected by Iona was rolled out after construction on 7 September 1966 and registered N2735R to the Fairchild-Hiller Corp and retained by the manufacturer for engineering tests. On 22 November 1972 it was delivered to Nordair, Canada and registered C-FNAK, operating for a US Air Force contract to service distant radar sites in harsh environments, with extremes of weather, around the Arctic in Alaska, Canada and Greenland. It continued this role for sixteen tough years until it was sold to Malmo Aviation, Sweden and registered to them on 15 March 1988 as SE-KBR. Malmo required them to fulfil a nightly Malmo – Stockholm Swedish Post Office contract. They were modified to accommodate up to 48 passenger seats. After three years, in October 1991, Malmo lost the contract to Falcon Aviation and the FH-227 was offered for sale. Iona acquired the aircraft with only 23,500 hours on the airframe in 25 years of operation. It was delivered on 19

September 1991 in Swedish marks, SE-KBR. Over the following weekend it received its Certificate of Airworthiness and was registered to Iona National Airways Limited on 23 September 1991 as EI-CAZ (see Table 33). The same day it entered service on the Cork – Shannon – Dublin DHL contract, the final An-26 service being on 20 – 21 September 1991. EI-CAZ became the first FH-227 to grace the Irish register. The Fairchild had passenger interior as well, and Iona planned to use it on daytime passenger charters. Iona had intended a series of six Dublin – Blackpool charters for the illuminations on the weekend of 25 – 28 October 1991 using the FH-227, EI-CAZ. Unfortunately, all the necessary approvals for the use of the aircraft for passenger work had not been received in time and the flights had to be operated with a combination of Bandeirantes and hired-in aircraft from Ryanair and Aer Lingus Commuter. Similarly, Iona were contracted for charters to Jersey over the 1991 Christmas period and because the approval for EI-CAZ to carry passengers was not received, Iona had to request Aer Lingus Commuter to operate these flights. At times of maintenance overhauls other similar aircraft including F-GCPZ, F-GCPX and F-GCPT replaced EI-CAZ.

From 14 October 1991, Iona lost the Federal Express Dublin – Birmingham operation to BAC Charter using a Shorts 330, because loads had again outgrown the Bandeirante. However, on the plus side, a second Federal Express Cessna 208A Caravan I was delivered. In this instance the chosen aircraft was a 1985 Wichita built model. It later obtained the Swedish registration SE-KRX on 14 August 1980 to Euroflight, Sweden on behalf of Federal Express and, bearing those marks, it arrived at Iona on 21 October 1991. It entered the Irish register jointly to Iona National Airways Limited and Federal Express as EI-FEX on 5 December 1991 (see Table 34). It commenced service on 9 December 1991 on a Dublin – Shannon – Waterford – Dublin rotation, while the other 208 Caravan, EI-FDX, operated Dublin – Cork – Dublin. In order to cope with extra business caused by Christmas, Iona leased an FH-227, SE-KBP, from Malmo Aviation for the period 4 December to 16 December 1991.

The first Fairchild FH-227D to join the Irish register was acquired by Iona for use on the DHL contract and was registered EI-CAZ. It bore the Iona logo top of fuselage forward of wings, and DHL logo below rear side windows.

Photograph courtesy Paul Duffy

aircraft; the Leinster Aero Club with a Cessna 152; plus a host of privately owned aircraft with others in the hangar for maintenance and repair. All in all, it was a busy location and could conceivably have housed as many as fifty aircraft. It was a far cry from the situation sixty years previously when Hugh Cahill obtained the licence to operate Ireland's first commercial aerodrome at Kildonan.

FOOTNOTE (*xv)
Cessna 150 / 152s: EI-BMM, EI-BMN, EI-BNC, EI-BRO, EI-BVU, EI-BVW, EI-CCJ, EI-CCK, EI-CCL and EI-CCM / Cessna 172s: EI-BGH and EI-BRM / Cessna 182: EI-BCL / Cessna 310s: EI-ATC, EI-BEO and EI-BMK

This period at the end of 1991 could probably be regarded as the pinnacle of Iona's commercial operations. Iona operated the second largest aircraft fleet in Ireland, second only to Aer Lingus, the national carrier. Ryanair had at that time been operating for almost seven years and their fleet numbered eight aircraft. Had Pearse decided to walk his domain at Dublin and Cork on the occasion of his seventy-fifth birthday – 26 January 1992, and photograph the entire fleet, he would have developed twenty-six photographs. The cargo and contract fleet comprising two Cessna 404 Titans (EI-BUM and EI-BVA), two Bandeirantes (EI-BPI and EI-BVX), two Cessna 208 Caravans (EI-FDX and EI-FEX), one Fokker F-27 Friendship (EI-FEA) and three Fairchild-Hiller FH-227s (EI-CAZ, SE-KBP and F-GCPT). In addition, sixteen Cessnas were available for the approximately 400 members of the Irish Aero Club (*xv). The Iona ramp was also home to the Dublin Airport Flying Club, with six

Cessna 208A Caravan, EI-FEX, jointly registered to Iona and Federal Express 5 December 1991

Photograph via Pearse Cahill collection

Table 32

Registration	EI-FEA
Aircraft Type	Fokker F27-600 Friendship
Constructors Serial Number	10385
Place & Year of Manufacture	Schiphol, Holland, 1968
Previous Registrations	OO-FEA; PH-FNH; OY-KAC; VH-TQN
Registered to	Iona National Airways Ltd, 14 March 1991
Delivery date	15 February 1991
Remarks.	It first flew on 28 November 1968 and was delivered 6 December 1968 to T.A.A. as VH-TQN. It was taken out of service on 3 October 1982 and stored at Melbourne, Australia until 11 June 1984 when sold to SAS. Between 11 and 25 July 1984 it was ferried to Norwich for overhaul by Air UK. Registered OY-KAC and delivered to SAS on 30 November 1984. On 28 September 1989 it was ferried Copenhagen-Woensdrecht where it was converted to freighter configuration by Fokker for Federal Express. On 8 December 1989 the F27, using test registration PH-FNH, was ferried Woensdrecht - Maastricht for repainting returning on 15 December. On 19 December 1989 it was ferried to Servisair, Brussels as OO-FEA, carrying the name *Brecht*. The marks OO-FEA were cancelled on 8 March 1991 and became Irish as EI-FEA on 14 March 1991.
	Following withdrawal of FedEx from Europe, it was ferried to Brussels and handed back to Federal Express. It was removed from the Irish register 4 May 1992 and reverted to Federal Express Corporation, Memphis, Tennessee, adopting the marks N729FE. It was recorded as current to them in early 2004.

Table 33

Registration	EI-CAZ
Aircraft Type	Fairchild-Hillier FH-227D
Constructors Serial Number	519
Place & Year of Manufacture	Hagerstown, USA, 1966
Previous Registrations	SE-KBR; C-FNAK; N701U; N2735R
Registered to	Iona National Airways Ltd, 23 September 1991
Delivery date	19 September 1991
Remarks	The machine selected by Iona was rolled out after construction on 7 September 1966 and registered N2735R to the Fairchild-Hiller Corp and retained by the manufacturer for engineering tests. On 22 November 1972 it was delivered to Nordair, Canada and registered C-FNAK, operating for a US Air Force contract to service distant radar sites in harsh environments, with extremes of weather, around the Arctic in Alaska, Canada and Greenland. It continued this role for sixteen tough years until it was sold to Malmo Aviation, Sweden and registered to them on 15 March 1988 as SE-KBR.

On 12 August 1992, the aircraft went unserviceable at Cork. It was ferried to Norwich on 27 July 1994 and later donated to the Fire Service at Norwich airport for training purposes. Cancelled from Irish register 15 December 1994.

Table 34

Registration	EI-FEX
Aircraft Type	Cessna 208A Caravan
Constructors Serial Number	208-0016
Place & Year of Manufacture	Wichita, USA, 1985
Previous Registrations	SE-KRX; N804FE; N9342F
Registered to	Iona National Airways Ltd, 5 December 1991
Delivery date	21 October 1991
Remarks	Its previous American registration was N804FE to Federal Express. It later obtained the Swedish registration SE-KRX on 14 August 1980 to Euroflight, Sweden on behalf of Federal Express and, bearing those marks, it arrived at Iona on 21 October 1991.

Following the withdrawal of Federal Express from Europe, the aircraft was to be returned to FedEx. At 3pm on Saturday, 25 April 1992, along with EI-FDX, the two aircraft taxied out from the Iona ramp, for the last time and together they took off for Prestwick, Scotland, on the first leg of their three-day return journey to Wichita, Kansas. It was cancelled from the Irish register on 23 April 1992.

The following day, 24 April 1992, the aircraft was placed on the US register becoming N835FE in the name of Federal Express Corporation, Memphis, Tennessee and is recorded as current to them early 2004.

Chapter

8

TERMINAL TROUBLE

The loss of some prestigious contracts resulted in a reduction in the Iona fleet of aircraft and a decrease in staff levels. The outcome was the demise of Ireland's first commercial aviation operator

Chapter Eight

TERMINAL TROUBLE

Although Iona began the year of 1992 on a high note, there was trouble ahead. Federal Express decided to withdraw its European operation back to the United States. The announcement came on Saint Patrick's Day 1992. The Federal Express announcement, to take effect from 4 May 1992, came as a direct result of their reported operating losses of US$250.6 million in the third quarter of 1991. As the company's president stated:

> 'The operations needed to support our inter-European service have been extremely costly, and we have not generated adequate revenues to cover our costs. In addition, the market in Europe has not developed express traffic as quickly as we had expected.'

This withdrawal potentially affected the 7,000 Federal Express employees throughout Europe, including 125 in Ireland. FedEx would be bringing all their aircraft back to the United States.

In August 1990 Iraq invaded Kuwait and this led to the outbreak of the Gulf War in January 1991. The aviation industry worldwide suffered serious consequences as a result of fuel price rises. One report stated that of the World's twenty largest airlines, only British Airways, Cathay, Singapore Airlines and Swissair made a profit in each year between 1991 and 1993, with US airlines suffering most. Passenger numbers were reduced in every part of the world, with airlines closing routes and an escalating number of redundancies.

The withdrawal of Federal Express signalled the beginning of financial and trading difficulties for Iona. For a start, it meant the termination of Iona's operation of the Cessna 208 Caravans. EI-FDX had been with Iona since August 1988 and EI-FEX had only been with the company since December 1991 – three months prior to the Federal Express announcement. Both aircraft performed their last rotation on 21 April 1992. After their return to Dublin they were taken to the Iona hangar for maintenance checks prior to their ferry back to the United States. Both Caravans reverted back to their original US marks, with EI-FDX becoming N833FE and EI-FEX becoming N835FE to Federal Express. The two Caravans were ferried across the Atlantic by American ferry pilots. At 3pm on the evening of Saturday, 25 April 1992, the two aircraft taxied out from the Iona ramp, for the last time, to the holding point of Runway 28 at Dublin. Together they took off for Prestwick, Scotland, on the first leg of their three-day return journey to Wichita, Kansas.

Cessna 208A Caravan bears registration marks N835FE (formerly EI-FEX). It is shown above taxing out from the Iona ramp on 25 April 1992 at commencement of its ferry flight back to Wichita, Kansas following termination of the Federal Express contract. It was joined by sister ship N833FE, formerly EI-FDX

Photograph courtesy Simon Nolan

Fokker F-27 Friendship, EI-FEA would soon finish the Shannon – Dublin – Brussels – Dublin – Shannon rotation. Its last flight for Iona was operated just over a year after commencement of service in Ireland. On the evening of 30 April 1992, it routed Shannon – Dublin – Brussels for the last time as 'IONA 015Y'. At Brussels it was handed back to Federal Express. It was removed from the Irish register 4 May 1992 and reverted to Federal Express adopting the marks N729FE. In the United States it was placed with Empire Airlines, of Coeur d'Alene, Idaho, a company that operates F-27s and Cessna 208s for FedEx – just as Iona did. Iona had been involved with FedEx for four years.

At the beginning of April 1992 the night Post Office contract, which had been operating on a Dublin – Luton – Manchester – Dublin rotation by the Bandeirante, was changed to a simplified Dublin – Coventry – Dublin rotation. The British Post Office established a hub at Coventry, hence the reason for the change. From 5 May 1992 the Bandeirante, EI-BPI, was replaced on this operation by Fairchild FH-227, EI-CAZ, which flew Cork – Shannon – Dublin each weekday evening as the 'IONA 109' for DHL, then Dublin – Coventry – Dublin as the 'IONA 970' / '971' carrying the Express Mail before returning Dublin – Shannon – Cork in the early morning, again for DHL. It lay over in Cork all day, before commencing another rotation. An additional Reed Aviation freight contract had also been secured.

With the general scale-down in business, Iona had to dispose of some resources, which regrettably meant letting a number of staff go, as well as taking two aircraft out of service for sale. The 'Bandit' EI-BPI had remained with Iona for three years and was ferried Dublin – Staverton on 12 May 1992 for disposal. It was not removed from the Irish register until May 1993 and subsequently returned to Denmark and resumed its previous marks OY-ASY with Muk Air of Copenhagen. Cessna 414A Chancellor, EI-BGP, was also ferried to Staverton on 12 May 1992 for disposal. For EI-BGP this was just over thirteen years, to the week, since it arrived at Iona.

The finances of another Irish aviation company came to the fore around the same time. Having traded successfully and profitably for 17 years, Guinness Peat Aviation (GPA), opted to float the company on the World Stock market. Scheduled floatation date was 18 June 1992. The entire outcome was a financial disaster for the Shannon based one time leader in aircraft leasing and the company eventually collapsed - at a time when it had book debts of US$11 billion. The company later cleared these debts, though its founder, Tony Ryan, is reported to have lost US$300 million through the collapse.

On a positive note, Iona secured a new Kerry – Dublin schedule service on 23 June 1992 using Cessna 404 Titan aircraft. The service was to be run as an experiment underwritten by Kerry airport to test the market reaction to an early morning Kerry – Dublin and evening Dublin – Kerry schedule. The service complimented the Aer Lingus Commuter Saab 340B schedule, with an early morning Kerry – Dublin flight arriving Dublin at 8.30am and returning to Kerry at 6.30pm, using flight numbers 'IND741' and 'IND742' respectively. The Aer Lingus schedule was geared to connecting flights with Dublin departures at 12.05pm and 4pm. Unfortunately the optimism was short lived; after a trial period of three months the passenger demand was insufficient to sustain a viable operation and the service terminated on 25 September 1992.

The fortunes of Iona received another blow in the late summer of 1992. With effect from 1 September 1992, Iona announced they would be ceasing the Shannon – Dublin – Cologne service for UPS. The EI Air Exports Lockheed L188 Electra, EI-CET, would take over the contract. On 12 August 1992, the Fairchild FH-227, EI-CAZ, operated the Dublin – Shannon – Cork feeder service for DHL. While at Cork it developed a technical problem with an engine and was grounded. Iona was forced to sub-charter Channel Express Heralds to fulfil its obligations to DHL ('IND 109' / 'IND 110') and also to the Post Office in respect of the Dublin – Coventry Express Mail Service contract ('IND970' / 'IND971').

Iona would, in the meantime, continue with the UPS contract serving Cork – Dublin – Cork feeder service using the remaining Bandeirante, EI-BVX. Following the loss of the UPS contract to Cologne, the leased Fairchild FH-227, F-GCPT, was returned to TAT at Dinard, France. Its last service was the 'IND1912' returning from Cologne to Dublin and Shannon on the morning of 1 September 1992. It was ferried to Dinard on 5 September 1992. To maintain their contracts with UPS and the Post Office, Iona leased a Fairchild FH-227B, F-GCJO from the French carrier ACE Transvalair. The aircraft arrived in Dublin on delivery from Dinard on 8 September 1992. On Monday, 14 September it positioned to Cork and then commenced operating the nightly 'IND109' Cork – Shannon – Dublin for DHL, followed by the 'IND970' Dublin – Coventry for the Post Office. Iona wanted to ensure they could fulfil their contractual obligations. This released the Channel Express Heralds that had operated the service since 12 August 1992, when EI-CAZ went unserviceable at Cork. On the evening of 29 September, the Fairchild also developed technical problems at Cork, and another Channel Express Herald was drafted in until F-GCJO was restored to service the following day. On 1 March 1993 an Iona crew ferried the Fairchild EI-CAZ from Cork to Norwich, where Air UK would perform work on the aircraft and place it in storage pending sale. In September 1994 Aviation Tech Services of Norfolk advertised it for sale in a non-flyable condition 'as spares' in *Flight* magazine. It was transferred to the ownership of Nordanic Fly, who donated it to the Norwich Airport Fire Service for rescue training purposes, with the Irish registration marks removed. EI-CAZ was cancelled from the Irish register 15 December 1994.

The setbacks continued when, on 28 June 1993, DHL required an aircraft larger than the Iona FH-227 and the contract was awarded to Hunting Cargo using an Electra. In February 1993 a new company called Hunting Cargo Airlines (Ireland) Limited had been formed and was granted operating authority in April 1993. The Lockheed L188 Electra, EI-CET, was subcontracted from EI Air Exports to the new company.

The involvement of Hunting Cargo in Irish cargo business increased steadily over the summer months. From 28 June 1993, DHL revised their pattern of operation to take account of the growing volume of business from the southwest of Ireland. Hitherto, Iona's FH-227, F-GCJO, was used to feed Cork and Shannon cargo to Dublin for onward transportation to the DHL hubs at East Midlands and Brussels. With the revised operation an Electra (or substitute Merchantman) would operate East Midlands – Dublin – Shannon as BCS969 (European Air Transport call sign), arriving at Dublin at 1.20am GMT departing at 4.15am, awaiting the existing service from Brussels and

East Midlands, and arriving Shannon at 5am GMT. The reciprocal flight would then depart Shannon at 7.40pm, proceeding non-stop to East Midlands. The DHL freight from Cork would be trucked to Shannon to join the flight. The existing Brussels – East Midlands – Dublin Merchantman service continued as well, so DHL were substantially increasing their capacity in the Irish market. Due to the fact DHL required an aircraft larger than the FH-227 to fulfil their requirements with the increasing loads of freight, the last DHL feeder service operated by Iona routing Cork – Shannon – Dublin by the FH-227, F-GCJO, was on 25 June 1993. The FH-227 continued the nightly service 'IND970' / 'IND971' Dublin – Coventry – Dublin for the Express Mail Service of the Post Office / Reed Aviation.

Iona discovered that substantial cost savings could be achieved by replacing the FH-227, on lease from ACE Transvalair, by a smaller Fairchild F-27. F-GCJO was returned on 28 November 1993 and was replaced on 10 December 1993 by a leased Fairchild F-27J, F-GDXT, from Stellair. The intervening period was filled using Bandeirante, EI-BVX, Titan EI-BUM and Cessna 310, EI-BEO.

The Cahill family continued to receive recognition and acknowledgement for their efforts at developing and fostering aviation in Ireland. Hugh Cahill was posthumously awarded the Sean O'h-Uadhaigh Cup by the Aviation Trailblazers of Ireland at a presentation accepted by Pearse on the 17 April 1993. The award is granted to recipients for pioneering achievements in Irish Aviation and the citation read: *'Ireland's first Commercial Aviator.'*

Another aviation operator was also experiencing trading difficulties. The national carrier, Aer Lingus, declared a loss of £188 million for the financial year ended 31 March 1993. For the second year in succession, favourable results from the Aer Lingus services, hotels, commercial holdings and other non-core activities did not compensate for losses in air transport. The annual accounts reflected the worst financial results in the history of the Group. The airline announced, on 15 June 1993, that it was seeking to make 1,200 of its staff redundant and to lay-off a further 200 staff in

TEAM Aer Lingus as part of its rescue plan. Internationally, the airline industry worldwide had endured the toughest five years between 1989 and 1994, which had serious effects on fiscal returns while restricting growth and development plans. Another Cahill, Bernie, was at the helm of this aviation company, in the role of Chairman since August 1990.

In July 1993, the two Cessna 310s EI-ATC and EI-BMK were sold to Preferred Aircraft Parts, Cleveland, Ohio for spares. They were dismantled in the Iona hangar and loaded into two containers. The containers departed Dublin on 28 July 1993 for shipment to the United States. EI-ATC had been with Iona for 25 years since its undercarriage collapsed on landing runway 17, adjacent to the Iona hangar, on 3 August 1968. Many of EI-ATC's years were spent languishing in the Iona hangar awaiting repairs. On 5 March 1982 EI-BMK arrived at Iona. Both aircraft were cancelled from the Irish register in August 1993. The Cessna T.303 Crusader, EI-BVP, was also a victim of the reduction of the Iona fleet. It was removed from the Irish register in August 1993 following sale to Casper Air Services, Wyoming, USA and delivered Dublin to Jersey on 18 August 1993 as N7079U. Two days later it routed Jersey – Glasgow – Reykjavik. It had been ferried across the Atlantic for delivery to Iona on 16 April 1988. The Cessna 404 Titan, EI-BVA, was sold to Business Air of Bennington, Vermont as N404BA and was cancelled from the register in June 1993. It had joined the Iona fleet on 26 July 1987.

Things were not all doom and gloom at the Iona hangar. The small package business was continuing to expand and Iona was still involved. With effect from 1 October 1993, Channel Express had secured the Shannon – Dublin – Cologne UPS contract from Hunting Cargo. Channel Express operated the contract under licence from Iona, using Iona's Aircraft Operators Certificate (AOC). The aircraft used for the contract was a Lockheed Electra using Iona's name. The aircraft was a 1959 vintage Lockheed L. 188AF Electra. Manufactured at Burbank, it was first registered as N5535 to Eastern Airlines and delivered to them on 9 July 1959. It remained with Eastern for 18 years serving the company's short and medium passenger routes throughout the eastern United States. American Jet Industries converted it to freighter configuration in January 1978. This involved installing an entirely new floor, stressed to accept a 300 pounds per square inch load, a 6 foot 9 inch by 11 foot 10 inch cargo door in the forward fuselage, and a pallet loading system that would handle 7,000-pound pallets. It was sold to Evergreen International Airlines in April 1978 for use on freight and US military contract work. N5535 passed through Shannon for the first time on 2 June 1978.

In March 1987 Evergreen placed the Electra in storage at Marana, Arizona, for three and a half years. It was sold to Channel Express Air Services Limited, Hurn, on 10 October 1990. A lengthy overhaul followed and it was not ferried across the

The largest aircraft ever to join the Iona fleet was the Lockheed L. 188A Electra, EI-CHO. It carried the full Channel Express colour scheme and is seen landing at Dublin Airport 15 June 1994.

Photograph courtesy Paul Cunniffe

Atlantic until 22 August 1992. It was not placed on the UK register. In late September 1993 it was with Air UK in Norwich undergoing preparatory work for its lease to Iona. On 25 September 1993 it entered the Irish register as EI-CHO to Iona National Airways Limited (see Table 35). This was the largest aircraft ever to join the Iona fleet. It carried the full Channel Express colour scheme and included the Iona titles. The hirers were listed as Dart Group plc, Bournemouth. It commenced the UPS Shannon – Dublin – Cologne contract 1 October 1993. EI-CHO remained on the UPS contract until 8 October and was then redeployed on other Channel Express contract work, at which stage N341HA took over. EI-CHO rarely visited Dublin thereafter. On 1 November 1993, UPS based three of their own Boeing 727-100s at Cologne. This left Channel Express with two UPS routes, the Irish and another Scandinavian route, Helsinki – Stockholm – Cologne. From 1 November, EI-CHO operated the Scandinavian service each weekday evening.

The following summer, Channel Express found a way to continue to operate the Electra without Iona's involvement. On 25 June 1994, ownership was changed to Tonella Limited, Hurn and the hirers were listed as Channel Express (Air Services) Limited. On 1 November 1994, EI-CHO appeared on the United Kingdom register to Channel Express (Air Services) Limited with the new marks G-CHNX. It was cancelled from the Irish register the same date, having spent over one year on the Irish register in the name of Iona. Its last flight with Channel Express was 30 October 2001 following which it was withdrawn from use at Hurn, and slowly stripped of components.

On 28 June 1994, EI-BEO suffered a propeller blade failure – with the number one propeller detaching on take-off at Carrickfin, County Donegal. It remained there with the port engine and propeller missing. At this stage it had 4,775 hours on the airframe.

The local *Fingal Independent* of 12 November 1993 carried a front page article titled *'Iona Airways closure threat shock.'* The article referred to a

Cessna 310Q, EI-BEO, lay in the hangar at Carrickfin, Co Donegal for several years following failure of the port propeller on 28 June 1994

Photograph courtesy Hugo Wilhare

controversial planning decision by Brian Cowen, Minister for Transport. The issue regarding the erection of the hangar and facilities was again on the agenda at Iona. The company stated that they could create sixty new jobs if they were granted permission to proceed with their application – ongoing since 1980. Pearse Cahill lashed the decision and hoped the Minister would change his mind. Their forty-year-old hangar failed to comply with the Government's new JAR-145 regulations and they would be forced to vacate it in two months time. Pearse Cahill was quoted as saying *'We understand this happened because of objections from Aer Rianta on the grounds of noise and security.'* Local Senator G. V. Wright represented Iona to the Minister and on 14 July 1994 he received the following correspondence:

'I am pleased to inform you that following bilateral consultations between Aer Rianta and Iona National Airways, the matter has now been satisfactorily resolved. Accordingly, my Department has written to the planning authorities withdrawing our objections in this case.'

Signed: Brian Cowen, TD, Minister for Transport, Energy and Communications.

Notification of Grant of Permission, dated 21 September 1994, was issued from the Planning Department, Fingal County Council in respect of *'Light aircraft assembly and maintenance building with* *aviation school, offices and separate house and septic tanks at Huntstown, Cloghran.'* This signified success for Pearse - after fourteen years perseverance! However, matters were to move in a different direction, and Pearse's aspirations to develop the land across the road never gained any further momentum. In June 1998 the site, comprising approximately ten acres was advertised for sale by tender by Ganly Walters(*xvi).

Iona's remaining Cessna 404 Titan, EI-BUM, stayed with the company for over a year after the departure of the other Titan, EI-BVA. That aircraft had been ferried back to the United States on 18 September 1993. EI-BUM was the first Cessna 404 acquired by Iona and was delivered on 4 May 1987. On 7 October 1994 it was ferried from Dublin by an Iona crew as 'IND404' for pre-sale overhaul by SCA at Dinard, France. On 19 October 1994 the Bandeirante, EI-BVX, was repositioned to Light Aircraft Park 'C' at Dublin airport, having been repossessed by Woodchester Finance, due to unpaid rental agreements on the aircraft.

Iona's financial difficulties continued towards the end of 1994. On 21 October 1994, an application to the High Court to have an interim Examiner appointed was refused because the Revenue Commissioners, a substantial creditor, had not been notified of the application. However, on 27 October 1994, a successful application for the appointment of an Examiner was made to the High Court. At the hearing, it was stated that Iona had debts of IR£2,300,000, including £670,000 owed to the Revenue Commissioners. The latter had opposed the application, but in view of the assessment that creditors would be worse off if the company went into Liquidation, they withdrew their opposition. Included in the figure of £2,300,000 was a substantial amount relating to lease/rental agreements in respect of the larger

commercial aircraft, that were not utilised by Iona for the full term. It was stated in Court that Iona were in negotiation for two new cargo contracts, one with Reed Aviation and the other with UPS, and these would together make a profit of £370,000 for Iona. The company's directors had expressed the view that the freight contract business was profitable and that the company should be able to discharge its trade and revenue liabilities as they fall due, during the period of the Examinership. During this term of Examinership, Iona would have a period of protection from its creditors, to endeavour to restructure its business and come to an arrangement with its creditors. The Court granted the appointment of Craig Gardner, accountants, as Examiner on 27 October 1994.

A new company, Iona Airways (Freight) Limited was established on 11 November 1994. It was allocated Certificate of Registration number 223108. The intended purpose of this company was to segregate freight contract work from other Iona aviation business. Little business was conducted and this company was formally dissolved on 3 March 2000.

The start of Iona's financial and trading difficulties could be traced back to the Federal Express decision to withdraw its European operation back to the United States, with effect from 4 May 1992, at a time when the Iona fleet of aircraft and its staff were at an all time high. Another factor was when UPS changed its contract to the EI Air Export's Lockheed Electra from 1 September 1992. On 28 June 1993, DHL required an aircraft larger than the Iona FH-227 and the contract was awarded to Hunting Cargo using an Electra. On the flying school side, the involvement of the US Government embargo on trade with Libya resulted in the loss of a potentially lucrative contract to train Libyan pilots. At the peak of the small package business

FOOTNOTE(*xvi).
The annotation read: 'This land which extends to about 4.05 Ha / 10 acres, is situated in a strategic location adjoining Dublin airport, near the *Boot Inn*. Planning permission was granted for a light aircraft assembly and maintenance unit which offers a unique opportunity to develop aircraft facilities beside the airport. Planning permission was granted on 21 September 1994 for a light aircraft assembly and maintenance building with aviation school, offices and septic tanks. Planning reg ref – 92a / 1376.'

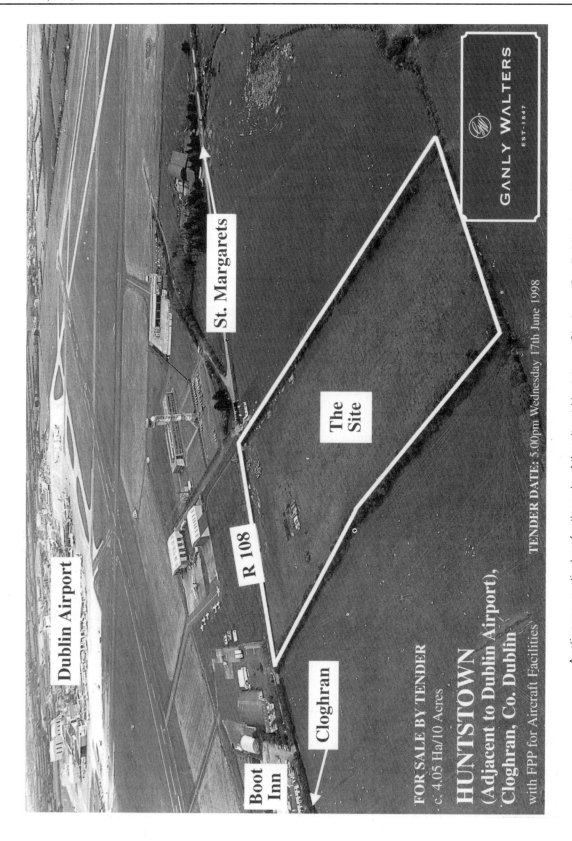

FOR SALE BY TENDER
c. 4.05 Ha/10 Acres

HUNTSTOWN
(Adjacent to Dublin Airport),
Cloghran, Co. Dublin

with FPP for Aircraft Facilities

TENDER DATE: 5.00pm Wednesday 17th June 1998

GANLY WALTERS
EST·1847

Dublin Airport

Boot Inn

Cloghran

R 108

The Site

St. Margarets

Auctioneers particulars for the sale of the site at Huntstown, Cloghran, Co. Dublin, June 1998

the company employed upwards of 130 staff. At the time of the appointment of the Examiner, the staff levels were quoted as 32 employees.

An almost vacant and empty Iona hangar towards the end of 1994

Photograph courtesy Simon Nolan

During the period of the Examinership the company continued to trade. It had two remaining contracts on its books. The Fairchild F-27, F-GDXT, on lease in lieu of the Bandeirante EI-BVX, that remained impounded at Dublin airport, continued to operate the UPS contract on the Dublin – Cork – Dublin service and the Post Office, Dublin – Coventry – Dublin, Express Mail Service.

The Examiner went back to the High Court on 8 December 1994. At a hearing in front of Justice Costello he advised the Court it would be impossible to obtain investment within the time allocated under the Companies Act, 1990. He requested Examinership cease from that day. In making the order to cease protection of the Court and thus discharge the Examiner, Justice Costello expressed his regret that matters ended in this manner. This left the company at the mercy of its creditors. Operations continued for a further week.

On the afternoon of Thursday, 15 December 1994, the company again went back to the High Court

seeking a petition to appoint a provisional Liquidator. The High Court appointed Dublin accountant, Liam Dowdall as provisional Liquidator to Iona National Airways Limited. The company ceased trading that day; ten days before Christmas. Liam Dowdall took possession of the company hangar and offices at Dublin airport and these were closed down. Any light aircraft at the facility had been removed in the interim. The busy Iona ramp referred to above at the end of 1991, three years previously, now lay quiet, idle and somewhat derelict.

On the morning of 15 December 1994, the Fairchild F-27, F-GDXT flew as 'IND514' from Shannon to Cork on behalf of UPS. This was the last revenue flight for Iona. That evening the Fairchild positioned from Cork to Dublin using its registration as its call sign, and for the first time not using an Iona trip number. This confirmed the demise of the Iona operation.

The principle creditor of Iona's was the Revenue Commissioners. On 16 January 1995 they petitioned the High Court for unpaid taxes amounting to £623,977.

The official Liquidator, Liam Dowdall, of BDO Binder, Chartered Accountants, Setanta Centre, Nassau Street, Dublin 2 appointed Hamilton Osborne King, 32 Molesworth Street, Dublin 2 to offer the assets of Iona National Airways Limited (in Liquidation) for sale by Tender. The tender date was Friday, 21 April 1995 at 12 noon. A tender document was produced that contained 525 lots. Robert McKay, Asset Valuers and Auctioneers, 4 Blackbourne Square, Rathfarnham Gate, Dublin 14 acted on behalf of Hamilton Osborne King in the disposal of the assets. The first twelve lots referred to aircraft, which were disposed of as follows:

Lot 1. Cessna Reims F152-II single engine aircraft

Current registration:	EI-BNC
Serial No:	F152-1894
Date of Manufacture:	1982
C of A Expiry Date:	21.10.1995
Airframe hours:	1,050

Lying: Waterford Regional Airport, Killowen, County Waterford. (*xvii)

Notes: French built, last flight February 1995. EI-BNC was sold through the auctioneer and remained at Waterford until 4 May 1995 when it was delivered to the UK. On 15 June 1995, it was registered G-BWEU to Sky Pro Limited, 5 Park Road, Bawtry, Doncaster, S. Yorks. It was cancelled from the Irish register on the same day. EI-BNC was delivered to Iona from Reims on 22 February 1982.

Lot 2. Cessna 152-II single engine aircraft

Current registration:	EI-BVU
Serial No:	152-83182
Date of Manufacture:	1979
C of A Expiry Date:	25.11.1995
Airframe hours:	6,684

Lying: Waterford Regional Airport, Killowen, County Waterford. (*xvii)

Notes: Last flight February 1995. EI-BVU was sold through the auctioneer to Haimoss Limited, Old Sarum Flying Club, The Portway, Sawsbury, Wiltshire and acquiring the registration G-BWEV on 28 June 1995.

Lot 3. Cessna 152-II single engine aircraft

Current registration:	EI-BVW
Serial No:	152-85123
Date of Manufacture:	1981
C of A Expiry Date:	3.12.1994
Airframe hours:	5,680

Lying: Waterford Regional Airport, Killowen, County Waterford. (*xvii)

Notes: Last flight February 1995. EI-BVW was sold through the auctioneer to Marnham Investments Limited, Northern Ireland and was flown to Woodgate Air Maintenance Ltd, Belfast International Airport, and took up the registration G-IAFT on 20 June 1995.

Lot 4. Cessna 152 single engine aircraft

Current registration:	EI-CCM
Serial No:	152-82320
Date of Manufacture:	1979
C of A Expiry Date:	28.07.1995
Airframe hours:	7,700

Lying: Weston airport, Leixlip, County Kildare.

Notes: EI-CCM was not sold at auction. On 18 November 1999 ownership was transferred to Eric Hopkins, Newcastle, County Wicklow in flying condition. This machine was one of a batch of four machines sent from the western United States of America to Dublin in crates arriving at Dublin port in August 1990.

FOOTNOTE (*xvii)
All three Waterford based Cessnas were cancelled from the Irish register on 15 June 1995. These latter Cessnas, EI-BVU and EI-BVW, were two of the three aircraft that arrived in crates from Wichita to Iona in early July 1988. The third being EI-BVV that was involved in the fatal crash near Mulhuddart, 27 September 1988.

Lot 5. Cessna 310Q twin engine aircraft

Current registration:	EI-BEO
Serial No:	310-Q0233
Date of Manufacture:	1971
C of A Expiry Date:	04.07.1994
Airframe hours:	4,775

Lying: Donegal International airport, Carrickfin, County Donegal

Notes: Aircraft last flew 28th June 1994 and suffered damage when the No. 1 propeller detached prior to take-off. Left engine and propeller missing. EI-BEO was purchased through the auctioneer by Christopher Keane, Saggart, County Dublin. It was cancelled from the Irish register on 17 November 1995, and registered to the new owner on 19 January 1996. It was cancelled by him on 27 November 2000 and removed to the United States as N7733Q for possible restoration to flying status. It was registered to Mid Atlantic Aircraft Inc on 9 February 2001. This aircraft was purchased in Germany and ferried to Iona on 3 April 1978.

Lot 6. Cessna F152-II single engine aircraft

Current registration:	EI-CCK
Serial No:	79610
Date of Manufacture:	Not known
C of A Expiry Date:	Expired
Airframe hours:	Not known

Lying: Newcastle airfield, County Wicklow
Notes: Suffered heavy landing, largely disassembled, no engine, (Lot 201 being offered separately may be a suitable engine block).

Notes: EI-CCK was not sold at auction and remained at Newcastle, County Wicklow. This aircraft was another of a batch of four machines sent from the western United States of America to Dublin in crates arriving at Dublin port in August 1990.

Lot 7. Auster J1N single engine aircraft

Current registration:	EI-AMK
Serial No:	Not known
Date of Manufacture:	c.1944
C of A Expiry Date:	Expired
Airframe hours:	Not known

Lying: Newcastle airfield, County Wicklow
Notes: Wings removed but available, no engine. Possible restoration project.

Notes: EI-AMK was not sold at auction. It never flew again following its forced landing at Birr, County Offaly on 1 June 1979. It was originally acquired 30 years previously on 9 October 1964.

Lot 8. Cessna F152-II single engine aircraft

Current registration:	EI-BMM
Serial No:	F152-1899
Date of Manufacture:	1981
C of A Expiry Date:	Expired
Airframe hours:	6,547

Lying: Iona hangar, Dublin airport
Notes: Hangared since April 1993 with time expired engine. Tail removed but available. NavCom, ADF, HSI and turn co-ordinator missing.

Notes: EI-BMM was acquired through the auctioneer by Peter Redmond, Clondalkin, Dublin 22. It was registered to him on 16 May 1996 and its base was given as Weston. This was one of two Cessna 152s ferried from Reims on 4 April 1982.

Lot 9. Cessna F152-II single engine aircraft

Current registration: EI-CCJ
Serial No: 152-80174
Date of Manufacture: 1978
C of A Expiry Date: Expired
Airframe hours: 4,773
Lying: Iona hangar, Dublin airport
Notes: Hangared since April 1993. Engine removed, spare time expired engine available. No propeller. One fuel tank, NAV/COM and turn co-ordinator missing.

Notes: EI-CCJ was purchased through the auctioneer by Nalson Aviation Limited, Willey Park Farm, Standstead Road, Caterham, Surrey. It was originally purchased by Iona along with EI-CCK, EI-CCL and EI-CCM.

Lot 10. Cessna F152-II single engine aircraft

Current registration: EI-BRO
Serial No: F152-18957
Date of Manufacture: 1982
C of A Expiry Date: Expired
Airframe hours: c. 5,000
Lying: Iona hangar, Dublin airport
Notes: Aircraft is effectively a shell. Last flew 26 February 1992 when suffered left wing damage in mid-air collision. Repairs commenced but aircraft rather incomplete. Time expired engine available.

Notes: EI-BRO was purchased through the auctioneer by Nalson Aviation Limited, Willey Park Farm, Standstead Road, Caterham, Surrey. It was subsequently sold to East Midlands Aircraft Hire Limited based at East Midlands and registered to them on 11 October 1995 as G-IBRO. It was cancelled from the Irish register on 25 August 1995. It was delivered new from Reims to Iona 18 November 1985. This was the aircraft involved in the fatal accident in County Cork with Cessna 172, EI-BRM on 26 February 1992.

Lot 11. Scrap Cessna 152.

Registration No. EI-AUH.
Fuselage and wings (This aircraft was a Cessna 172 and not a 152 as stated by auctioneer.)

Notes: EI-AUH was purchased through the auctioneer by Christopher Keane, Saggart, County Dublin. It was originally ferried to Iona on 5 August 1970. It was involved in an accident at Kilkenny in May 1972. Its wings and fuselage were used in the rebuild of EI-AVA and it was removed from the Irish register 28 August 1986.

Lot 12. Scrap Cessna 152.

Registration No. EI-BIA as lotted.

Notes: EI-BIA was purchased through the auctioneer by Christopher Keane, Saggart, County Dublin. It was delivered to Iona on 19 September 1980. Nine days later it crashed at an air display at Holycross, near Thurles, County Tipperary. The new aircraft was written-off and was cancelled from the register on 16 June 1981.

By August 1995 Aer Rianta had secured the former Iona facilities at Cloghran from the Liquidator. Iona received no recompense for the buildings they had progressively erected and developed over a period of forty years. Subsequently, the hangars were listed as unfit for any commercial or other use, though Aer Rianta has since been using some of the hangars for storing the airport snow clearing vehicles.

In March 1996, the Liquidator revealed that Iona had collapsed leaving debts of £2 million. He stated that Iona was insolvent as far back as March 1992, and that the deficiency in the company was as high as £1 million by March 1993. The Liquidator applied to commence proceedings against the former directors of Iona National Airways Limited for reckless trading. This action was not proceeded with through the Courts. Iona's directors had

vigorously opposed the Liquidator's application, saying that at all stages the company's directors acted responsibly and honestly, and that, had they secured one big contract, the situation would have improved dramatically. Pearse was mindful of the fact that Iona never obtained any financial assistance from taxpayers, unlike other aviation organisations that received grants to assist with development of their aviation business.

The Liquidator completed the task of finalising the affairs of Iona National Airways Limited and the company was dissolved on 29 May 2000. During the course of five and a half years, the Liquidator had £563,633.25 available for disposal. The following table (amounts in Irish pounds) summarises how the Liquidator disposed of this amount:

BDO Binder, Liquidators fees	234,428.43
Eugene F. Collins, solicitor for Liquidator, legal fees	130,288.25
Collector General	48,849.07
Craig Gardner, Examiner's fees	35,361.89
Employee entitlements	27,151.57
Auctioneers valuer's fees	24,924.46
Insurance	17,701.22
Chief Clerk-Dublin Metropolitan District Court	16,989.86
Revenue solicitor	10,498.91
Security costs	9,870.34
Accountant's fees	1,579.05
Coyle Hamilton, Liquidator's bond	1,524.00
Wages and expenses	1,332.31
Coyle Hamilton, insurance	1,226.20
Telecom Eireann, telephone	548.07
Maintenance costs	430.08
Storage costs	497.51
Transport costs	360.00
Bank of Ireland, bank charges	48.27
Sundries	23.76
TOTAL	563,633.25

Iona Garage and Engineering Works Limited was formally dissolved in the Companies Office on 26 March 1999. By a set of coincidences the dissolution of Iona National Airways Limited, at the end of May 2000, was simultaneous with the placing of the garage property on the market for sale. The property at the junction of Prospect Road and Whitworth Road, Cross Guns Bridge, Glasnevin, comprising 815 square metres, was advertised for sale by Ganly Walters, at a public auction to be held on 12 July 2000(*xviii).

The vendors, Arc Hire, anticipated the building might be demolished for development. I visited the site on 19 June 2000 for research purposes in the company of Ronan Lee and Pearse Cahill. Pearse referred to the stained-glass windows and wondered as to their whereabouts. We removed the wooden sheeting at the upper portion of the large windows to reveal, much to our amazement and delight, the stained-glass windows that were inserted by his father, Hugh, seventy years earlier. We returned a few weeks later and the three of us carefully removed all fourteen sections, completely intact – 'IONA NATIONAL AIRWAYS LIMITED, ACCESSORIES, TAXIS, DAY AND NIGHT.'(See photograph in colour section). To see a man, in his eighties, working up a ladder in an effort to preserve a portion of his legacy and patrimony, makes you realise how proud this man was of his family heritage. In early 2004 the building was refurbished and converted to the licensed premises, *Porterhouse.*

The collapse of Iona was a very sad affair, leaving a gap in the marketplace. The company had been an integral part of the aviation scene in Ireland for sixty-five years – almost forty of them at Dublin airport, and as Pearse Cahill was fond of reminding everyone: *'Iona was Ireland's oldest airline, and Kildonan was Ireland's first commercial airport.'* What is not in doubt is that many hundreds of airline crew throughout the world owe their careers to the Cahill family. The zeal, enthusiasm and dedication of Hugh and Pearse Cahill undoubtedly helped shape the path of aviation in Ireland.

FOOTNOTE (*xviii)
The auctioneers' particulars stated that: 'The property is located on a strategic corner position at the junction of Prospect Road and Whitworth Road. The property is within 3 minutes walk of both Phibsboro and Drumcondra. Cross Guns Bridge is a popular central location with established businesses including Des Kelly Carpets, ADT Alarms and Cross Guns Bakery. The site is within easy reach of the Mater Hospital, Kings Inn, Croke Park and is adjacent to Mountjoy Square and North Circular Road. The property comprises a warehouse / industrial type structure, which has been partly converted to retail, office and ancillary uses. The structure comprises concrete walls with smooth external render, steel framed roof trusses and double skinned asbestos roof. Included in the boundary of the site is the old railway station, which is accessed via Whitworth Road entrance. The property boasts over 60m of road frontage. In addition to the net area of 815 sq. m, there may be possibilities to extend the area of the site, to include adjoining ownerships, subject to agreement and the necessary consents.'

Pearse Cahill and Catherine Greene beside the port engine of EI-BGP pose for a photograph along with Iona ground staff about 1981

Photograph via Catherine Greene collection

Embraer EMB. 110P1 Bandeirante, EI-BPI operating on behalf of An Post's Express Mail Service.
Photographed at Dublin airport 31 May 1991

Photograph courtesy Paul Cunniffe

Embraer EMB. 110P1 Bandeirante, formerly EI-BPI and now operated by Scan Con Airways in Denmark as OY-ASY.
Above photograph taken at Fagernes-Leirin, Norway on 1 February 2004.

Photograph courtesy Eirik Langas Nilsen

Fokker F.27-600 Friendship, EI-FEA photographed at Dublin airport 25 April 1992- 9 days before it was removed from the Irish register and returned to Federal Express, Memphis, Tennessee.

Photograph courtesy Paul Cunniffe

Fairchild-Hillier FH-227D, EI-CAZ displaying the joint DHL and Iona logos.

Photograph courtesy Leo Murray / Military Aircraft Photographs

Cessna 208A Caravan, EI-FEX, photographed on the Iona ramp, 5 April 1992-
3 weeks before its return to USA.

Photograph courtesy Mark Richardson

Lockheed L188A Electra, EI-CHO in the colours of Channel Express.
The Iona logo is inscribed forward of the rear exit door.

Photograph courtesy Leo Murray / Military Aircraft Photographs

Arthur Wignall was a colourful and charismatic individual who frequented Iona for over 25 years. During that period he was renowned for his aerobatic performances in his HARP Lager sponsored Pitts S-2A, EI-BKA. He is photographed over Blessington Resevoir, Co. Wicklow on 24 May 1983 by Paul Duffy from Iona's Cessna 182P, EI-BCL

Photograph courtesy Paul Duffy

The Iona fleet available for charter work was photographed at Iona ramp 12 March 1984 to promote the inauguration of the Dublin to Sligo scheduled route

Photograph courtesy Paul Duffy

The above series of photographs captures Iona engineers working through the night to perform an engine change on one of the Cessna 208's operated on behalf of Federal Express. As dawn breaks through the roof lights the final touches are applied

Photographs via Pearse Cahill collection

The above photograph captures the four Cessna 152-II's that were imported from United States of America for pilot training use at Iona. They arrived in crates in August 1990 and were registered in sequence EI-CCJ, EI-CCK, EI-CCL and EI-CCM.

The recovery of the 70-year-old stained glass panes from the premises at the junction of Prospect Road and Whitworth Road, 27 July 2000. Left to right: Ronan Lee, Michael Traynor and Pearse Cahill

Photograph from author's collection

Never lost the touch!! Pearse navigates the *'Iona Special'* round the street circuit at Newtownards to mark the 75th anniversary of the Tourist Trophy races on 20 June 2003. It was 50 years since Pearse raced competitively

Photograph courtesy Esler Crawford, Belfast, via Pearse Cahill collection

37 Lower Baggot Street,
Dublin 2, Ireland.

Tel: 01 662 3255 Fax: 01 661 8235
Email: mail@ganlywalters.ie
Website: www.iavi.ie/ganlywalters

Also at Kilkenny. Tel: 056 64833

GANLY WALTERS
est - 1847

FOR SALE BY PUBLIC AUCTION
(Unless previously sold)

in our salesroom at 37 Lower Baggot Street, Dublin 2
at 3pm on Wednesday 12th July 2000.

LANDMARK DEVELOPMENT OPPORTUNITY
(Subject to the necessary consents)
AT CROSS GUNS BRIDGE,
GLASNEVIN, DUBLIN 9.

(DUE TO CLIENT RELOCATING)

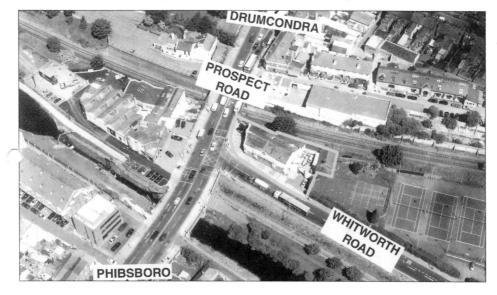

Landmark Site with superb high profile corner position.

At the junction of Prospect Road and Whitworth Road.

Site area c. 815 sq. m. (8,773 sq. ft.)

Auctioneers particulars for the sale of the property at Cross Guns Bridge, July 2000

Table 35

Registration	EI-CHO
Aircraft Type	Lockheed L.188A Electra
Constructors Serial Number	1068
Place & Year of Manufacture	Burbank, USA, 1959
Previous Registrations	N5535
Registered to	Iona National Airways Ltd, 25 September 1993
Delivery date	October 1993

Remarks

It was first registered as N5535 to Eastern Airlines and delivered to them on 9 July 1959. It remained with Eastern for 18 years. It was sold to Evergreen International Airlines in April 1978 for use on freight and US military contract work. In March 1987 Evergreen placed the Electra in storage at Marana, Arizona for three and a half years. It was sold to Channel Express Air Services Limited, Hurn on 10 October 1990. A lengthy overhaul followed and in late September 1993 it was with Air UK in Norwich undergoing preparatory work for its lease to Iona. It remained on the UPS/Iona contract for one week and relocated to a Scandavian route. Registered to Tonella Limited 31 May 1994 with the hirers noted as Channel Express (Air services) Limited, Hurn. On 1 November 1994 it was cancelled from the Irish register and became G-CHNX, remaining with Channel Express. It was withdrawn from use at Bournemouth-Hurn on 31 October 2001.

It was de-registered as G-CHNX on 12 May 2003 with the annotation *'permanently withdrawn from use'*. The fuselage was scrapped at Hurn but the nose section survived and was moved to John Morgan's collection at Pershore, Worchester on 1 October 2003. It is anticipated it will be repainted in its 1959 style Eastern Airlines colours as N5535, its original registration.

Chapter

9

UP, UP AND HOORAY!

Alongside the commercial operations of Iona National Airways Limited, were the pilot training and club activities at the Irish Aero Club

Chapter Nine

UP, UP AND HOORAY!

The story of the Irish Aero Club runs parallel to that of Iona and, although the two stories intersect at many points, the flying club deserves a chapter of its own. Like that of Iona, the story of the Irish Aero Club is intrinsically linked to the Cahill family. By the mid 1960s Iona Engineering Works Ltd were becoming well established in the light aviation business. The aircraft purchased to date were registered to a company whose name did not reflect its role at Dublin airport. It was time to consider a name that would portray the operations of the company. Pearse reflected on an aviation organisation that existed in his youth – The Irish Aero Club.

In 1909 a group of aviation enthusiasts got together and formed themselves into a body called The Irish Aero Club, later changing its name to The Aero Club of Ireland. Little activity was recorded for the club during its first years in existence, the First World War having some bearing on this. Many efforts were made to inject vitality into the club, but the incident that gave the club its lifeline was the *Bremen* Atlantic crossing in April 1928. In the months that followed, one of the *Bremen* crew, Colonel James Fitzmaurice, was instrumental in giving impetus to the band of enthusiasts. On 15 August 1928 a revitalised group of aviators formed a new aero club, again taking the name the Irish Aero Club. The club set about raising funds to purchase an aircraft, which was achieved in a relatively short period of time. Within seven weeks they took possession of an Avro Avian. It was the first aircraft to be placed on the Irish civil aircraft register as EI-AAA on 5 October 1928. Flying instruction commenced from Baldonnel on 12 January 1929. During its first two years of operation the club flourished, it had two aircraft and an abundance of members. 1931 saw an improvement in the clubs fortunes, additional aircraft were purchased and the Air Corps afforded civil aviation greater facilities at Baldonnel. In 1933 the club was instrumental in co-ordinating the tour

of Ireland by Sir Alan Cobham and his aerial circus. 1933 was also a tragic year for the Irish Aero Club and these events are described elsewhere in this publication.

In October 1933 the club opened a branch at Sligo and followed this the next year with a branch at Cork. A club meeting in October 1935 referred to symptoms of financial problems. In 1936 Killarney was included in the venues for training by the club and there were signs of an increase in activities. 29 May 1937 saw the club suffer its third fatal accident, when another of its Gipsy Moths crashed into the Little Sugar Loaf mountain in County Wicklow, killing the pilot, Reginald Good, the only occupant. This left the club with one remaining aircraft, Gipsy Moth EI-AAU. The King's Cup air race in September 1937 was a major boost to the morale of the club but an even larger financial headache and placed a high strain on already stretched resources. At a rather sombre club meeting on 26 November 1937, the Irish Aero Club Limited resolved to cease trading and a Liquidator was appointed to wind up the company. The resulting litigation became a reference case for constitutional law, based on the newly enacted Constitution of Ireland that came into force that year. As a result, legal precedent was created when it was determined that claims by the State stood side by side with the claims of all other creditors.

The ethos of the Irish Aero Club Limited was to make the Irish public air minded and, for its members, it provided them with the opportunity to fly and obtain the licences at a reasonable cost. Within a couple of years another World War affected civil aviation in Ireland. One can only speculate as to the fortunes of the club had they survived until the 'Emergency' and afterwards. This chapter is in no way intended to cover the history of the Irish Aero Club prior to its ceasing operations in 1938. Instead, it continues the story after the war years.

The name of the Irish Aero Club Limited was in the mind of one man twenty eight years after the meeting held to dissolve the club. In 1965 Iona Garage and Engineering Works Limited had been giving flying instruction at its base at Cloghran,

Dublin airport. To segregate the activities of the maintenance base from the flying instruction, Pearse Cahill decided to form a separate company to handle and oversee the flying instruction. He investigated the name of the Irish Aero Club Limited to find it was struck off the register of limited companies. On 6 December 1965 the name of the Irish Aero Club Limited appeared again on the Irish aviation scene, when the company was registered with Certificate of Registration number 23272. To formalise the arrangement and determine which aircraft were doing what, it was decided to transfer all aircraft involved in flight training to the new company.

This chapter in no way details the full extent of activities of The Irish Aero Club at Iona, but is merely an overview of the aircraft involved. Perhaps a reader someday will be inspired to tell the full story and bring to the fore the many tales and exploits associated with this club and it's members over 30 years.

My intention is to give the reader an account of the movements of the 40 plus aircraft associated with the flying club and allow former members to reminisce fondly about events - some of which could not even be printed in a book such as this! It might take another publication to cover all these anecdotes.!!

The first aircraft to be transferred from Iona Garage and Engineering Works Limited to the new club was the Cessna 150E, EI-AOO (see Table 16). It was registered to the Irish Aero Club Limited on 18 February 1966. The aircraft was intended for use by the Galway Flying Club Limited but was not formally transferred to them until 14 November 1967.

The second aircraft to be transferred from Iona Garage and Engineering Works Limited to the flying club and become part of the Irish Aero Club Limited was Cessna 172G, EI-AOK. That transfer is recorded as 29 March 1966 (see Table 18).

On 16 March 1966, Arthur Wignall ferried Iona's first Cessna 172 from the Cessna factory in Reims, France to Dublin airport. This new Cessna 172G was registered EI-AOK

Photograph courtesy George Flood

Iona used Auster J/1 Autocrat, EI-AMK, for pilot training purposes for fifteen years since its acquisition in 1964

Photograph courtesy George Flood

EI-AOK had its moment of glory when it featured in a 1967 film *Robbery* starring Stanley Baker. The aircraft is seen, towards the end of the film, purporting to take-off from an airstrip in England. The airstrip was in fact at Gowran Grange; other locations were in Counties Carlow and Meath, including the car chase and shots of the train respectively. Pearse was the pilot during the filming. The film portrays the efforts of a criminal gang to rob the overnight mail train from Glasgow. Similarities have been drawn with the Great Mail Train robbery in England, 8 August 1963, some years previous.

Auster J/1 Autocrat, EI-AMK, painted in RAF camouflage scheme and serial number VF523, for film purposes. Paddy Robinson, pictured at front of aircraft, was the pilot during the film work

Photograph via Pearse Cahill collection

A further administration exercise saw Auster J/1 Autocrat, EI-AMK, transfer across to Irish Aero Club on 11 October 1966 (see Table 15). During the summer of 1969 it was advertised for sale at £1,000. Fortunately nothing materialised and EI-AMK was to prove a valuable asset and workhorse at Iona for fifteen years. Not to be outdone by EI-AOK, at one stage EI-AMK was painted in Royal Air Force combat colours for use in a film. The scene was shot at Ballyfree and involved the Iona aircraft taxing beside some blazing hay on the night of 8 July 1969. For the occasion it wore green camouflage and RAF roundels and bore the marks MT355. Iona's Chief Flying Instructor, Paddy Robinson, piloted it. Other films featuring Iona aircraft were *Three Little Indians, McKenzie Break,* starring Brian Keith and *Fu Man Chu.*

The second of the two new Cessnas ordered from the Brussels based Cessna representatives in 1965 was a Cessna 150G model. This new aircraft was delivered from Reims, France via United Kingdom on 28 January 1967 and was registered EI-APF (see Table 36).

On 4 November 1967, the Irish Aero Club Limited took possession of their third new Cessna 150. This time a 150H model. Prior to delivery from Reims, France, it was placed on the register on 23 October 1967 as EI-ARY. This aircraft was leased by Iona to the Kerry Aero Club (see Table 37).

Photographed January 1967 in front of the hangar are the first three Cessnas registered to Iona. Left to right: Cessna 172G, EI-AOK, Cessna150E, EI-AOO and Cessna 150G, EI-APF

Photograph courtesy Paul Duffy

Iona accepted delivery of 3 new Cessna 150s within a 12 month period January 1967 to January 1968. In foreground is EI-APF, leading the formation is EI-AST and in the rear is EI-ARY

Photograph courtesy Paul Duffy

Iona hangar, 16 August 1968, following extension to original hangar. Clubhouse is under construction. In the foreground are a Tripacer, an Avro Anson and Iona's Cessna 150, EI-APF (on left)

Photograph courtesy Paul Duffy

Cessna were certainly very pleased with Pearse when he placed an order for yet another new Cessna aircraft. The sixth since the arrival of EI-AOO in April 1965. Pearse's logbook shows a delivery flight totalling five hours 45 minutes on 11 February 1968 from Reims, France to Dublin, routing via Liverpool and Valley. The aircraft in question was a Cessna 150H, bearing the registration EI-AST, having been registered to the Irish Aero Club Limited on 30 January 1968 in advance of the ferry flight (see Table 38). Training and instruction at the Irish Aero Club was flourishing towards the end of the 1960s. To end the decade on a positive note, a new Cessna 150J was ordered. On 5 March 1969 EI-ATH was placed on the register and delivered from Reims on 22 March 1969. Pearse's log book records the test flight on 27 March 1969 (see Table 39).

To commemorate the fiftieth anniversary of the trans-Atlantic flight of Alcock and Brown in 1919, a celebration took place at the site of the memorial in Clifden, County Galway on 15 June 1969. An account of the flight was read to those that gathered and was followed by a fly-past of three Iona aircraft – EI-AOK, EI-AST and EI-ATH. Two

Canadian pilots, Captain Gene Locke and Tom Lee arrived at Shannon from St. Johns, Newfoundland, the previous day in a Piper PA-31 Navajo in an effort to retrace the flight of Alcock and Brown.

The 30 August 1969 marked the official opening of Farranfore airport, County Kerry. It was called Kerry's second airfield, as one was already in existence at Killarney Race Course. It was a 2,400 foot grass runway. The first sod to mark the construction of Kerry County Airport at Farranfore was turned on 14 March 1969. The first official aircraft to use the airport was a light aircraft piloted by Captain Milo Carr of the Department of Transport and Power on 25 August 1969. There had, however, been an earlier, unofficial, movement at Farranfore when Iona's Cessna 172, EI-AOK landed on the partly completed runway on 23 August 1969. On board were John Byrne, Pearse Cahill, Captain Carr and Tom Ryle (Chairman and Director of the airport). Brian Lenihan, the Minister for Transport and Power on 30 August 1969, performed the official opening ceremony. The first commercial aircraft landed shortly after the ceremony was complete and carried the twenty three entrants for the International Rose of Tralee Festival. It was a Shorts Skyvan chartered, on their behalf, by Pearse and flew the 'Roses' from Shannon to Farranfore to publicise the occasion.

The 1970s were to continue in the same positive vein as the 1960s had ended. A new Cessna 150K Aerobat was registered on 10 April 1970 to the Irish Aero Club as EI-AUC. It was delivered from Reims, France on 23 April 1970 in its orange and white colours (see Table 40).

Tragically, Cessna 150H, EI-ARY, on lease to Kerry Aero Club from Iona, failed to get airborne from Farranfore, County Kerry on 14 June 1970 and hit a tree stump, killing the student pilot, Karl Hissenauer (41) and seriously injuring his instructor, Christopher Gallagher (24). The wreckage was removed to the Iona hangar at Dublin airport and the registration was removed from the Irish register on 20 July 1972.

Iona ordered a new Cessna 172H in 1970. This was the second new Cessna 172 ordered by Iona, the first being EI-AOK in 1966, subsequently transferred to the Irish Aero Club. The latest 172 was registered on 28 July 1970 as EI-AUH. Delivery from Reims was the following week, 5 August 1970. Since the transfer of EI-AOO to the Irish Aero Club in 1965, all aircraft purchased for the following five years were registered in the name of the flying club. The exception, in this instance, was EI-AUH that was registered to Iona National Airways Limited (see Table 41).

Another new Cessna 150K Aerobat was purchased and registered as EI-AUO on 2 March 1971, to the Irish Aero Club Limited (see Table 42). It was a Reims built machine. Reims Aviation temporarily mis-painted it as EI-ALL prior to delivery. On 5 March 1971, Pearse commenced the ferry flight to Dublin at 4.30pm. One hour 50 minutes later he arrived at Le Touquet where he overnighted. The following day, departing at 1.20pm he flew the 40 minute second leg across the Channel to Lympne, England, overnighting there. Next morning, 7 March 1971, at 11.15am he departed Lympne for

Liverpool, touching down two hours 55 minutes later. After a stopover lasting one hour 45 minutes, Pearse was airborne again on the final leg to Dublin, arriving at 5.30pm.

Orders for new Cessnas continued in 1971 with another new Cessna reserved, this time the newer version 172K. It was registered to Iona National Airways Limited on 1 July 1971 as EI-AVA (see Table 43). Pearse was getting well acquainted with the ferry flights from Reims and yet again volunteered to bring the new aircraft to Dublin. Another evening departure at 6pm on 2 July 1971 from Reims, reaching Le Touquet one and a half hours later. He did not get out of there until the afternoon of 4 July, when he flew to Ashford, Kent in 35 minutes. After a four-hour stopover he continued flying for a further two hours to arrive at East Midlands airport at 7.30pm; another overnight stay and he was on his way the next morning at 11.30am to complete the final leg of the ferry flight in two hours.

The investment in new aircraft continued with the purchase of a further Reims built Cessna 150L. On 3 March 1972 this aircraft was registered to the Irish Aero Club Limited as EI-AVM. It was to be the final aircraft to grace the Irish register in the name of Irish Aero Club Limited. It was delivered to Dublin on 9 March 1972 (see Table 44).

Cessna 150K Aerobat photographed at the Reims plant in France. The registration EI-ALL was erroneously painted by Reims Aviation. For the ferry flight on 5 March 1971 it bore the correct registration EI-AUO

Photograph via Paul Duffy collection

Cessna 172H EI-AUH spent a considerable time operating for Iona until it failed to take off from Kilkenny airfield in May 1972. It overran the runway, crashed through the boundary hedge and came to rest with its nose in the ground and tail up. The three occupants, including two editors from *Flying* magazine were uninjured. The wreckage was removed to the Iona hangar where the wings and fuselage were used in the rebuild of EI-AVA some years later. As a consequence, EI-AUH was cancelled from the register on 28 August 1986.

This photograph taken on 17 March 1972, the week after delivery of EI-AVM, displays some of the range of aircraft available to members of the Irish Aero Club for pilot training or leisure flying. Left to right: at rear, EI-AVA, EI-ATH, EI-APF, EI-AUO, EI-AVM, EI-AUC, EI-AST and in front, EI-AVF, EI-AVC and EI-AOD

Photograph courtesy Paul Duffy

1973 opened with an order for another Reims built Cessna 150; on 22 February 1973 as EI-AWE (see Table 45). It was ferried via Le Touquet and Liverpool to Dublin on 25 March 1973. The registration of Cessna 150, EI-AWE, in February 1973, was to Iona National Airways Limited as opposed to the flying school trading as Irish Aero Club. Instruction continued at the Irish Aero Club but all future aircraft acquired for pilot training were registered in the name of Iona National Airways Limited, except the occasional registration in Pearse's own name. Iona National Airways Limited was the name formerly used by Pearse's father, Hugh, in 1931. It was Pearse's intention in 1965 to segregate flying instruction with other activities of the Iona organisation and therefore any aircraft associated with pilot training would be registered to the Irish Aero Club Limited. Management at Iona decided, in 1973, not to continue with this policy and opted to register future aircraft to Iona National Airways Limited, this, however, did not in any way reflect the demise

of the flight training operations. Quite the contrary, in fact this side of the business was flourishing. While Iona purchased many new aircraft for onward sale to other clubs and private owners throughout Ireland, they did retain some for pilot training purposes. It became a policy of Iona to purchase new aircraft from Cessna, use them for pilot training with the Irish Aero Club and then sell them to flying clubs second-hand, thus allowing flying clubs in Ireland to acquire reasonably new training aircraft at an affordable price. A typical example was Cessna 150F, EI-APF, used for pilot training at Dublin airport from January 1967 until its sale to Midland Flying Club, Birr, County Offaly in March 1973.

Iona purchased two new Cessnas in early 1974. The first to arrive was a Cessna 182J, manufactured at the Cessna factory Wichita, United States of America. From Wichita it was flown across the Atlantic, bearing registration marks N52229 and arriving at the Iona hangar on 25 March 1974. This

A group of Irish Aero Club instructors photographed in 1973. Left to right: Brian Murphy, Terry Rowan, John Colton, Paddy Robinson and Eugene Higgins. In the background are David Abrahamson and Kevin Conway

Photograph courtesy Paul Duffy

a Cessna 150L Aerobat. It was registered on 26 March 1974 as EI-AYF to Iona National Airways Limited. The aircraft was delivered to Iona from Reims, France via Cardiff on 4 April 1974 (see Table 46). In May 1974, the Irish Aero Club appointed Jack Reid as its Chief Flying Instructor. He replaced Paddy Robinson who took up a position in Aer Arann.

In March / April 1974 Iona took delivery of two new aircraft in ten days. Pearse was to go one better. On 5 May 1975, two new aircraft left Reims and flew to Hurn, north of Bournemouth, Dorset. The following day they continued their journey until they arrived at the Iona ramp. Both aircraft had been placed on the Irish register

was the second Cessna 182, the first one being EI-ANC in September 1965. On 21 March 1974 the latest Cessna 182 was registered to Iona National Airways Limited as EI-AYJ (see Table 47). Ten days after the delivery of EI-AYJ, yet another new Cessna aircraft arrived at the Iona hangar. This time

on 2 May 1975 in the name of Iona National Airways Limited. The first was EI-BAS, a Cessna 172M (see Table 48). The second aircraft was a Cessna 150L bearing registration EI-BAT (see Table 49).

Members of the Irish Aero Club with families and friends at Iona, 1973

Photograph courtesy Paul Duffy

The first delivery of a new aircraft for 1976 occurred when a new Cessna 150M was handed over at Reims on 29 April and arrived at Dublin airport the next day. On 27 February 1976 it was registered as EI-BBN to Iona National Airways Limited (see Table 50). After only eight days with Iona, the aircraft was damaged in a training accident at The Ward, County Dublin on 8 May 1976 and removed to Rogers Aviation at Cranfield, Bedfordshire, north east of Milton Keynes, in late August 1976 for rebuilding.

On 19 September 1976 ex-Iona Cessna 172, EI-AVA, then owned by Patrick Parke, was severely damaged at Kilbrittain, County Cork when it overran the wet grass runway to crash into the hedge at the end of the field. An Iona aircraft, Cessna 182J, EI-AYJ, followed some minutes behind EI-AVA. Pearse was piloting and was temporarily blinded by bright sunshine. Likewise, braking efficiency was reduced due to the wet grass surface. In its attempt to go around it collided with a fire engine, setting off a number of fire extinguishers, it then struck the starboard wing of EI-AVA, and ended its journey in a hedge having crossed a road at the end of the field. The wings folded back snagging the doors. Amazingly, Pearse and Tom Farrington, the front seat passenger, sustained no serious injuries. Catherine Greene, Secretary of Iona, was a rear seat passenger and was taken to hospital and detained for observation. Pearse's only complaint was he lost his glasses in the crash and couldn't see all the food at a party hosted by Russell Winn later that evening. Unfortunately, the only person to sustain injury resulting from the accident was a local man who had climbed up a tree expecting a better view of EI-AVA following its impact with the hedge. He was knocked from the tree following impact from Pearse's aircraft. He was treated in hospital for minor injuries. Both aircraft were returned to Dublin the following weekend. EI-AYJ was a 'write-off' and was removed from the official register on 16 June 1981. EI-AVA was sent to Rogers Aviation at Cranfield, England and was restored to flying condition using the wings from EI-AUH that crashed in Kilkenny in May 1972.

Patrick Parke's Cessna 172, EI-AVA and Iona's Cessna182, EI-AYJ, (through the hedge and across the road), following both aircraft coming to grief at Kilbrittain, Co. Cork, 19 September 1976. The rear windscreen was smashed by Oliver 'Sammy' Bruton to enable the 3 occupants escape from EI-AYJ

Photograph via Pearse Cahill collection

The above incident at Kilbrittain was not as serious as another accident that weekend. Morane Rallye, EI-BBP, departed Kilbrittain at 7.50am on the following morning, 20 September 1976. It was routing Kilbrittain – Abbeyshrule and did not file a flight plan, as none was required due to the special conditions made for the Kilbrittain Fly-in. It was not observed as overdue and an alert was not raised until 2.30pm; several aircraft took part in the search, including Iona's Cessna 172, EI-BAS, (Rescue 5). The Rallye was located in the Galtee Mountains. It struck the mountain near the ruins of O'Loughran's Castle on the Mitchelstown – Cahir road and appeared to have been climbing steeply at the moment of impact, as if the pilot saw the mountain too late and made a vain attempt to clear the summit. The weather conditions at the time were very bad and this hindered the search. All three people on board were killed, they were: Tom Gannon (aircraft owner and pilot), Richard Reilly and James Byrne, who owned the land on which Abbeyshrule airfield was built. All 3 were directors of Longford Aviation. Following the accident, Jim Byrne's wife requested the flying club at Abbeyshrule to vacate the field. A project, headed by Paul Duffy, successfully secured a site about half a mile away.

Within two months a replacement for the Cessna 182, EI-AYJ, along with another new 172 were ordered from Cessna. Pearse did not like to let the grass grow under his feet. Both new aircraft were registered on 22 November 1976 to Iona National Airways Limited. The Cessna 172N was registered EI-BCK (see Table 51), with marks EI-BCL allocated to the Cessna 182P (see Table 52). The first of the two to reach Iona was the Cessna 182P, arriving on 20 January 1977. Prior to delivery it bore the American registration N1366M. It was bearing this registration as it was a European demonstrator of this type and had clocked up 100 hours in this role. Cessna 172N, EI-BCK, was delivered via Jersey on 5 March 1977.

During February 1977 some of Iona's aircraft were advertised for sale:

Cessna 150s	EI-AVM	£6,000
	EI-BBN	£13,000
	EI-AWE	£7,000
	EI-BAT	£10,000
Cessna 172s	EI-AVA	£9,000
	EI-BCK	£21,000
Cessna 182	EI-BCL	£30,000

Eleven days after the arrival of EI-BCK another new Cessna 150 was ordered by Iona and placed on the Irish register on 16 March 1977. The latest Cessna 150M to the fleet bore the marks EI-BCV (see Table 53). On Friday, 3 June 1977 it was ferried from Reims to Dublin via Birmingham, with Pearse flying to Reims in the Cessna 182, EI-BCL, to facilitate the ferry flight.

Cessna 150M EI-BBN was delivered to Dublin 26 July 1977 after rebuild resulting from its accident on 8 May 1976 at The Ward, County Dublin.

The pilot training activity was continuing well, and in 1976 / 1977 Iona turned out 45 licensed pilots. The total flying hours for the Iona fleet increased by

almost 900 hours in 1977 compared with 1976.

EI-AVC	Cessna 337	387 hours
EI-ATC	Cessna 310	218 hours
EI-BAT	Cessna 150	800 hours
EI-AVM	Cessna 150	770 hours
EI-BBN	Cessna 150	305 hours
EI-BAS	Cessna 172	540 hours
		(during last 5 months)
EI-BCK	Cessna 172	405 hours
EI-BCL	Cessna 182	504 hours

EI-AWE was replaced by EI-BCV mid year and between them they clocked up 634 hours.

The total hours for 1976 were 3,690, and the total hours for 1977 were 4,563. As regards pilot training, Iona's philosophy was *'keep the aeroplanes up, keep the pilots up and a huge 'hooray' when a licence or rating was achieved.'*

A short time after the delivery of EI-BCV a new Cessna 152 was ordered from Reims. On 11 November 1977 it was registered to Iona National Airways Limited as EI-BDO (see Table 54). On 26 January 1978 it commenced its delivery flight from Reims, piloted by Allan Dagg and Peter Cahill. It overnighted at Jersey, Channel Islands, following a flight time of 3 hours 20 minutes. The following day it completed its second leg to Dublin in a flight time of 3 hours.

The first Cessna 150 came off the production line in September 1957. In 1960, Cessna acquired a 49% interest in Avions Max Holste, France. The company changed its name to Reims Aviation SA. From then, single-engine models, and the push-pull Cessna 337, were produced at Reims. The first major external design modification appeared in the mid-1960s. Earlier models had a vertical tail and the change resulted in a swept-back fin. After producing approximately 24,000 models of the 150, Cessna changed to a 152 version in 1977. This upgrade resulted in the fitting of an Avco-Lycoming 0.235 engine producing at 110HP, a 10-horse power increase in power, and which can use 100 Octane low-lead fuels. Other improvements included a new propeller and cowling changes to reduce noise and vibration. The first Reims built Cessna 152 to appear on the Irish register was EI-BDO delivered to Iona on 27 January 1978.

At approximately 4.15pm on 15 March 1979 Cessna 150M, EI-BDO, made a successful forced landing in a field near Baltinglass, County Wicklow. A number of civil and Air Corps aircraft assisted in the search to locate the Cessna. At 4.45pm Dublin Air Traffic Control received a phone call from the pilot confirming his location and that he was unharmed. The aircraft took off and returned to Dublin later that evening.

On 1 June 1979 with Pearse at the controls, Auster J/1 Autocrat, EI-AMK suffered an engine failure while flying at 300 feet above the ground. He made a successful forced landing south of Birr, County Offaly. Fortunately, no one was injured in the incident. It was returned to the Iona hangar at Dublin airport but never flew again.

1979 was to prove a bumper year for the Cessna order books, with Iona placing orders for seven new aircraft and a one-year-old 414 Chancellor in a ten-month period. The first three of these aircraft had sequential marks reserved for them on 22 January 1979. First to be registered that year was a Cessna 172N. On 30 March 1979 it acquired the marks EI-BGH (see Table 55). On 14 May 1979, two new Reims built Cessna 152s entered the register in the name of Iona National Airways Limited as EI-BGI (see Table 56) and EI-BGJ (see Table 57). EI-BGI was delivered from Reims on 15 June 1979 with Pearse again at the controls. Having adequately recovered from the incident with EI-AMK, and, routing via Bournemouth, he proceeded to Enniskillen, County Fermanagh to attend a fly-in, where he received the award for the longest journey to reach the event. On the same day, 15 June 1979, EI-BGJ was also ferried to Iona from Reims. EI-BGI was then leased to Waterford Aero Club for the period to 16 April 1985. Four

years earlier Pearse presented two new aircraft to the Iona ramp on the same day. That occasion was 6 May 1975 when EI-BAS and EI-BAT were delivered.

To further enhance pilot training facilities, an Analog Training Computers Incorporated model ATC-610K flight simulator was acquired at a cost of £7,000 at the end of January 1980. Installed in a caravan adjoining the clubhouse, the new simulator was made available for use to groups and individuals as well as to members of the Irish Aero Club. Its rate was £11.00 per hour. This compared favourably with the hourly rate for the Cessna 152 of £18.00 and £21.00 for the Cessna 172. Up to 20 hours could be validated towards an Instrument Rating. The unit is controlled by pre-programmed magnetic tape cassettes of the standard C60/C90 type and consists of a basic instrument panel and control layout representative of a modern light aircraft and a basic visual presentation consisting of a diagram against which a model aircraft moves. Movement of the model is keyed to the controls and the instructor has a separate printout of the pupil's progress. This was the first light aircraft simulator for the Irish Republic. Pearse used to joke about flying a 152 upside down in the clubhouse until people realised what he was talking about! Following the demise of Iona in 1995, Aerial Advertising Limited, Weston, acquired the simulator.

Four further registrations, almost sequential, had marks reserved for them on 5 November 1979. The first two were new Cessna 152s. The first of this line to have its details recorded on the register on 30 November 1979 was an Aerobat becoming EI-BIA (see Table 58). It was delivered to Iona via Liverpool on 19 September 1980. Nine days later Pearse flew it to attend an air display at Holycross, near Thurles, County Tipperary. During the display, with Ray Di Mascio at the controls, it failed to recover in sufficient time from a manoeuvre and crashed in a field adjoining the display field. The pilot was seriously injured but survived the crash. The new aircraft was 'written-off' and was cancelled from the register on 16 June 1981.

A distressed Pearse Cahill (centre photo) leaves the scene of the accident involving new Cessna 152, EI-BIA, at the Thurles Air Display, 28 September 1980. The pilot, Ray Di Mascio, though seriously injured in the accident survived to continue his career in commercial aviation. The aircraft was delivered new to Iona nine days prior to this accident

Photograph courtesy Liam Byrne via Ronny Vogt

The second of these two Cessna 152s also registered on 30 November 1979, was EI-BIB (see Table 59). It appeared at Iona on 14 March 1980, six months prior to the arrival of EI-BIA. EI-BIB was delivered the following day to Carnmore for use by the Galway Flying Club. It was one year later when it was formally registered to them on 13 March 1981. A deal involving EI-ATH formed part of the sale. EI-BIB remained in service with the Galway club until it overran the runway on landing at Carnmore in November 1981 and was extensively damaged. The severely damaged aircraft was brought to Abbeyshrule, County Longford for repair and the club had the use of Rallye EI-BMA. EI-BIB returned to Galway following repairs. The third in this particular sequence was a Cessna 172N, EI-BIC (see Table 60). EI-BIC was placed on the register on 15 February 1980 and was ferried from Reims via Jersey on 15 March 1980.

The seventh and final new Iona aircraft to be ordered in 1979 was a Cessna 152 Aerobat, EI-BIE (see Table 61). It was registered on 28 February 1980 and delivered to Iona on the same day as EI-BIC and the day after EI-BIB reached Iona. A truly historic period in the life of Iona – three new aircraft arriving from Reims, France within two days of each other. Cessna 310, EI-BEO, piloted by Peter Cahill, was flown to Reims carrying the ferry pilots.

While much of the previous paragraphs reflects new aircraft registered to Iona, there was also a considerable amount of second-hand aircraft changing hands through the auspices of Iona. Also, Iona supplied many of the flying clubs throughout Ireland with new Cessna single-engine aircraft. The name of Iona did not appear on official records, and the registration marks were allocated directly to the club, organisation or individual.

In 1980, Pearse celebrated the fiftieth anniversary of the commencement, by his father, of commercial aviation in Ireland. It was the fifteenth year since he reactivated the business. In that fifteen year period 426 aircraft had been entered on the Irish civil aircraft register. Of that total, 47 were registered to Iona – most of these being Cessnas. This represents 11% of all aircraft, civil and commercial on the Irish register. This does not include aircraft sold by Iona directly to clubs and individuals that were registered directly by the respective owners. The staff at Iona after fifteen years had increased to twenty, including clerical staff, pilots and engineers. A visitor to the Iona clubhouse in April 1980 was General Adolf Galland, former General of Fighter Arm, the Luftwaffe. He was on a lecture tour and delivered a talk titled *'Thunderbolt – The Channel Dash'* to members of the Royal Aeronautical Society at their Annual General Meeting in Dublin on 21 April 1980.

Resulting from an accident at an airstrip on Lambay Island, off north County Dublin on 5 May 1980, Cessna 172N, EI-BGH suffered extensive damage. There were no injuries. Iona had the contract with James Baring – Lord Revelstroke – to fly him over and back from the mainland. The damaged aircraft was ferried by boat to the mainland and onwards to Iona by road. In late June 1980 it was shipped to Rogers Aviation, Cranfield, England for repairs. Following its return to service, over a year later, it remained with Iona for a further twelve years.

General Adolf Galland, on left, on a visit to the Iona clubhouse in the presence of Pearse Cahill and Tom Farrington, on right, during the course of his lecture tour of Ireland in April 1980

Photograph via Pearse Cahill collection

On 21 September 1980, two days after the delivery of Cessna 152 Aerobat, EI-BIA, another new Cessna 152 Aerobat arrived at the Iona ramp. It was registered on 18 September 1980 to Iona National Airways Limited and was for use by Leinster Aero Club Limited. It was a Wichita built aircraft, previously registered to the Egyptian Air Force, but not taken up. It lay in Brussels for a while pending further sale. When the deal was completed with Iona, it was delivered from Brussels to Birmingham on 19 September 1980 and onward to Dublin arriving 21 September 1980. The ferry pilots were Bobby Power and Eamon Shiel. The aircraft in question was EI-BJM (see Table 63). It was the first American built Cessna 152 to appear in Irish marks, it was also the first American rather than French built Cessna single for some time. It was not formally registered to the Leinster Aero Club Limited until 26 August 1981.

In 1964, the Leinster Aero Club moved from Weston to the Iona hangar at Dublin airport. For a short while they moved to Westpoint, also at Dublin airport and then back to the Iona ramp. For their early years of operation the Leinster Aero Club operated Auster J/1 Autocrat, EI-AGJ, registered to them 13 May 1958; Beagle A.61 Terrier, EI-AMB, registered to

General Adolf Galland, on a visit to Iona clubhouse in conversation with Iona's Secretary, Catherine Greene, during the course of his lecture tour of Ireland in April 1980

Photograph via Catherine Greene collection

them 28 October 1961 and Morane Sauliner MS880B, EI-AMD, registered to them 17 April 1962.

Pearse was in no way concerned about competition from another club, as his primary interest was to encourage aviation, regardless of source. Around the same time, Iona were also providing accommodation to the Dublin Airport Flying Club. At the end of 1990 the Leinster Aero Club and the Dublin Airport Flying Club re-located to the adjoining Venair strip. EI-BJM remained there until the Leinster Aero Club returned to their former home base at Weston airport, Leixlip, County Kildare, in March 2004.

By 1981 Reims Aviation SA were offering four versions of the Cessna 152 to customers. The standard version. The 152-II, with factory installed avionics and extra instrumentation. The 152 Trainer with the most frequently ordered equipment extras as standard – intercom and headset, flight hour recorder, refuelling steps, hand grips, tinted windows, sun visors, Cessna 300 Nav/Comm, transponder and some extra instrumentation. The 152 Aerobat, structurally strengthened to carry loads of +6G and –3G.

Another new Cessna 152 was added to the Iona fleet. On 10 February 1981 marks were reserved for a Reims built model that was delivered to Iona by Peter Cahill on 31 March 1981 and routed via Birmingham. It was allocated the registration EI-BIN (see Table 62). This registration had the distinction of holding Irish Certificate of Registration No. 1,000. At the time 730 aircraft had carried Irish civil registrations, some held two or more, mainly due to changes of ownership.

On 10 March 1982, the week after registering Cessna 310Q, EI-BMK, Iona added yet two more new Cessna 152s to the Irish register. Like many of their predecessors, they were Reims built aircraft. The ferry pilots were flown to Reims on 2 April 1982 in Cessna 337, EI-AVC. Both new aircraft were delivered Reims – Dublin on 4 April 1982. The first of the two entries on the register to Iona National Airways Limited was EI-BMM (see Table 64). The second of these two was next in sequence, EI-BMN

(see Table 65). The third new Cessna 152 ordered by Iona in 1982 was registered to Iona National Airways Limited on 5 August 1982 as EI-BNC (see Table 66).

Some past members will recall enjoyable social evenings in the clubhouse around the early 1980s, like the Halloween Fancy Dress Ball. Parties would generally be held to celebrate members that had attained aviation milestones, for example, 'first solos', private pilot's licence flight tests and other achievements. In order to continue the interest throughout the winter months, Iona installed a television and video recorder to show aviation related films. Private pilot licence classes usually commenced in September and extended through the winter months. A regular feature of the club bar was a 'Happy Hour' from 9pm to 10pm; sometimes a bar extension to 2am would be obtained for some of the social occasions. Music would be provided and there was never a scarcity of singers.

On the evening of Tuesday, 18 June 1985, Cessna 152, EI-BDO, operated by the recently formed Lismore Aero Club, County Waterford, was lost in the sea five miles south of Youghal, County Cork. The aircraft had taken-off from Lismore about 9pm and was on a pleasure flight until it encountered difficulties and ditched into the sea. The passenger managed to cling to a buoy until a trawler picked him up. The pilot, Raymond Sheane, (32), was not so fortunate and lost his life following the accident. The aircraft was on lease to Lismore Aero Club from Iona. The wreckage was never recovered from the sea bed and was cancelled from the register on 22 August 1986.

On the weekend of 14 to 16 June 1985, Iona held an air rally at Edenderry, County Offaly. Many competitions were arranged, including an aerial treasure hunt, flour bombing, spot landing competition, timed circuit. All members who travelled to Edenderry partook in a most successful and enjoyable weekend.

While some members were deeply involved in the social activities of the club, two members were planning a more ambitious activity. To raise funds for the Matt Griffin Memorial Fund, for a research centre at Our Lady's Hospital for Sick Children, Crumlin, Dublin, two members planned to create a record for the number of landings at different fields throughout Ireland. The aircraft used in the attempt was the Iona Cessna 182, EI-BCL. The attempt commenced at 6am and finished at 9.30pm The *Irish Aviator* in its August 1985 issue carried an account of the attempt. The following are extracts from that article:

'Jim Duggan and Terry O'Neill were fortunate indeed that they did not choose the longest day for their attempt on a record number of landings at different fields around Ireland. The longest day was also perhaps the wettest day of the year and Monday the 24th of June 1985 turned out to be far more suitable.

'Their target of 55 Irish airfields was reduced to 52 by a number of unusual circumstances. The airfield at Bantry was not available to them because of the search and rescue operations for the Air India 747 disaster, while Clonmel turned out to have been invaded by sheep, allowing no room for an aircraft to do anymore than a low pass. Gay Tracy's field near Roscrea was just coming up to the harvest and the grass there was too long to allow 'Charlie Lima' to do a touch and go. All-in-all, the flight took a total of 16 hours and 30 minutes.

'The whole event was organised by the INTO (Irish National Teachers Organisation), of which Jim Duggan is a member and Terry O'Neill's connection arose through his wife Finola. The 'Flyathon' was sponsored by Ola fuel, who provided the fuel, and Iona National Airways who provided the aircraft and back-up services free of charge, and is estimated by INTO to be likely to raise up to £75,000 for their charity.

'The total flight time was 14 hours, and about 2½ hours were involved in the stopovers. Refuelling took place at Cork, Galway, Sligo and Abbeyshrule (provided free of

charge at Abbeyshrule by Gabriel McGoey). INTO had arranged for observers to be present at each of the landing fields, and in many cases supporters also turned up.

'Included in the flight was the first official landing at Knock Airport, where Jim and Terry were met by Monsignor Horan. It seems that their victory will be entered in the Guinness Book of Records next edition.'

It subsequently transpired that the duo did a touch and go at another airfield missed in their first check of the airfields and from a target of fifty six the final tally was fifty three. While there were several landings at the new airport at Knock, this event was recorded as the first officially sanctioned landing at the airport, hence the large number of well-wishers that greeted them on arrival. Monsignor James Horan warmly welcomed them. Earlier, at dawn on the Iona ramp, Michael Healy

Jim Duggan and Terry O'Neill are warmly greeted by their families following their record breaking flight around Ireland for charity on 24 June 1985 in Iona's Cessna 182, EI-BCL. Left to right: Noleen Duggan, Barry and Clíodhna are in the arms of their father, Jim Duggan. Finola O'Neill is holding Laura while Claire is in her father, Terry's arms

Photograph courtesy Jim Duggan

tossed a coin to determine which of the pilots would be in command for the historic landing. Jim won the toss, but graciously relinquished the honour and both aviators shared the privilege – a rare occasion when a single engine aircraft was landed as a two man crew operation!!. The record featured on RTE News bulletins that evening, and the *Irish Times* the following morning carried a front page report headed *'Knock plays part in world record.'*

The purchase of new aircraft for club use continued in 1984, with the order for a Cessna 172Q Cutlass and a Cessna 152. The 172 bore the registration N97033. It was first flown from Wichita to King Avionics for a full avionics fit out. On completion of this work it was ferried across the Atlantic, arriving in Dublin 7 April 1984. It was based at Iona for over one year before it was registered EI-BRM to Iona National Airways Limited, on 17 June 1985 (see Table 67). The Cessna 152 was registered EI-BRO (see Table 68). On 18 November 1985 it was delivered by Peter Cahill from Reims to Dublin, routing via Luton. Both legs of the ferry flight were 2 hours 20 minutes duration. It was about mid-1985 that Cessna ceased production of the 152s at its Reims plant. The 1985 new Schedule of Prices for the new Cessna 152 quoted a manufacturer's suggested list price of US$ 30,900. EI-BRO was the last Reims-built Cessna registered to Iona.

Following its lease to Waterford Aero Club after delivery in June 1979, Cessna 152, EI-BGI, was cancelled from the Irish register on 6 November 1985. The following day it was registered as G-BMHI to Bevelhurst Limited and delivered by Peter Cahill, via Leeds, to Manchester on 28 November 1985. On 29 August 1991 it was destroyed over Cargo, near Newtown, Powys, Wales when it was involved in a mid-air collision with a Royal Air Force Jaguar XX843. The pilot, and sole occupant, of G-BMHI was killed, as was one of the two crew of the Jaguar. The other ejected successfully.

In 1988, Iona purchased three Cessna 152s for pilot training. At this stage Cessna had ceased manufacturing at the Reims factory. These three were second-hand and were crated from Wichita to Dublin. The three aircraft were in USA marks N47184, N6467P and N6093Q. They were placed on the Irish register on 7 June 1988 as EI-BVU (see Table 69), EI-BVV (see Table 70) and EI-BVW (see Table 71) respectively. It was initially intended they be used for pilot training at Cork airport when Iona's plans for pilot training there materialised. EI-BVU and EI-BVW later operated pilot training at Dublin for many years clocking up many hundreds of hours.

The Irish Aero Club fleet of training aircraft was increased by three when Cessna 152's, EI-BVU, EI-BVV and EI-BVW arrived at Iona in crates in July 1988. The above photograph, taken 18 April 1993, shows EI-BVU with the markings of the Iona Flight Training School.

Photograph courtesy Paul Cunniffe

At 3.06pm on Tuesday, 27 September 1988, Cessna 152, EI-BVV departed from Runway 23, Dublin airport. The pilot was 26-year-old Kenneth Daly, Road One, Park Drive, Castleknock, Co. Dublin. He had obtained his Private Pilot's Licence with the Irish Aero Club on 12 May 1988 and had accumulated 103 hours total flying time. On board was John Collins, Glasnevin Park, Glasnevin, Dublin. John was on a first time familiarisation flight to be conducted in the Maynooth, County Kildare area. At 3.11pm the Air Traffic Controller relayed some military traffic information to EI-BVV and EI-BVW. EI-BVW acknowledged. There was no response from EI-BVV after six calls. The aircraft impacted the ground at speed near Kilmore House, Kilshane, adjacent to Dolly's public house, near Mulhuddart, County Meath. Both occupants were killed instantly. The Department of Tourism and Transport conducted an investigation into the accident. Some of its comments were:

'The aircraft was loaded within the maximum weight for the aircraft.....the aircraft was properly maintained and was serviceable prior to the accident.....the maintenance history of the aircraft was properly documented.....weather conditions at the time of the accident were quite good.....the aircraft attitude at impact was about 30 degrees below the horizontal in the upright position.....the main wreckage came to rest approximately 60m from the initial impact in a jumbled heap.....the fuselage was destroyed at impact, the complete cabin disintegrated.....the engine separated from its mounting frame aft of the engine mounting dampers in severe overload.....the RPM indicator as recovered showed a reading of 3400 RPM with the needle jammed between the glass and the instrument facia bevel.....there was no evidence that either pilot or passenger were suffering from any medical condition which might have had a bearing on the accident.....the cause of death in both cases was identified as resulting from severe and multiple injuries.....there was no fire.....the accident was not survivable"*incapacitation of the pilot, either overt or subtle, temporary or permanent, cannot be ruled out as a possible cause of this accident*" the definitive cause of the accident could not be determined from the available evidence. No indication was found from the evidence that the accident was caused by a defect in the aircraft or an error on the part of the pilot.'

The aircraft was destroyed and cancelled from the register 3 August 1991.

The wreckage of Cessna 152, EI-BVV, lies in a field near Mulhuddart, Co. Dublin following the fatal crash that claimed two lives on 27 September 1988

Photograph courtesy *Irish Times*

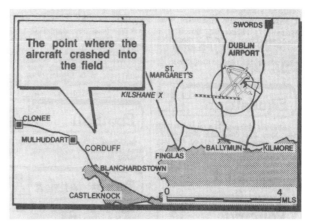

The point where the aircraft crashed into the field

Site map indicating location of crash of EI-BVV

Courtesy *Irish Times*

By 1989 the flight training operations were continuing to develop. Iona decided to present a more professional approach and set about establishing a school that would train pilots to full commercial standard. Traffic at Dublin airport was increasing, particularly with the opening of the new runway 10 / 28. It became evident at Iona's planning stage that Dublin airport and the Control Zone had the potential to cause delays to training in light aircraft and the decision was made to establish the training facility at Cork airport. Initially the two Cessna 152s, EI-BVU and EI-BVW, were utilised for the purpose at Cork when the operation commenced in June 1989.

Cork airport offered all the facilities of a modern international airport, combined with, for the most part, uncongested airspace. Iona Flight Training School took over the former Joyce Aviation hangar at Cork. Its first Chief Flying Instructor was Michael Flavin. Classrooms, briefing rooms and administrative offices were added. In May 1990 they moved to their own complex about half a mile from the airport. The new school attracted media attention when Siona Meighan undertook her Private Pilot's Licence flight test while still sixteen years of age. She was presented with her licence on her seventeenth birthday. Iona Flight Training School Limited was officially registered on 25 July 1990 and was allocated Certificate of Registration No. 162294. In Cork, Joe Ryan was the operations manager and Denis Joyce was responsible for maintenance. Michael Goss was initially responsible for ground school training of students and when Michael Flavin returned to Dublin, Michael Goss took over the mantle of Chief Flying Instructor. The operations at Cork were managed by Enda Hopkins, only daughter of Pearse Cahill. Enda was assisted by her husband, Eric.

Enda, only daughter of Pearse Cahill, managed the Iona Flight Training School at Cork airport

Photograph courtesy Enda Hopkins

Eric Hopkins, a former airline captain with Laker Airways, British Airways and BOAC, frequently travelled to Cork at assist his wife Enda at the Iona Flight Training School

Photograph courtesy Eric Hopkins

Pilot training facilities were enhanced at Dublin when four additional Cessna 152s were purchased. As production of new aircraft had ceased at Reims, France, the aircraft acquired were all second-hand machines. They were crated and sent from the western United States of America to Dublin arriving at Dublin port in August 1990. They were transported by road to Dublin airport where assembly took place at the Iona hangar, recently vacated by the Dublin Airport Flying Club. The four aircraft were placed on the register to P. Cahill on 9 October 1990 in sequential form and were allocated the marks EI-CCJ, EI-CCK, EI-CCL and EI-CCM (see Tables 72 to 75 respectively). Their previous American identities were N24251, N757BM, N24791 and N68679 respectively. The first three were manufactured in 1978 and EI-CCM was a 1979 model. All were manufactured at Cessna's factory at Wichita. The four provided the Irish Aero Club with many hundreds of hours of pilot training. The cost of annual membership of the Irish Aero Club was £120.00, and hourly instruction was £67.40 in the Cessna 150/152s.

The first newsletter for Iona National Airways was circulated in April 1991. Its editor was Jeanne Scully. In April 1991 courses available included Private Pilot's Licence (PPL) Instrument Rating (IR) Multi-Engined Rating and Commercial Pilot's Licence (CPL). The basic training aircraft were the Cessna 152 and Cessna 172. When required at Cork a Cessna 182 or 310 would be dispatched from Dublin. The 310s were now more available for pilot training in twin-engine aircraft, as the Cessna 414, EI-BGP, and the Cessna 303 Crusader, EI-BVP, were utilised for air taxi and charter work. Iona were then in a position to offer a full PPL course completed in three to four months, subject to the candidate successfully completing the written examinations and flight test. They were then advertising the course at £4,500, to include ground school, books, Department fees and forty hours flying. It did not include accommodation, though Iona provided a mini-bus service in Cork for students.

PPL training was also available in Dublin though most students attending Cork were there for the CPL course. Four courses a year were planned, with a maximum of twelve students on each CPL course, with a CPL course taking approximately twelve to fifteen months to complete. The cost then was quoted as £30,865, which included 750 hours of ground school and 210 hours flying, broken down into 135 hours basic flying training in the Cessna 152, forty five hours IFR in the Cessna 172, five hours airways flying in the Cessna 182 and twenty five hours multi-engine in the Cessna 310.

Students undertaking this level of expenditure would have intended to make flying their career, and graduates from the school have gone on to serve with Aer Lingus, Ryanair and other commercial operators. It was also Iona's policy to employ, where possible, pilots from the school for their own rapidly expanding commercial operations. In this way, students had a very real prospect of employment immediately they attained their licences or ratings.

In the early months of 1991 Iona were progressing satisfactorily with talks involving Libyan Arab Airlines for the training of cadet pilots by Iona Flight Training School at Cork airport. By the summer, discussions had reached an advanced stage, so much so, that both parties drafted contract documents for approval. The contract would involve Iona providing ground school from 9.30am to 5.30pm daily for three months, thereafter, the

Promotional photograph showing
interior of Iona lounge and bar at Dublin airport

Photograph via Pearse Cahill collection

students would sit the written Commercial Pilot's Licence examination. A course in Morse would be included. A total of 205 hours flying would be given to each student comprising 135 hours on the Cessna 152, forty five hours on the Cessna 172 and 25 hours on the Cessna 310, leading to an Irish Commercial Pilot's Licence with Instrument Rating and Multi-Engine Rating. The first class was planned for June 1991. Students must have passed a medical examination prior to coming to Ireland. Libyan Arab Airlines would be responsible for return flights, accommodation, subsistence and recreation during the students stay in Cork. For this, the airline agreed to pay to Iona the sum of £27,896 for each student. The fee was to include all Government written examinations, flight tests and medical examinations. The proposal was to train twenty students per class, with three classes per year. The initial contract covered 120 student pilots, worth a potential £5 million to Iona plus the unquantified financial spin-off for the Cork region.

Word of the impending contract reached the United States Embassy in Dublin. The *Cork Examiner* 16 July 1991 carried a heading *'Libyan pilots: no plan to intervene.'* Another paper's banner was *'Iona faces wrath of US.'* The Embassy was reported as saying that America opposed commercial trade with Libya because it supported terrorism. The then Chief Flying Instructor at Cork, Michael Goss, was contacted by the United States Embassy in Dublin and requested to attend a meeting at the Embassy. The meeting was convened in a secure area within the Embassy. Those in attendance to meet Michael Goss included the most senior officials representing the Federal Bureau of Investigation in Ireland; the Central Intelligence Agency in Ireland and the Chancellor acting in the absence of the American Ambassador to Ireland. The United States position regarding Iona's training of Libyan pilots was made clear to Michael and Iona were left in no doubt about the future of the Federal Express, DHL and UPS contracts held by Iona should the company continue with its plans to implement the training programme. Michael Goss defended the programme and was quoted as saying:

'The company won the contract against stiff competition. The Americans haven't baulked at our trade in beef to Libya. We're a school. We teach commercial pilots – not fighter pilots. Aer Lingus had a long record of providing Libyan nationals with training as airline mechanics and engineers.'

Deputy Denis Lyons, Junior Minister for Tourism, Transport and Communications said the contract would provide an important jobs boost for Cork, but added he did not expect the Irish Government to intervene in the matter between the American Government and Iona. A statement from Iona said they would axe the project if the Irish Government urged them to do so. Belfast Unionist MP Cecil Walker was quoted as saying:

'It is absolutely outrageous that these pilots, who may be potential terrorists under the Gaddafi (correct spelling Qaddafi) regime are being trained on Irish soil. Guns and bombs supplied by Libya have brought suffering to all Irish people North and South of the border.'

Following the murder of Police Constable Yvonne Fletcher in London in 1984, the British Government severed its links with Libya. The Americans had also urged its allies not to engage in trade with Libya. On 21 December 1988, Pan American flight 103 was brought down over Lockerbie, Scotland with the loss of 270 persons. While no suspects had been charged at the time, the finger of suspicion for planting the bomb on board the airliner was, by the summer 1991, being pointed in the direction of the Libyan Government. Could this suspicion have provoked the American Government to react to the Iona proposal in relation to the pilots the way they did? One can only surmise. (In April 2003, the Libyan Government agreed to a compensation package for relatives of those that lost their lives in the tragedy. In September 2003, the United Nations consented to the lifting of trade sanctions imposed against Libya since the incident).

Tragically, Cessna 172, EI-BRM and Cessna 152, EI-BRO, were involved in a mid-air collision near Bandon, County Cork at approximately 1.55pm UTC on Wednesday, 26 February 1992. The instructor, Aidan Murray and student Shay O'Riordan in the 152, EI-BRO, were able to return to Cork airport. Regrettably, the 172, EI-BRM, crashed three nautical miles southwest of Bandon

killing the instructor, Seamus Campbell (38) and his student pilot James Kennedy (28). The 172 was destroyed and subsequently cancelled from the register. The 152 was transported to the Iona hangar at Dublin. It never flew again in Ireland. In this instance the Department of Tourism and Transport did not publish an official report into the circumstances involving this tragedy, consequently, it would be inappropriate to comment further.

Firemen examine the wreckage of Cessna 172, EI-BRM following the fatal crash near Bandon, Co. Cork that claimed the lives of the instructor and student pilot on 26 February 1992

Photograph courtesy *Irish Examiner*

Site map indicating location of crash of EI-BRO and EI-BRM

Early 1992 saw a downturn in the contract work at Iona National Airways, after the loss of the Federal Express contract, announced 17 March 1992, three weeks after above fatal crash. Meanwhile, affairs at the Irish Aero Club were not at this stage showing decline and two additional Cessna 172P Skyhawks arrived for pilot training four days before the departure from the Iona hangar of Bandeirante EI-BPI. Both were eleven - year-old Wichita manufactured machines. They were flown across the Atlantic routing Casper (Wyoming) – Wichita – Bangor, Maine – Goose Bay – Reykjavik – Dublin arriving in Dublin 8 May 1992. The first to be entered on the register was EI-CFM, on 19 May 1992, having the registration N53000 for the ferry flight (see Table 76). The second aircraft was consecutively registered EI-CFN, having borne registration N5446K (see Table 77). Both Irish registrations had been previously reserved. In this instance both 172s were registered personally to M. P. Cahill. Following the acquisition of these two Cessna 172s the Iona fleet reached its peak. The strength of the fleet of aircraft available to members of the Irish Aero Club was 16 aircraft – nine Cessna 152s, (BMM, BMN, BNC, BVU, BVW, CCJ, CCK, CCL and CCM) three Cessna 172s, (BGH, CFM and CFN) one Cessna 182 (BCL) and the three twin-engine Cessna 310s (ATC, BEO and BMK).

In August 1992 a notice appeared in the newspapers seeking planning permission for *'the construction of a light aircraft assembly and maintenance building with aviation school facilities'* across the road from the Iona complex at Cloghran. The location of the facility would have been on lands personally owned by the Cahill family. By this time Iona had relocated the Cork flight training facility back to Dublin. The closure of Iona at Cork followed the collapse of the European College of Aeronautics, Cork. Around the end of 1992, the school were placing advertisements in *Flight* magazine for commercial pilot training for IR£35, 000. The price included a six month flying / ground work experience in the company's own operation. Iona claimed that 98% of its students were then working with Irish or foreign airlines and that over 1,000 pilots have been trained to date.

On 4 May 1993, Cessna 152 EI-CCL made a forced landing, following engine failure 2,000 feet over Bray Head. The Cessna came down in a cornfield at Half Moon near Windgates, beside the Bray to Greystones road. The two on board were slightly injured and taken to Loughlinstown Hospital. The pilot was Louisa Hopkins, a granddaughter of Pearse Cahill and her instructor was Patricia O'Brien, from Co. Clare. The Cessna was severly damaged and never flew again.

Mr. Michael Lowry, Minister for Transport, Energy and Communications with Ms. Louisa Hopkins, the first woman to fly 737 aircraft for Ryanair, and Mr. Ray MacSharry, chairman of Ryanair. Photograph taken 1995

Photograph courtesy Pearse Cahill collection

Louisa later joined the Aer Lingus flight crew.

The financial affairs of Iona came to a head at the end of 1994. Matters referred to in chapter eight had a consequence for the Irish Aero Club when the Examiner was appointed to Iona National Airways Limited on 27 October 1994. This had repercussions for the aero club - even though it continued to flourish. Pilot training continued until the appointment of the Liquidator on 15 December 1994 and it was compelled to cease operations with effect from that date.

Following the demise of Iona the Cessna 172P, EI-CFN, was transferred to Liam Kane, Weston on 12 January 1995, where it has remained since, though under a variety of owners. It arrived at Iona on 8 May 1992, along with EI-CFM, following their ferry flight across the Atlantic. In February 1995 three of the Iona Cessna 152s were flown to Waterford Regional Airport for storage pending sale by the Liquidator. They were EI-BNC, EI-BVU and EI-BVW. Cessna 152 EI-CCK suffered damage in a landing accident at Cork. It was subsequently removed by road to Newcastle, County Wicklow and never flew again. It was offered for sale by the Liquidator but was not sold at auction in April 1995 and continued to lie in a dismantled state at Newcastle. Iona Flight Training School Limited, established in Cork and registered in July 1990 was officially dissolved on 3 May 1996.

During the period of over thirty years covered by the above chapter, there were forty five single-engine aircraft available for the students of the flying club at Iona. This does not include any twin-engine aircraft also available, such as the three Cessna 310s. Of these, thirty five were new Cessna 150 / 152s, 172s and 182s; nine were imported second hand from the US; and the remaining aircraft was the Auster EI-AMK. The operations of the Irish Aero Club were transferred to Eric Hopkin's airfield at Newcastle, County Wicklow where they continue in business at time of publication – continuing a name that has been synonymous with aviation in Ireland since 1909.

On Saturday, 3 April 2004, Pearse was honoured at a function hosted by the *Aviation Trailblazers of Ireland* in the Officer's Mess, Casement Aerodrome, Baldonnel for his lifetime contribution to aviation in Ireland.

It is fitting that Pearse Cahill should have the last word. During the course of one of the many interviews Pearse kindly gave for this publication, we interviewed him on the Iona ramp on 5 July 2000, five years after its closure. At the conclusion of that interview he gave us his thoughts as we pondered the now idle area that was once the centre of so much aviation activity for many years:-

'Now that I look around and see the expanse of ground and all that was put into it, I am sorry to say I could not hand the business, after forty years, to my family to carry on. Sad to think we had to pack up and get out. How the buildings that are left here behind me were not turned into monetary value towards the debt of Iona. The only legacy I know is that our staff is now with Aer Lingus, ... with Ryanair, with every flying organisation here in Dublin airport .... and eh, Shannon have some of our staff. That is the only legacy I have left .... That's it'.

Louisa Hopkins (foreground) becomes the fourth generation of Cahills involved in aviation in Ireland. Pictured with Louisa in 1989 are her grandfather, Pearse, and her uncle, Peter. Inset is her great-grandfather, Hugh Cahill

Photograph courtesy Pearse Cahill collection

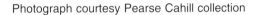

Former Iona ramp, now idle and once a hive of considerable aviation activity from arrival of Iona in 1957 to cessation of their operations in 1995. Above photograph taken October 2004

Photograph from authors collection.

IRISH AERO CLUB - CHIEF FLYING INSTRUCTORS

NOTE: No records are available and the following information was obtained through the grateful assistance of Chief Flying Instructors contacted by the author. In some instances dates are approximate based on best available information.

1.	THOMPSON BOYES	1962-1965
2.	TERRY ROWAN	1965-06.67
3.	PADDY ROBINSON	06.67-06.70
4.	BRIAN MURPHY	06.70-01.71
5.	EUGENE HIGGINS	01.71-04.73
6.	PADDY ROBINSON	04.73-05.74
7.	JACK REID	05.74-1975
8.	JOHN COLTON	1975-1976
9.	TONY DOYLE	1976-1978
10.	BILLY GARDINER	1978-1979
11.	PETER CAHILL	1979-1980
12.	GERRY KIRWAN	1980 -11.85
13.	TERRY O'NEILL	11.85-11.87
14.	MICHAEL FLAVIN	11.87-11.89
15.	MICHAEL GOSS	11.89-02.90
16.	OLLIE O'NEILL	02.90-12.94

CORK

1.	MICHAEL FLAVIN	06.89-11.89
2	MICHAEL GOSS	11.89-02.93
3	BO VAN ULSEN	02.93.12.94

The efforts of the numerous Instructors at the Irish Aero Club are recognised by all concerned. Unfortunately, as no records exist, it has proven impossible to list them here. Their contribution is in no way diminished by this omission

TABLES

FOR AIRCRAFT

ASSOCIATED WITH

THE

IRISH AERO CLUB LIMITED

Table 36

Registration	EI-APF
Aircraft Type	Cessna F.150G
Constructors Serial Number	150-0112
Place & Year of Manufacture	Reims, France, 1966
Previous Registrations	New aircraft
Registered to	Irish Aero Club Ltd, 6 March 1966
Delivery date	28 January 1967

Remarks

The aircraft originally ordered was serial number 0066. This aircraft was never delivered to Dublin; instead it went to Helsinki, Finland as OH-CEU. In its place a Cessna 150G, serial number 0112, was allocated the registration EI-APF on 6 March 1966. On 3 August 1969, at the Stradbally Steam Traction Rally, Co. Offaly, its nose wheel and the underside of the front fuselage were damaged in a heavy landing. There were no injuries to the occupants. It was repaired and after returning to service with Iona it was later sold to Midland Flying Club, Birr, Co. Offaly on 1 March 1973.

On 29 October 1981 its ownership transferred to L. O. Kennedy, Nenagh with Birr given as its base. On 18 June 1998 it became part of the Sligo Aero Club Limited. On 26 December 1998, during a storm, part of the hangar collapsed on it at Sligo, resulting in the aircraft being 'written-off'. It was dismantled and the fuselage was removed to Carrickfin, Co. Donegal. It never flew again.

Cessna F.150G, EI-APF, landing at Birr, Co. Offaly

Photograph courtesy George Flood

Cessna F.150G, EI-APF, at Iona 1970

Photograph courtesy Paul Cunniffe

Table 37

Registration	EI-ARY
Aircraft Type	Cessna F.150H
Constructors Serial Number	150-0239
Place & Year of Manufacture	Reims, France, 1967
Previous Registrations	New aircraft
Registered to	Irish Aero Club Ltd, 23 October 1967
Delivery date	4 November 1967
Remarks	This aircraft was leased to Kerry Aero Club. Tragically, it failed to get airborne from Farranfore, Co. Kerry on 14 June 1970 and hit a tree stump, killing the student pilot and seriously injuring his instructor, Christopher Gallagher. The wreckage was transported to the Iona hangar at Dublin airport and the registration was removed from the Irish register on 20 July 1972.

Cessna F.150H, EI-ARY at Iona, 1968

Photograph courtesy Paul Cunniffe

Cessna F.150H, EI-ARY at Farranfore, Co. Kerry, 1970

Photograph courtesy Liam Byrne via Ronny Vogt collection

Table 38

Registration	EI-AST
Aircraft Type	Cessna F.150H
Constructors Serial Number	150-0273
Place & Year of Manufacture	Reims, France, 1968
Previous Registrations	New aircraft
Registered to	Irish Aero Club Ltd, 30 January 1968
Delivery date	11 February 1968
Remarks	On 9 March 1973 ownership of, EI-AST, transferred to the Garda Flying Club, based at Weston, Co. Kildare. On 9 January 1979 it changed hands to Liberty Flying Limited, Cork, until it moved to Carnmore, Co. Galway when Peter McKenna registered it on 25 July 1996. Seamus Coghlan, Athenry, Co. Galway took ownership on 14 February 2001. On 16 April 2002, its new owner became Ormond Flying Club Limited, Birr, Co. Offaly. It is recorded as current with them in early 2004.

Cessna F.150H, EI-AST at Iona, 12 July 1969

Photograph courtesy Paul Cunniffe

Cessna F.150H, EI-AST at Iona, 1971

Photograph courtesy Liam Byrne via Ronny Vogt collection

Table 39

Registration	EI-ATH
Aircraft Type	Cessna F.150J
Constructors Serial Number	150-0426
Place & Year of Manufacture	Reims, France, 1969
Previous Registrations	New aircraft
Registered to	Irish Aero Club Ltd, 5 March 1969
Delivery date	22 March 1969

Remarks

Following the damage to the nose section of EI-AOO in a heavy landing at Galway in September 1969, a deal was struck with the Galway Flying Club, whereby EI-AOO was taken back to the Irish Aero Club and the Galway Flying Club received EI-ATH, registered to them on 9 September 1969. It was delivered to Galway on 12 September 1969.

As part of the sale by Iona of Cessna 152, EI-BIB, to Galway Flying Club it was agreed in March 1980, to return EI-ATH to Iona. It transferred to Hibernian Flying Club, Cork on 16 January 1981. Blown over in a storm at Cork airport on 10 March 1982 and extensively damaged. Removed to Abbeyshrule, Co. Longford and was cancelled from the register 16 May 1986.

Cessna F.150J, EI-ATH at Iona, 24 June 1969

Photograph courtesy George Flood

Cessna F.150J, EI-ATH at Iona, 13 July 1969

Photograph courtesy Paul Cunniffe

Table 40

Registration	EI-AUC
Aircraft Type	Cessna FA.150K Aerobat
Constructors Serial Number	150-0040
Place & Year of Manufacture	Reims, France, 1970
Previous Registrations	New aircraft
Registered to	Irish Aero Club Ltd, 10 April 1970
Delivery date	23 April 1970

Remarks

EI-AUC operated with Iona until it was registered to the Fifteen Flying Club Limited, Dublin on 7 September 1973. It remained with different companies under the umbrella of Dublin Airport Flying Club until it was blown over in a gale at Dublin airport on 17 January 1995. It was transported by road to Abbeyshrule, Co. Longford on 19 April 1995 and while undergoing repair there it was registered to Oliver (Sammy) Bruton 17 October 1996. Following completion of its repair work the next owner of the Aerobat was the Garda Aviation Club Limited, Weston, to whom it was registered on 14 August 1998. On 15 July 1999 on a flight from Weston, it crashed and overturned in a cornfield near Maynooth, Co. Kildare. The wreckage was removed to the military airfield at Gormanston, Co. Meath for scrutiny by accident investigators from the Department of Transport.

Following settlement with GAB Robins, Aviation Insurers, the wreckage was acquired by Nalson Aviation Limited, Willey Park Farm, Stanstead Road, Caterham, Surrey. In early 2004 it remains there and, though partly dismantled, could be a restoration project.

Cessna FA.150K Aerobat, EI-AUC at Birr, Co. Offaly, 23 August 1970

Photograph courtesy George Flood

Cessna FA.150K Aerobat, EI-AUC, at Iona ramp, while operated by Dublin Airport Flying Club, 26 August 1978

Photograph courtesy Paul Cunniffe

Table 41

Registration	EI-AUH
Aircraft Type	Cessna F.172H
Constructors Serial Number	172-0727
Place & Year of Manufacture	Reims, France, 1970
Previous Registrations	New aircraft
Registered to	Iona National Airways Ltd, 28 July 1970
Delivery date	5 August 1970
Remarks	EI-AUH operated for Iona until it failed to take off from Kilkenny airfield in May 1972. It overran the runway, crashed through the boundary hedge and came to rest with its nose in the ground and tail up. The three occupants, including two editors from *Flying* magazine were uninjured. The wreckage was removed to the Iona hangar where the wings were used in the rebuild of EI-AVA some years later. As a consequence, EI-AUH was cancelled from the register on 28 August 1986. At the Liquidators auction the remains were purchased by Christopher Keane, Saggart, Co. Dublin but not placed on the Irish register by him.

Cessna F.172H, EI-AUH

Photograph courtesy Paul Duffy

Cessna F.172H, EI-AUH at Abbeyshrule, Co. Longford, 15 August 1971

Photograph courtesy George Flood

Table 42

Registration	EI-AUO
Aircraft Type	Cessna FA.150K Aerobat
Constructors Serial Number	150-0074
Place & Year of Manufacture	Reims, France, 1971
Previous Registrations	New aircraft
Registered to	Irish Aero Club Ltd, 2 March 1971
Delivery date	7 March 1971
Remarks	Reims Aviation temporarily mis-painted it as EI-ALL prior to delivery.

EI-AUO served Iona until it was registered on 22 May 1975 to Kerry Airways Limited, Farranfore, Co. Kerry. On 15 June 1976 the registered owner became Kerry Aero Club Limited. In early 2004 it was still flying with them.

Cessna FA.150K Aerobat, EI-AUO at Iona on its delivery date, 7 March 1971

Photograph courtesy Paul Cunniffe

Cessna FA.150K Aerobat, EI-AUO at Iona, April 1972

Photograph courtesy George Flood

Table 43

Registration	EI-AVA
Aircraft Type	Cessna F.172K
Constructors Serial Number	172-0762
Place & Year of Manufacture	Reims, France, 1971
Previous Registrations	New aircraft
Registered to	Iona National Airways Ltd, 1 July 1971
Delivery date	5 July 1971
Remarks	EI-AVA was sold to Patrick Parke on 21 June 1974. On 19 September 1976 it was severely damaged at Kilbrittain, Co. Cork when it overran the wet grass runway to crash into the hedge at the end of the field. Iona's Cessna 182J, EI-AYJ, collided with it. Both were removed to Dublin. EI-AVA was sent to Rogers Aviation at Cranfield, and restored to flying condition using the wings from EI-AUH that crashed in Kilkenny in May 1972. EI-AVA flew after the rebuild on 3 August 1978. It was registered to M. P. Cahill on 23 August 1978. It crashed six weeks later on 19 September 1978, at Castlebridge, Co. Wexford. EI-AVA was cancelled from the register 11 July 1979. In May 1980 its fuselage was removed to the UK and used in the rebuild of G-AYTH. On 19 February 1982 it was observed on a trailer outside the British Airways European Division maintenance base at Heathrow airport.

Cessna F.172K, EI-AVA at Abbeyshrule, Co. Longford 15 August 1971, 6 weeks after delivery to Iona

Photograph courtesy George Flood

Cessna F.172K, EI-AVA at Iona, 17 April 1976, while owned by Patrick Parke

Photograph courtesy Liam Byrne via Ronny Vogt collection

Table 44

Registration	EI-AVM
Aircraft Type	Cessna F.150L
Constructors Serial Number	150-0745
Place & Year of Manufacture	Reims, France, 1972
Previous Registrations	New aircraft
Registered to	Irish Aero Club Ltd, 3 March 1972
Delivery date	9 March 1972
Remarks	The Victor Mike Flying Group based at Dublin airport purchased the Cessna 150L, EI-AVM, from Iona on 16 March 1979. On 13 January 1983 it was advertised for sale in *The Irish Times*. Between 1984 and 1996 it had three registered owners at Abbeyshrule, Co. Longford; George Farrar, 7 June 1984; Patrick Kearney, 17 December 1985; Oliver Bruton, 9 July 1996. On 18 December 1996 it moved to John Cowell at Castlebar, Co. Mayo and while still based there it changed hands to Tom Carter et al on 11 February 2000. On 9 September 2003 ownership changed to John Logan, Ballynacargy, Co. Westmeath and Tony Bradford, Portlaoise, Co. Laoise. On 9 February 2004 the registration was transferred to Tojo Air Leasing Limited, Ballynacargy, Co. Westmeath. Its base was given as Abbeyshrule, Co. Longford.

Cessna F.150L, EI-AVM landing at Weston, Co. Kildare.

Photograph courtesy George Flood

Cessna F.150L, EI-AVM landing at the first Air Spectacular Air Display, Fairyhouse racecourse, Sunday, 27 August 1978

Photograph courtesy George Flood

Table 45

Registration	EI-AWE
Aircraft Type	Cessna F.150L
Constructors Serial Number	150-0877
Place & Year of Manufacture	Reims, France, 1972
Previous Registrations	New aircraft
Registered to	Iona National Airways Ltd, 23 February 1973
Delivery date	25 March 1973
Remarks	The Third Flight Group Limited, on 1 June 1977, purchased Cessna 150L EI-AWE. Its Certificate of Airworthiness was completed on 2 June 1977. This group formed part of the Dublin Airport Flying Club and was based at the Iona ramp. It was removed to Abbeyshrule for maintenance in the early 1990s, but this became more permanent and the aircraft languished inside the gates of Midland Aviation Limited, Abbeyshrule, Co. Longford until it was transferred to David Bruton, Abbeyshrule on 1 July 1999. In April 2001 it was sold to Philip Maguire, Santry, Dublin and subsequently sent to the UK for rebuild. It was cancelled from the Irish register on 6 February 2004 and placed on the UK register in the name of Philip Maguire as G-IAWE on 9 February 2004. In early 2004 it was in Shrewsbury, Shropshire under-going restoration.

Cessna F.150L, EI-AWE at Iona, 7 April 1973 - 2 weeks after delivery

Photograph courtesy Paul Cunniffe

Cessna F.150L, EI-AWE at Iona, 18 July 1973

Photograph courtesy George Flood

Table 46

Registration	EI-AYF
Aircraft Type	Cessna FRA.150L Aerobat
Constructors Serial Number	150-0218
Place & Year of Manufacture	Reims, France, 1974
Previous Registrations	New aircraft
Registered to	Iona National Airways Ltd, 26 March 1974
Delivery date	4 April 1974
Remarks	EI-AYF remained in use at Iona for almost two years. On 20 February 1976 it was transferred to Harley Harold, Dublin. On 13 October 1978 it was registered to Garda Flying Club Limited, Weston. It remained at Weston for its next owner, Kieran A. O'Connor to whom it was registered 30 January 1996. It next moved to the mid-west and was based at Coonagh in the ownership of Limerick Flying Club (Coonagh) Limited on 28 May 2001. It has not flown since Summer 2002 and was moved to Abbeyshrule, Co. Longford pending possible sale.

Cessna FRA.150L Aerobat, EI-AYF at Iona, 28 March 1981.

Photograph courtesy Leo Murray

Cessna FRA.150L Aerobat, EI-AYF at Iona. In the background are Cessna FA.150K Aerobat, EI-AUC (on left) and Cessna F.150L, EI-AWE

Photograph courtesy George Flood

Auster 5 Series J/1 Autocrat, EI-AMK, was to spend fifteen years working for Iona. Seen here in its original all-white livery at Iona 20 April 1968

Photograph courtesy
Paul Cunniffe

Cessna 182A Skylane, EI-ANC was only with Iona for a few weeks from September 1965 pending sale to a client in UK.

Photograph courtesy
Paul Cunniffe

Cessna 175A Skylark, EI-AND, was the first of its type on the Irish register. Photographed 11 May 1975 - 3 months after registration to Pearse Cahill

Photograph courtesy
Paul Cunniffe

Cessna F172G, EI-AOK, was the first new Cessna purchased by Iona and delivered to them on 16 March 1966. This photograph was taken in 1970

Photograph courtesy Paul Cunniffe

Cessna 150E, EI-AOO, was the first Cessna registered to Iona and performed its first flight on 20 May 1965. It was also the first Cessna 150 to grace the Irish register. Photographed at Iona 22 August 1970

Photograph courtesy Paul Cunniffe

Cessna F150G, EI-APF, was the second of the new Cessnas purchased by Iona for pilot training and delivered as new 28 January 1967. It remained at Iona for 6 years

Photograph courtesy Paul Cunniffe

Cessna F150H, EI-ARY, was delivered to Iona 4 November 1967. It was later leased by Iona to Kerry Aero Club.

Photograph courtesy Paul Cunniffe

Cessna F150H, EI-AST, photographed at Iona. It was delivered new to Iona 11 February 1968 and remained at the club until 9 March 1973

Photograph courtesy Paul Cunniffe

Cessna F150J, EI-ATH, only spent 6 months at Iona from March 1969 before moving to Galway Flying Club. Photographed at Dublin airport in 1969

Photograph courtesy Paul Cunniffe

Cessna FA150K Aerobat, EI-AUC, photographed 17 May 1970 - 3 weeks after delivery to Iona. It remained with Iona until September 1973

Photograph courtesy Paul Cunniffe

Cessna F172H, EI-AUH, photographed 29 August 1970 - 4 weeks after delivery to Iona. This aircraft was the second Cessna 172 purchased by Iona since EI-AOK in March 1966

Photograph courtesy Paul Cunniffe

Iona's second Aerobat was Cessna FA150K Aerobat, EI-AUO delivered on 7 March 1971. It was photographed 17 March 1971- 10 days after delivery

Photograph courtesy Paul Cunniffe

Cessna F172K, EI-AVA, was delivered to Iona 5 July 1971 and was photographed at Gowran Grange 20 June 1976. It was then owned by Patrick Parke.

Photograph courtesy
Paul Cunniffe

Cessna F150L, EI-AVM, photographed at Iona 12 March 1972 - 3 days after delivery. It remained at Iona until 16 March 1979

Photograph courtesy
Paul Cunniffe

Cessna F150L, EI-AWE, photographed at Castlebridge, Co. Wexford, 23 September 1973. It was delivered 25 March 1973 and remained with Iona until 1 June 1977. It was the last aircraft registered in the name of the Irish Aero Club

Photograph courtesy
Paul Cunniffe

Cessna FRA150L Aerobat, EI-AYF, was delivered to Iona 4 April 1974. It was captured on film 3 days later

Photograph courtesy Paul Cunniffe

Cessna 182J, EI-AYJ, was flown across the Atlantic from the Cessna plant in Wichita, and arrived at Iona 25 March 1974. This photograph was taken 27 April 1975

Photograph courtesy Paul Cunniffe

This photograph of Cessna F172M, EI-BAS, was taken at Iona 11 May 1975 - five days after its ferry flight from Reims

Photograph courtesy Paul Cunniffe

Cessna F150L, EI-BAT, was delivered to Iona on 6 May 1975- the same day as EI-BAS and was photographed at Iona 11 May 1975. It served Iona for 4 years.

Photograph courtesy
Paul Cunniffe

Following rebuild Cessna F150M, EI-BBN, was returned to Iona on 26 July 1977 and was photographed on Iona ramp 4 days later. It was sold to Sligo North West Aero Club in April 1981

Photograph courtesy
Paul Cunniffe

Cessna F172N, EI-BCK, was ferried from Reims, France via Jersey on 5 March 1977. This photograph was taken on the Iona ramp 16 December 1978. It spent ten years at Iona

Photograph courtesy
Paul Cunniffe

4 April 1981

Photograph courtesy
Paul Cunniffe

4 October 1986

Photograph courtesy
Paul Cunniffe

Photograph courtesy
Simon Nolan

Cessna 182P, EI-BCL was delivered to Iona 20 January 1977. It was to serve the club for 17 years before sale to Frank Doherty in February 1994. The above sequence of photographs shows the various colour schemes the aircraft adopted

Table 47

Registration	EI-AYJ
Aircraft Type	Cessna 182J
Constructors Serial Number	182-62470
Place & Year of Manufacture	Wichita, Kansas, USA, 1974
Previous Registrations	N52229 (for ferry flight)
Registered to	Iona National Airways Ltd, 21 March 1974
Delivery date	25 March 1974
Remarks	EI-AYJ was involved in an accident at Kilbrittain, Co. Cork on 19 September 1976 where it was extensively damaged. (See EI-AVA). It was a 'write-off' and was removed from the official register on 16 June 1981.

Cessna 182J, EI-AYJ at Iona 28 March 1974 - 3 days after ferry flight from Wichita, Kansas, USA

Photograph courtesy Paul Cunniffe

Cessna 182J, EI-AYJ at Iona 17 April 1976

Photograph courtesy Liam Byrne via Ronny Vogt collection

Table 48

Registration	EI-BAS
Aircraft Type	Cessna F.172M
Constructors Serial Number	172-1262
Place & Year of Manufacture	Reims, France, 1975
Previous Registrations	New aircraft
Registered to	Iona National Airways Ltd, 2 May 1975
Delivery date	6 May 1975
Remarks	EI-BAS remained registered to Iona until it transferred to Frank Fahey and Brendan Fitzgerald, Abbeyshrule on 24 October 1978. On 14 August 1981 it was registered back to Iona National Airways Limited. From 16 September 1984 its new base was Waterford and on 4 July 1985 it was sold to Falcon Aviation Limited, Waterford. It remained with this company for 18 years. On 18 October 2002 it arrived at City of Derry airport, Eglington, where, on 2 November 2002, it was caught by strong winds, thrown on its back and was damaged beyond repair. It was deregistered on 6 March 2003. Subsequently it was dismantled and on 30 April 2003 it reportedly departed on a low loader for Bournemouth where it may be used as spares.

Cessna F.172M, EI-BAS in Iona hangar, 24 May 1975 - 18 days after delivery

Photograph courtesy George Flood

Cessna F.172M, EI-BAS at Iona, 17 April 1976

Photograph courtesy Liam Byrne via Ronny Vogt collection

Table 49

Registration	EI-BAT
Aircraft Type	Cessna F.150L
Constructors Serial Number	150-1196
Place & Year of Manufacture	Reims, France, 1975
Previous Registrations	New aircraft
Registered to	Iona National Airways Ltd, 2 May 1975
Delivery date	6 May 1975
Remarks	On 18 April 1979, EI-BAT, was transferred to the newly formed Twentieth Air Training Co. Limited. This company formed part of the Dublin Airport Flying Club and was located at the Iona ramp. It moved to Donegal where it was registered to John A. Barrow, Crolly, Co. Donegal on 26 August 1987. On 9 January 1992 it was damaged by fire on start-up at Carrickfin, causing all the area forward of the firewall to be destroyed. It was repaired and returned to service. On 15 October 1992 it was registered to the Carrickfin based Donegal Aero Club Limited. It returned to the Dublin area, this time to be located at Weston in the name of Kieran A. O'Connor on 6 March 1997. A report in *Air Britain News* October 1999 reported that EI-BAT was air tested by YLA at Leeds/Bradford on 27 August 1999 and returned to Ireland after a protracted stay. In early 2004 it was current at National Flight Centre, Weston Airport, Co. Kildare.

Cessna F.150L, EI-BAT at Iona, 11 May 1975 - 5 days after delivery

Photograph courtesy Paul Cunniffe

Cessna F.150L, EI-BAT at Iona, 17 April 1976

Photograph courtesy Liam Byrne via Ronny Vogt collection

Table 50

Registration	EI-BBN
Aircraft Type	Cessna F.150M
Constructors Serial Number	150-1281
Place & Year of Manufacture	Reims, France, 1976
Previous Registrations	New aircraft
Registered to	Iona National Airways Ltd, 27 February 1976
Delivery date	30 April 1976
Remarks	After only eight days with Iona, the new aircraft was damaged in a training accident at The Ward, Co. Dublin on 8 May 1976. It was removed to Rogers Aviation at Cranfield, Bedfordshire, north east of Milton Keynes, in late August 1976 for rebuilding. It was redelivered to Dublin 26 July 1977 and returned to service.

On 30 April 1981 EI-BBN, moved to the northwest and was registered to Sligo North West Aero Club Limited. On Christmas Eve 1997 it suffered severe damage as a result of a storm at its base at Strandhill, Co. Sligo. It never flew again and was cancelled from the register 23 June 1998.

Cessna F.150M, EI-BBN at Iona, 3 May 1976 - 3 days after delivery. 5 days later it crashed at The Ward, Co. Dublin

Photograph courtesy George Flood

Cessna F.150M, EI-BBN at Iona, 26 August 1978 following re-build

Photograph courtesy Paul Cunniffe

Table 51

Registration	EI-BCK
Aircraft Type	Cessna F.172N
Constructors Serial Number	172-1543
Place & Year of Manufacture	Reims, France, 1977
Previous Registrations	New aircraft
Registered to	Iona National Airways Ltd, 22 November 1976
Delivery date	5 March 1977
Remarks	EI-BCK, having spent ten years with Iona since delivery on 5 March 1977, moved across the city to Weston, where it was transferred to Hugh Caulfield on 16 October 1987. It remained at Weston and was purchased by Kieran A. O'Connor on 11 May 1999. In early 2004 it was current at National Flight Centre, Weston Airport, Co. Kildare.

Cessna F.172N, EI-BCK in front of Iona clubhouse 12 March 1977 - 7 days after delivery

Photograph courtesy Paul Cunniffe

Cessna F.172N, EI-BCK at Abbeyshrule, Co. Longford, 13 August 1978

Photograph courtesy Liam Byrne via Ronny Vogt collection

Table 52

Registration	EI-BCL
Aircraft Type	Cessna 182P
Constructors Serial Number	182-64-300
Place & Year of Manufacture	Reims, France, 1976
Previous Registrations	N1366M (Demonstration aircraft)
Registered to	Iona National Airways Ltd, 22 November 1976
Delivery date	20 January 1977

Remarks

It was purchased by Iona in January 1977, to replace the Cessna 182, EI-AYJ, following its destruction at Kilbrittain on 19 September 1976. EI-BCL was the aircraft that successfully flew around Irish airfields for charity on 24 June 1985. Frank Doherty, Donegal, purchased EI-BCL on 14 February 1994. On 21 May 1998 it was transferred to Laurence Burke, Newcastle, Co. Wicklow and based at Kilrush, Co. Kildare.

On 15 February 2003 it was involved in a ground collision at Kilrush with Ian Valentine's CAP 10, G-GCXC.

Cessna 182P, EI-BCL at Iona 31 May 1978

Photograph courtesy Liam Byrne via Ronny Vogt collection

Cessna 182P, EI-BCL at Iona 2 April 1991

Photograph courtesy Simon Nolan

Table 53

Registration	EI-BCV
Aircraft Type	Cessna F.150M
Constructors Serial Number	150-1415
Place & Year of Manufacture	Reims, France, 1977
Previous Registrations	New aircraft
Registered to	Iona National Airways Ltd, 16 March 1977
Delivery date	3 June 1977
Remarks	After serving the flying club for five years, Cessna 150M, EI-BCV, was sold by Iona and Pearse delivered it to Cork on 26 March 1982. On 17 September 1982 it was registered to the Hibernian Flying Club Limited, Cork. On 23 November 1987 it was delivered Cork via Earls Colne, Essex and to Ipswich on 24 November 1987 following its sale to the United Kingdom. On 14 December 1987 it was registered as G-BOBV to L. E. Usher, c/o Suffolk Light Aircraft Maintenance, Ipswich. It was cancelled from the Irish register 11 December 1987. On 22 March 1996 it was registered to Sheffield Aero Club, Netherthorpe, Worksop, UK. At 31 December 2002 total hours were recorded as 10,954.

Cessna F.150M, EI-BCV at Iona, 14 July 1977

Photograph courtesy George Flood

Cessna F.150M, EI-BCV at Iona, 31 May 1978

Photograph courtesy Liam Byrne via Ronny Vogt collection

Table 54

Registration	EI-BDO
Aircraft Type	Cessna F.152
Constructors Serial Number	152-1457
Place & Year of Manufacture	Reims, France, 1978
Previous Registrations	New aircraft
Registered to	Iona National Airways Ltd, 11 November 1977
Delivery date	27 January 1978
Remarks	This was the first Reims built Cessna 152 to grace the Irish register.

EI-BDO ditched into the sea five miles south of Youghal, Co. Cork on the evening of Tuesday, 18 June 1985, while operated by Lismore Aero Club, Co. Waterford. The aircraft had taken off from Lismore at 9pm for a pleasure flight until it encountered difficulties and ditched into the sea. The passenger managed to cling to a buoy until a trawler picked him up. The pilot, Raymond Sheane (32) was not so fortunate and lost his life following the accident. The aircraft was on lease to Lismore Aero Club from Iona. The wreckage was never recovered from the sea bed and was cancelled from the register on 22 August 1986.

Cessna F.152, EI-BDO at Iona, 4 February 1978 - 8 days after delivery

Photograph courtesy Paul Cunniffe

Cessna F.152, EI-BDO

Photograph courtesy Paul Duffy

Table 55

Registration	EI-BGH
Aircraft Type	Cessna F.172N Skyhawk II
Constructors Serial Number	F172-1789
Place & Year of Manufacture	Reims, France, 1979
Previous Registrations	New aircraft
Registered to	Iona National Airways Ltd, 30 March 1979
Delivery date	12 April 1979
Remarks	On 5 May 1980 it suffered extensive damage during a landing accident on Lambay Island, off Dublin. It was transported to Rogers Aviation, Cranfield, England for repair. On several occasions throughout 1993, EI-BGH was flown to Carrickfin, Co. Donegal where many hours were clocked up doing parachute drops in the area.

EI-BGH was transferred to the Golf Hotel Group, Powerscourt, Co. Wicklow on 14 December 1993. It had been with Iona since 30 March 1979. It subsequently was transferred to the UK register as G- BZGH and cancelled from the Irish register 19 November 1998. On 1 December 1998 ownership transferred to Desmond Behan, 38 Derravaragh Road, Dublin 6W. It is recorded as current in early 2004 and based at Weston airport, Co. Kildare. |

Cessna F.172N, EI-BGH at Iona, 12 May 1979 - 4 weeks after delivery

Photograph courtesy Paul Cunniffe

Cessna F.172N, EI-BGH at Iona, 19 April 1983.

Photograph courtesy Simon Nolan

Table 56

Registration	EI-BGI
Aircraft Type	Cessna F.152
Constructors Serial Number	F152-1607
Place & Year of Manufacture	Reims, France, 1979
Previous Registrations	New aircraft
Registered to	Iona National Airways Ltd, 14 May 1979
Delivery date	15 June 1979
Remarks	After delivery, EI-BGI was leased to Waterford Aero Club for the period to 16 April 1985. Following return from its lease to Waterford Aero Club it was cancelled from the Irish register on 6 November 1985. The following day it was registered as G-BMHI to Bevelhurst Limited and delivered by Peter Cahill, via Leeds, to Manchester on 28 November 1985.
	On 29 August 1991 it was destroyed over Cargo, near Newtown, Powys, Wales when it was involved in a mid-air collision with a Royal Air Force Jaguar, XX843. The pilot, and sole occupant, of G-BMHI was killed, as was one of the two crew of the Jaguar. The other ejected successfully. It was removed from the UK register 23 January 1992 with the annotation: *'Destroyed'*.

Cessna F.152, EI-BGI at Iona, 16 June 1979 - the day following delivery

Photograph courtesy Paul Cunniffe

Cessna F.152, EI-BGI at Iona, 9 September 1979

Photograph courtesy Liam Byrne via Ronny Vogt collection

Table 57

Registration	EI-BGJ
Aircraft Type	Cessna F.152
Constructors Serial Number	F152-1664
Place & Year of Manufacture	Reims, France, 1979
Previous Registrations	New aircraft
Registered to	Iona National Airways Ltd, 14 May 1979
Delivery date	15 June 1979
Remarks	Kerry Aero Club acquired ownership of EI-BGJ, on 15 May 1980. It relocated further south to the Hibernian Flying Club Limited, Cork, registered to them on 24 August 1987. It remained there for nine years until Kevin Higgins, Galway, had it placed on the register in his name on 5 January 1996. Two years later it moved further up the west coast to become part of the Sligo Aero Club Limited on 23 March 1998. While still based at Strandhill it was registered to Sligo Aeronautical Club Limited on 28 November 2002. Current with the club in early 2004.

Cessna F.152, EI-BGJ at Iona, 29 August 1979

Photograph courtesy Paul Cunniffe

Cessna F.152, EI-BGJ at Iona, 22 April 1988 while operated by Hibernian Flying Club, Cork.

Photograph courtesy Hugo Wilhare

Table 58

Registration	EI-BIA
Aircraft Type	Cessna FA.152 Aerobat
Constructors Serial Number	FA152-0366
Place & Year of Manufacture	Reims, France, 1979
Previous Registrations	New aircraft
Registered to	Iona National Airways Ltd, 30 November 1979
Delivery date	19 September 1980
Remarks	Nine days after delivery, Pearse flew it to attend an air display at Holycross, near Thurles, Co. Tipperary. During the display, with Ray Di Mascio at the controls, it failed to recover in time from a manoeuvre and crashed in a field adjoining the display field. The pilot was seriously injured but survived the crash. The new aircraft was 'written-off' and was cancelled from the register on 16 June 1981. Following the Liquidation of Iona, the remains of EI-BIA were purchased through the auctioneer in April 1995 by Christopher Keane, Saggart, Co. Dublin.

Cessna FA.152 Aerobat, EI-BIA at Thurles, Co. Tipperary, Sunday, 28 September, 1980

Photograph courtesy Military Air Photos via Leo Murray

Cessna FA.152 Aerobat, EI-BIA performing a low-pass at Holycross air display, Thurles, Co. Tipperary, 28 September 1980. It was damaged beyond repair in an accident later that day

Photograph via Paul Duffy collection

Table 59

Registration	EI-BIB
Aircraft Type	Cessna F.152
Constructors Serial Number	F152-1724
Place & Year of Manufacture	Reims, France, 1979
Previous Registrations	New aircraft
Registered to	Iona National Airways Ltd, 30 November 1979
Delivery date	14 March 1980
Remarks	The day after delivery to Iona it was ferried to Carnmore for use by the Galway Flying Club Limited. It was one year later when it was formally registered to them on 13 March 1981. A deal involving EI-ATH formed part of the sale. EI-BIB remained in service with the Galway club until it overran the runway on landing at Carnmore in November 1981 and was extensively damaged. The severely damaged aircraft was brought to Abbeyshrule, Co. Longford for repair. It returned to service with Galway Flying Club and was current with them early 2004.

Cessna F.152, EI-BIB at Iona, 15 March 1980 - the day following delivery to Iona. This was the only day it spent at Iona as it was ferried to Galway Flying Club later that day

Photograph courtesy Paul Cunniffe

Cessna F.152, EI-BIB with Galway Flying Club at Carnmore, Co. Galway, 20 July 1980

Photograph courtesy George Flood

Table 60

Registration	EI-BIC
Aircraft Type	Cessna F.172N Skyhawk
Constructors Serial Number	F172-1965
Place & Year of Manufacture	Reims, France, 1980
Previous Registrations	OO-HNZ
Registered to	Iona National Airways Ltd, 15 February 1980
Delivery date	15 March 1980
Remarks	The aircraft scheduled for the marks was allocated the registration EI-BIN. However, it never took up these marks either and went on to become LN-LGF to Scancopter Aviation A/S/, Notodden, Norway on 22 April 1981. The aircraft that eventually took the marks was also a 172N Skyhawk model.
	The Oriel Flying Group Limited, Dundalk, Co. Louth acquired EI-BIC, and it was registered to them on 4 September 1981. On 13 April 1995 it overran the runway at Castlebar, Co. Mayo and overturned. The aircraft was badly damaged and taken to Abbeyshrule, Co. Longford. It remained there as 'scrapped' and was cancelled from the Irish register on 18 November 2002.

Cessna F.172N Skyhawk, EI-BIC in Iona hangar shortly after delivery in March 1980

Photograph courtesy Liam Byrne via Ronny Vogt collection

Cessna F.172N Skyhawk, EI-BIC at Iona, 22 March 1980 - 7 days after delivery

Photograph courtesy Paul Cunniffe

Table 61

Registration	EI-BIE
Aircraft Type	Cessna FA.152 Aerobat
Constructors Serial Number	152-0362
Place & Year of Manufacture	Reims, France, 1980
Previous Registrations	New aircraft
Registered to	Iona National Airways Ltd, 28 February 1980
Delivery date	15 March 1980

Remarks

On 4 February 1981, EI-BIE was transferred to D. F. McEllin, Castlebar, Co. Mayo. While there it was twice blown over in gales. On one occasion, in January 1984, it ended up in the car park of the *Travellers Friend* public house, Castlebar. On 25 May 1987, it was cancelled from the Irish register following its removal in January 1987 to Peartree Farm, Chelford, Cheshire and registered G-STAP on 10 June 1987 to Stapleford Flying Club Limited, Stapleford, Tawney, Romford, UK. It was de-registered by them 16 April 1991 following sale to Cyprus as 5B-CIC.

On 20 February 1992 it was registered to Mark Aviation Services, Albatros Flight College, Lakatamia airfield, Cyprus. Subsequently Albatros ceased trading and the Certificate of Airworthiness expired 5 years later on 19 February 1997. The airfield at Lakatamia is now out of use and the remains of 5B-CIC now lie scrapped at Larnaka airport, Cyprus.

Cessna FA.152 Aerobat, EI-BIE at Iona 29 March 1980 - 14 days after delivery

Photograph courtesy Paul Cunniffe

Cessna FA.152 Aerobat, EI-BIE at Abbeyshrule, Co. Longford, 25 May 1980

Photograph courtesy Paul Cunniffe

Table 62

Registration	EI-BIN
Aircraft Type	Cessna F.152
Constructors Serial Number	152-1843
Place & Year of Manufacture	Reims, France, 1981
Previous Registrations	New aircraft
Registered to	Iona National Airways Ltd, 10 February 1981
Delivery date	31 March 1981
Remarks	EI-BIN remained with Iona for approximately four years until its cancellation from the register on 21 February 1985. It was delivered to Yeadon, adjacent to Leeds / Bradford airport on 14 February 1985 and placed on the UK register as G-BLWV on 25 February 1985 following sale to Belverhurst Limited, Doncaster. On 2 July 1987 it went to Redhill Aviation Limited, Redhill Aerodrome, Surrey and was recorded as current in early 2004. G-BLWV is the aircraft featured on the home page for Redhill Aviation's web site.

Cessna F.152, EI-BIN at Iona, 15 August 1981

Photograph courtesy George Flood

Cessna F.152, EI-BIN at Iona, 15 August 1981

Photograph courtesy George Flood

Table 63

Registration	EI-BJM
Aircraft Type	Cessna 152 Aerobat
Constructors Serial Number	152-0936
Place & Year of Manufacture	Wichita, USA, 1980
Previous Registrations	N761CC (Egyptian Air Force)
Registered to	Iona National Airways Ltd. 18 September 1980
Delivery date	21 September 1980
Remarks	It was a Wichita built aircraft, previously registered to the Egyptian Air Force, but not taken up. It lay in Brussels for a while pending further sale. It was the first American built Cessna 152 to appear in Irish marks, it was also the first new American rather than French built Cessna single for some time. The Leinster Aero Club Limited took possession of the aircraft following its delivery to Dublin. It was not formally registered to the Leinster Aero Club Limited until 26 August 1981. It remained with the Leinster Aero Club based at Dublin Airport, until March 2004, when the club returned to their former base at Weston Airport, Co. Kildare.
	On 12 May 2004, EI-BJM was registered to Kieran A. O'Connor and is based at Weston Airport.

Cessna 152 Aerobat, EI-BJM at Iona, 31 January 1981

Photograph courtesy Paul Cunniffe

Cessna 152 Aerobat, EI-BJM owned by Leinster Aero Club, at Fairyhouse Air Spectacular, 16 August 1981

Photograph courtesy Liam Byrne via Ronny Vogt collection

Table 64

Registration	EI-BMM
Aircraft Type	Cessna F.152-II
Constructors Serial Number	152-1899
Place & Year of Manufacture	Reims, France, 1982
Previous Registrations	New aircraft
Registered to	Iona National Airways Ltd, 10 March 1982
Delivery date	4 April 1982
Remarks	On 8 July 1993 ownership of EI-BMM was transferred to Eric Hopkins, Newcastle, Co. Wicklow, for use by the Newcastle Flying Club based at Newcastle. In April 1995, the Liquidator for Iona sold it at auction. It was acquired by Peter Redmond, Clondalkin, Dublin 22 and placed on the register to him on 16 May 1996. At that stage it had a time expired engine and was minus its tail section. It has been a restoration project and the engine has been restored to flying condition with additional work performed on the airframe in an effort to have it air worthy.

Cessna F.152-II, EI-BMM at Iona, 12 April 1982 - 8 days after delivery

Photograph courtesy Paul Cunniffe

Cessna F.152-II, EI-BMM

Photograph courtesy Leo Murray

Table 65

Registration	EI-BMN
Aircraft Type	Cessna F.152-II
Constructors Serial Number	152-1912
Place & Year of Manufacture	Reims, France, 1982
Previous Registrations	New aircraft
Registered to	Iona National Airways Ltd, 10 March 1982
Delivery date	4 April 1982
Remarks	EI-BMN remained at Iona providing training for a number of years until it changed hands to Eric Hopkins on 8 July 1993. Following the Liquidation of Iona it moved to BMN Group, Abbeyshrule, Co. Longford on 3 November 1995. On 30 January 2003, it was registered to Sligo Light Aviation Club Limited, Strandhill, Co. Sligo. Recorded as current with the club early 2004.

Cessna F.152-II, EI-BMN at Iona, 9 September 1983

Photograph courtesy Liam Byrne via Ronny Vogt collection

Cessna F.152-II, EI-BMN at Abbeyshrule, Co. Longford, 7 June 1998

Photograph courtesy Simon Nolan

Table 66

Registration	EI-BNC
Aircraft Type	Cessna F.152-II
Constructors Serial Number	152-1894
Place & Year of Manufacture	Reims, France, 1982
Previous Registrations	N9097Y
Registered to	Iona National Airways Ltd, 5 August 1982
Delivery date	18 August 1982

Remarks

Having borne the marks N9097Y for pre delivery purposes it was ferried Reims to Brussels on 22 February 1982. On 18 August 1982 Peter Cahill brought it to Dublin from Brussels, routing via Birmingham. It provided good long service to members of the Irish Aero Club Limited for a considerable number of years.

Following the liquidation of Iona, EI-BNC was sold through the auctioneer and remained at Waterford until 4 May 1995 when it was delivered to the UK. On 15 June 1995, it was registered G-BWEU to Sky Pro Limited, 5 Park Road, Bawtry, Doncaster, S. Yorks. It was cancelled from the Irish register on the same day. On 17 October 2002 it was registered to Affair Aircraft Leasing, Boston Spa, Wetherby, Yorkshire.

Cessna F.152-II, EI-BNC at Iona, 22 October 1982 - 2 months after delivery

Photograph courtesy George Flood

Cessna F.152-II, EI-BNC at Iona, 4 July 1987 - minus its wheel spats

Photograph courtesy Paul Cunniffe

Table 67

Registration	EI-BRM
Aircraft Type	Cessna 172Q Cutlass
Constructors Serial Number	172-76147
Place & Year of Manufacture	Wichita, USA, 1984
Previous Registrations	N97033
Registered to	Iona National Airways Ltd, 17 June 1985
Delivery date	7 April 1984
Remarks	The 172 bore the registration N97033. It was first flown from Wichita to King Avionics for a full avionics fit out. On completion of this work it was ferried across the Atlantic, arriving in Dublin 7 April 1984. It was based at Iona for over one year before it was placed on the Irish register as EI-BRM.
	This aircraft was involved in a mid-air collision near Bandon, Co. Cork on 26 February 1992 with Cessna 152, EI-BRO. The instructor and student pilot in EI-BRM were killed. The aircraft was later removed from the Irish register on 6 June 1992.

Cessna 172Q Cutlass, N97033, operated for 14 months at Iona before becoming EI-BRM

Photograph courtesy Simon Nolan

Cessna 172Q Cutlass, EI-BRM at Iona, 31 August 1985

Photograph courtesy Paul Cunniffe

Notes & References

Another club training aircraft was Cessna F150M, EI-BCV. It was delivered to Iona 3 June 1977 and photographed the following day. It served the club for 5 years before going to Cork

Photograph courtesy
Paul Cunniffe

The first Reims built Cessna 152 to appear on the Irish register was Iona's EI-BDO. It arrived at Iona 27 January 1978 and was photographed there on 4 April 1981

Photograph courtesy
Paul Cunniffe

Cessna F172N Skyhawk II, EI-BGH, with the colour scheme Iona Flight Training School

Photograph courtesy
Paul Duffy

Two new Cessna 152's arrived at Iona ramp from Reims on 15 June 1979. One of them, Cessna F152, EI-BGI, is photographed at Castlebridge, Co. Wexford one month later on 15 July 1979. It remained with Iona until November 1985

Photograph courtesy
Paul Cunniffe

The other Cessna 152 to arrive at Iona 15 June 1979 was Cessna F152 EI-BGJ and was photographed on the Iona ramp 2 August 1980, while owned by Kerry Aero Club.

Photograph courtesy
Paul Cunniffe

Cessna F152, EI-BIB, was delivered to Iona 14 March 1980. The following day it was transferred to Galway Flying Club. Above photograph was taken at Abbeyshrule, Co. Longford 25 May 1980

Photograph courtesy
Paul Cunniffe

Photographed on the Iona ramp on 22 March 1980, one week after Cessna F172N Skyhawk, EI-BIC, was delivered from France.

Photograph courtesy Paul Cunniffe

The seventh new Cessna aircraft ordered by Iona in 1979 was Cessna FA152 Aerobat EI-BIE. It arrived at Iona 15 March 1980 - same day as EI-BIC.
It was photographed at Abbeyshrule, Co. Longford, 8 August 1982.

Photograph courtesy Paul Cunniffe

Iona's Cessna F152 EI-BIN holds the distinction of bearing Irish Certificate of Registration number 1,000. It arrived at Iona 31 March 1981 and was photographed 4 days later.

Photograph courtesy Paul Cunniffe

Cessna F152 Aerobat, EI-BJM, was delivered to Iona 21 September 1980 and was for use by the Iona based Leinster Aero Club. This photograph was taken 31 January 1981.

Photograph courtesy Paul Cunniffe

Two new Cessna F152-II's were ferried to Dublin from Reims on 4 April 1982. The first was EI-BMM photographed in Co. Cork on 20 July 1991 with the logo for Iona Flight Training School, Cork

Photograph courtesy Paul Duffy

The second Cessna F152-II to arrive at Iona on 4 April 1982 was EI-BMN. It is photographed at Iona 8 days later. It was later repainted in a similar colour scheme to EI-BMM (above) when used for pilot training at Cork

Photograph courtesy Paul Cunniffe

Another aircraft to give long service at Iona was Cessna F152-II, EI-BNC, that arrived there 18 August 1982. Photographed 11 September 1982. It remained with Iona until the demise of the company at the end of 1994.

Photograph courtesy
Paul Cunniffe

Cessna 172Q Cutlass, EI-BRM, after over a year of operation at Iona as N97033 was transferred to the Irish register 17 June 1985. Photographed at Strandhill, Co. Sligo 12 days later on 29 June 1985

Photograph courtesy
Hugo Wilhare

On 18 November 1985 the last Reims built Cessna purchased by Iona arrived at Dublin airport. It was Cessna F152-II, EI-BRO and was photographed 10 April 1986

Photograph courtesy
Hugo Wilhare

EI-BVU

Photograph courtesy
Simon Nolan

EI-BVV

Photograph courtesy
Hugo Wilhare

EI-BVW

Photograph courtesy
Hugo Wilhare

Iona purchased 3 Cessna 152-II's intending them for pilot training at their new establishment at Cork airport. They arrived in crates from USA in July 1988. The first on the register was EI-BVU and was photographed shortly after assembly. The second registered was EI-BVV and was photographed 22 September 1988. The third in sequence was EI-BVW and was photographed at Iona 11 March 1989

EI-CCJ

Photograph courtesy Hugo Wilhare

EI-CCK

Photograph courtesy
Hugo Wilhare

EI-CCL

Photograph courtesy
Hugo Wilhare

In August 1990 four Cessna 152-II's arrived in crates at Iona from United States of America. They were assembled and put into service with the Irish Aero Club. Top photograph shows the first in sequence, EI-CCJ, at Iona 15 January 1992. Middle photograph is EI-CCK at Iona 25 September 1991 and the bottom picture of EI-CCL was also at Iona on 15 January 1992. Over the page is the fourth aircraft in the sequence, EI-CCM.

EI-CCM

Photograph via Paul Duffy

EI-CFM

Photograph courtesy
Simon Nolan

EI-CFN

Photograph courtesy
Paul Cunniffe

The final two aircraft acquired for use by the Irish Aero Club at Iona were two Cessna 172P Skyhawk's. They were flown across the Atlantic and arrived at Iona on 8 May 1992. The first in sequence was EI-CFM and was photographed at Iona in June 1994. Second of the pair was EI-CFN and was photographed at Iona on 18 April 1993

Notes & References

Table 68

Registration	EI-BRO
Aircraft Type	Cessna F.152-II
Constructors Serial Number	152-1957
Place & Year of Manufacture	Reims, France, 1985
Previous Registrations	New aircraft
Registered to	Iona National Airways Ltd, 12 November 1985
Delivery date	18 November 1985
Remarks	On 26 February 1992 this aircraft was involved with Cessna 172Q Cutlass, EI-BRM, in a mid-air collision near Bandon, Co. Cork. EI-BRO was able to return to Cork airport but tragically both on board the Cessna 172 were killed.
	At the Iona liquidation auction in April 1995, EI-BRO was purchased by Nalson Aviation Limited, Willey Park Farm, Stanstead Road, Caterham, Surrey. It was subsequently sold to East Midlands Aircraft Hire Limited based at East Midlands and registered to them on 11 October 1995 as G-IBRO. It was cancelled from the Irish register on 25 August 1995. On 10 July 1998 ownership transferred to Leicestershire Aero Club, Leicester Airport and was recorded as current early 2004.

Cessna F152-II, EI-BRO, at Iona 11 January 1986

Photograph courtesy Paul Cunniffe

Cessna F152-II, EI-BRO, at Iona.

Photograph courtesy Derek Gannon via Leo Murray.

Table 69

Registration	EI-BVU
Aircraft Type	Cessna 152-II
Constructors Serial Number	152-83182
Place & Year of Manufacture	Wichita, USA, 1979
Previous Registrations	N47184
Registered to	Iona National Airways Ltd 7 June 1988
Delivery date	July 1988 (in crate)
Remarks	It was one of the aircraft used by Iona Flight Training School when established in Cork in June 1989. Following the liquidation of Iona, it was flown to Waterford in February 1995 and was included in the auction in April 1995. It was sold through the auctioneer to Haimoss Limited, Old Sarum Flying Club, The Portway, Sawsbury, Wiltshire and acquiring the registration G-BWEV on 28 June 1995. It was removed from the Irish register 15 June 1995

Cessna 152-II, EI-BVU at Iona, 15 October 1988

Photograph courtesy Paul Cunniffe

Cessna 152-II, EI-BVU, at Iona 22 September 1988

Photograph courtesy Hugo Wilhare

Table 70

Registration	EI-BVV
Aircraft Type	Cessna 152-II
Constructors Serial Number	152-85018
Place & Year of Manufacture	Wichita, USA, 1981
Previous Registrations	N6467P
Registered to	Iona National Airways Ltd, 7 June 1988
Delivery date	July 1988 (in crate)
Remarks	On 27 September 1988 the aircraft left Dublin airport on a familiarisation flight to the west of the Dublin Control Zone. Tragically it crashed near Mulhuddart, Co. Meath shortly afterwards killing both occupants. It was removed from the register 3 August 1991.

Cessna F152-II, EI-BVV, at Iona 22 September 1988

Photograph courtesy Hugo Wilhare

Cessna F152-II, EI-BVV, at Iona 18 September 1988

Photograph courtesy Paul Duffy

Table 71

Registration	EI-BVW
Aircraft Type	Cessna 152-II
Constructors Serial Number	152-85123
Place & Year of Manufacture	Wichita, USA, 1981
Previous Registrations	N6093Q
Registered to	Iona National Airways Ltd, 7 June 1988
Delivery date	July 1988 (in crate)
Remarks	It was one of the aircraft used by Iona Flight Training School when established in Cork in June 1989. Following the liquidation of Iona, it was flown to Waterford in February 1995 and was included in the auction in April 1995. EI-BVW was sold through the auctioneer to Marham Investments Limited, Ballabeg, Castletown, Isle of Man and was flown to Woodgate Air Maintenance Ltd, Belfast International Airport, and took up the registration G-IAFT on 20 June 1995. It was cancelled from the Irish register 15 June 1995. It was recorded as current in early 2004 in operation by the Ulster Flying Club, Newtownards, Co. Down.

Cessna F152-II, EI-BVW, at Iona in June 1989

Photograph courtesy Paul Cunniffe

Cessna F152-II, EI-BVW, at Shannon, 22 July 1990.

Photograph courtesy Paul Cunniffe

Table 72

Registration	EI-CCJ
Aircraft Type	Cessna 152-II
Constructors Serial Number	152-80174
Place & Year of Manufacture	Wichita, USA, 1978
Previous Registrations	N24251
Registered to	P. Cahill 9 October 1990
Delivery date	August 1990 (in crate)
Remarks	Following the liquidation of Iona, it was offered for sale by the Liquidator at an auction in April 1995 with comment *'not flown since Apr 1993 due to time expired engine.'* This aircraft was sold at the auction to Nalson Aviation Limited, Willey Park Farm, Standstead Road, Caterham, Surrey. The aircraft never flew again and was used as spares.

Cessna F152-II, EI-CCJ, at Iona.

Photograph via Paul Duffy

Cessna F152-II, EI-CCJ at Iona, 14 July 1991

Photograph courtesy Alan Dwyer

Table 73

Registration	EI-CCK
Aircraft Type	Cessna 152-II
Constructors Serial Number	152-79610
Place & Year of Manufacture	Wichita, USA, 1978
Previous Registrations	N757BM
Registered to	P. Cahill 9 October 1990
Delivery date	August 1990 (in crate)
Remarks	EI-CCK suffered damage in a landing accident at Cork. It was subsequently removed by road to Newcastle, Co. Wicklow and never flew again. It was offered for sale by the Liquidator with comment *'largely dis-assembled and had no engine.'* It was not sold at auction in April 1995 and continued to lie in a dismantled state at Newcastle, Co. Wicklow.

Cessna F152-II, EI-CCK, at Iona.

Photograph via Paul Duffy

Cessna F152-II, EI-CCK, at Iona, 14 July 1991

Photograph courtesy Alan Dwyer

Table 74

Registration	EI-CCL
Aircraft Type	Cessna 152-II
Constructors Serial Number	152-80382
Place & Year of Manufacture	Wichita, USA, 1978
Previous Registrations	N24791
Registered to	P. Cahill 9 October 1990
Delivery date	August 1990 (in crate)
Remarks	On 4 May 1993, EI-CCL made a forced landing, following engine failure 2,000 feet over Bray Head. The Cessna came down in a cornfield at Half Moon near Windgates, beside the Bray to Greystones road. The two on board were slightly injured and taken to Loughlinstown hospital. The pilot was Louisa Hopkins, a granddaughter of Pearse Cahill, and her instructor was Patricia O'Brien, from Co. Clare. The Cessna was severely damaged and never flew again.

Cessna F152-II, EI-CCL, at Iona, 15 January 1992

Photograph courtesy Hugo Wilhare

Cessna F152-II, EI-CCL, at Iona.

Photograph via Paul Duffy

Table 75

Registration	EI-CCM
Aircraft Type	Cessna 152-II
Constructors Serial Number	152-82320
Place & Year of Manufacture	Wichita, USA, 1979
Previous Registrations	N68679
Registered to	P. Cahill 9 October 1990
Delivery date	August 1990 (in crate)
Remarks	Following the liquidation of Iona this aircraft was offered for sale at auction in April 1990. It was not sold at the auction. On 18 November 1999 ownership was transferred to Eric Hopkins, Newcastle, Co. Wicklow in flying condition. Still current early 2004.

Cessna F152-II, EI-CCM, at Iona, 3 April 1991

Photograph courtesy Hugo Wilhare

Cessna F152-II, EI-CCM, in the hangar at Newcastle airfield, Co. Wicklow.

Photograph courtesy Leo Murray.

Table 76

Registration	EI-CFM
Aircraft Type	Cessna 172P Skyhawk
Constructors Serial Number	74656
Place & Year of Manufacture	Wichita, USA, 1981
Previous Registrations	N53000
Registered to	Matthew Pearse Cahill 19 May 1992
Delivery date	8 May 1992
Remarks	Along with EI-CFN, EI-CFM was ferried across the Atlantic routing Casper (Wyoming)-Wichita-Goose Bay-Reykjavik-Dublin arriving 8 May 1992. EI-CFM was registered to Hibernian Flying Club, Cork on 7 May 1996. Blown on top of Grob G115A, EI-CCN, during a gale at Cork on 27 December 1997. It was removed from the Irish register 25 July 2000. It was acquired by Kieran A. O'Connor and in early 2004 was in a hangar at Weston airport as a possible restoration project.

Cessna 172P, Skyhawk, EI-CFM, at Weston, 2 February 1995.

Photograph courtesy Hugo Wilhare.

Cessna 172P, Skyhawk, EI-CFM, at Iona.

Photograph courtesy Simon Nolan.

Table 77

Registration	EI-CFN
Aircraft Type	Cessna 172P Skyhawk
Constructors Serial Number	74113
Place & Year of Manufacture	Wichita, USA, 1981
Previous Registrations	N5446K; JA4172; N5446K
Registered to	Matthew Pearse Cahill 19 May 1992
Delivery date	8 May 1992
Remarks	Along with EI-CFM, EI-CFN was ferried across the Atlantic routing Casper (Wyoming-Kansas-Bangor-Goose Bay-Reykjavik-Dublin arriving 8 May 1992. Following the demise of Iona the Cessna 172P, EI-CFN, was transferred to Liam Kane, Weston on 12 January 1995, where it has remained since, though under a variety of owners. Current early 2004 and based at Weston airport, Co. Kildare.

Cessna 172P, Skyhawk, EI-CFN, at Weston, 6 February 2000.

Photograph courtesy Simon Nolan.

Cessna 172P, Skyhawk, EI-CFN,

Photograph courtesy Derek Gannon via Leo Murray.

APPENDIX 1

Charts indicating known locations of aircraft associated
with Iona National Airways / Irish Aero Club.
The number in the box refers to the table number associated with the aircraft registration.

 = Aircraft inactive. Indicates crash location;
where aircraft is believed scrapped;
or under restoration.

⬤▬ = Aircraft active early 2004.
Indicates current known location.

IRELAND

③ AAF	㊿ BBN
⑥ AJC	�51 BCK
⑫ ALY	�52 BCL
⑬ AMJ	�54 BDO
⑭ AMS	�55 BGH
⑮ AMK	�57 BGJ
㊱ APF	�58 BIA
㊲ ARY	�59 BIB
㊳ AST	�60 BIC
㊴ ATH	�63 BJM
㊵ AUC	�64 BMM
㊶ AUH	㊻ BMN
㊷ AUO	㊿⑦ BRM
㊸ AVA	㊀ BVV
㊹ AVM	㊁ BVW
㊺ AWE	㊂ CCK
㊻ AYF	㊃ CCL
㊼ AYJ	㊄ CCM
㊽ BAS	㊅ CFM
㊾ BAT	㊆ CFN

UK

① AAK
④ AAG
⑤ AAP
⑨ AJF
⑩ AJA
⑪ ALU
⑯ AOO
⑰ ANC
⑱ AOK
⑲ AND
㉒ AVC
�33 CAZ
�35 CHO
�53 BCV
�56 BGI
㉒ BIN
㊻ BNC
㊽ BRO
㊾ BVU
㋺ CCJ

USA

⑧ AJE
⑳ ATB
㉑ ATC
㉓ BEO
㉔ BGP
㉕ BMK
㉗ BVA
㉘ BVP
㉚ FDX
㉜ FEA
㉞ FEX

REST OF THE WORLD

② AAD
⑦ AJD
㉖ BUM
㉙ BVX
㉛ BPI
㊽ BIE

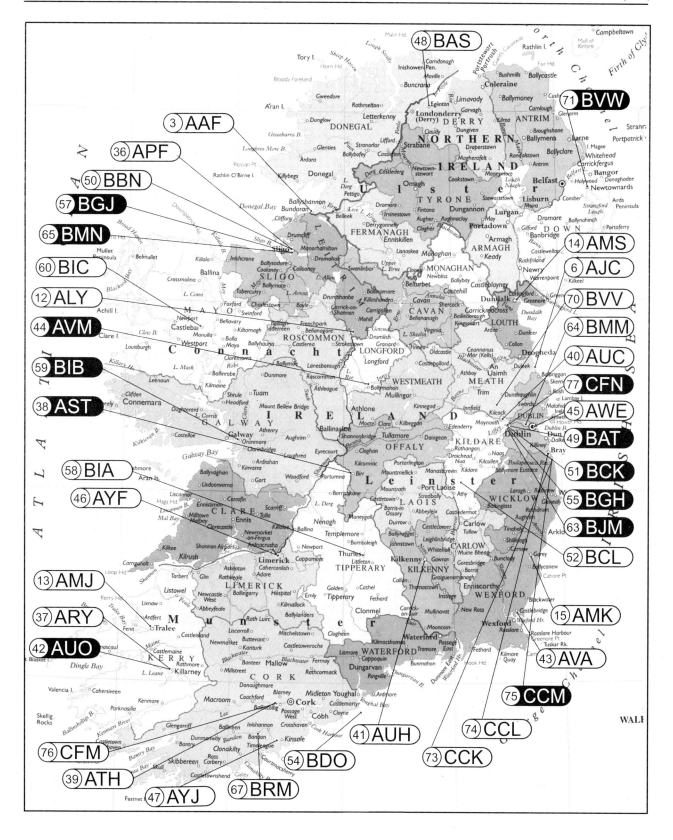

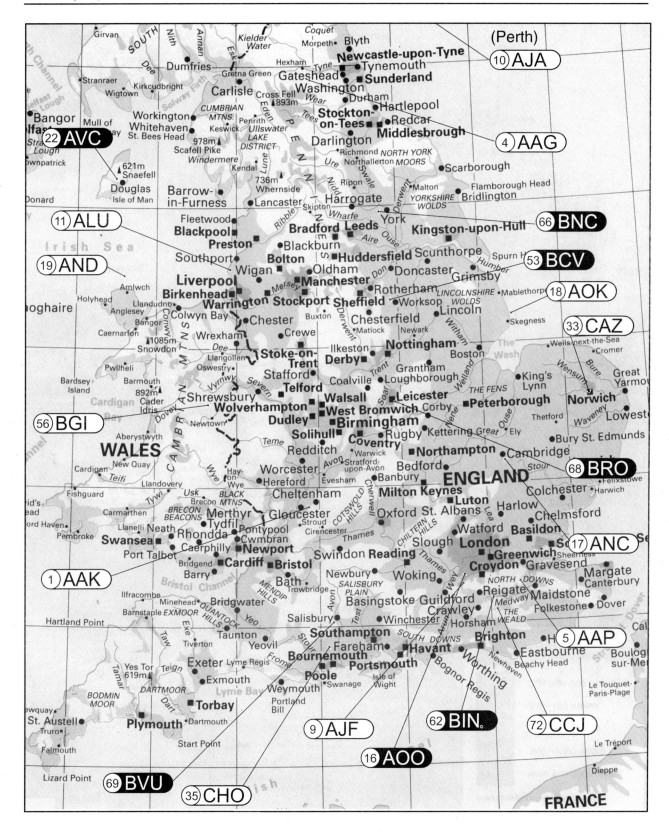

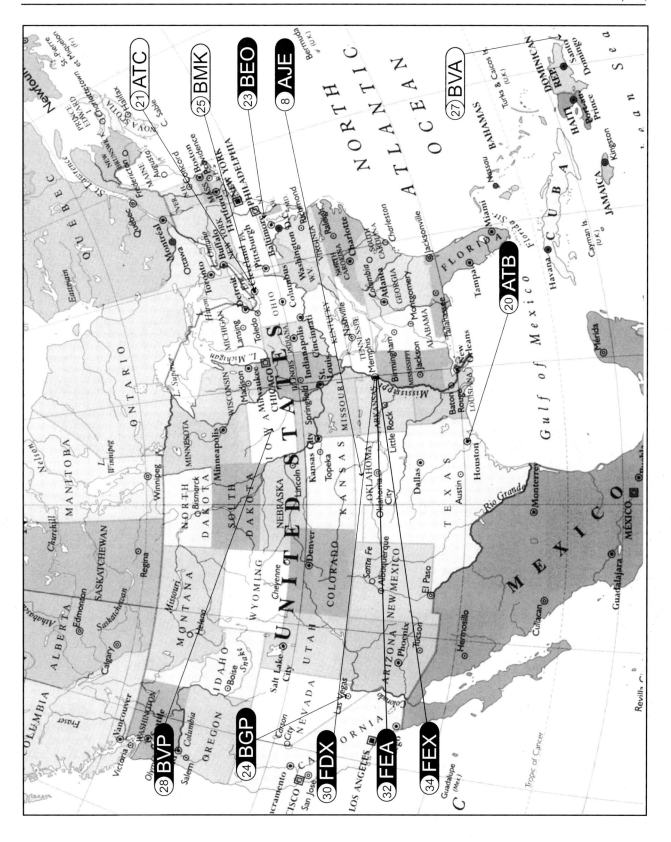

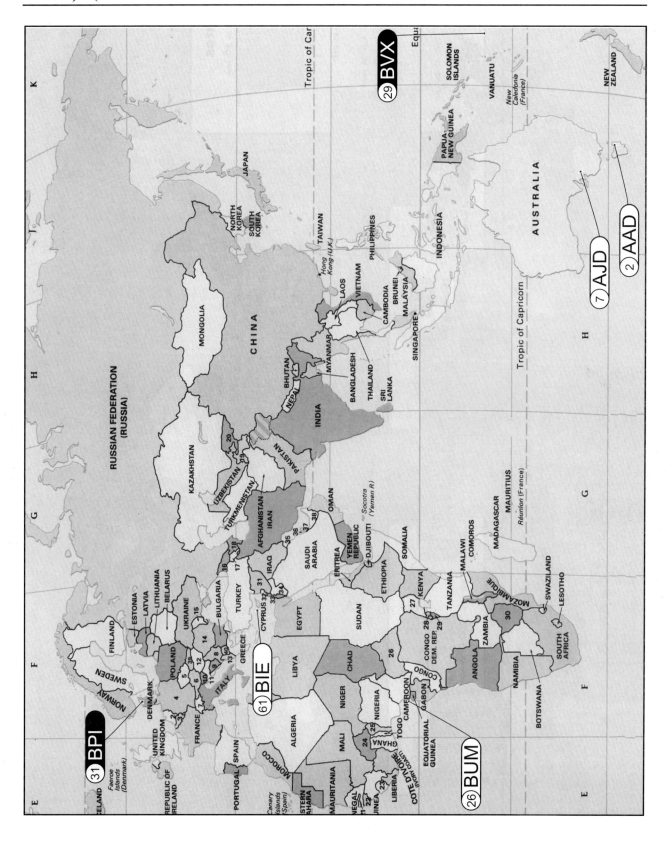

BIBLIOGRAPHY

Aero Ireland: Extracts from various articles

Aviation: Extracts from various articles

Aviation Ireland: Extracts from various articles

Butler, Philip H.: *Irish Aircraft*, Merseyside Aviation Society, 1972

Butler, Sr. Katherine: *Kildonan 1933 – 1936: A Memory*, Old Dublin Society, 18th January 1984, unpubl

Byrne, Capt K. and Tormey, Comdt P.: *A View from the Tower – Irish Air Corps*, Defence Forces Printing Press, 1991

Byrne, Liam: *History of Aviation in Ireland*, Blackwater, 1980

Carvill, Joan: *The Wicklow Motor Races 1950-1957*, Dreoilin Specialist Publications Ltd, 2003

Clegg, Peter: *Sword in the Sky-Midland & Scottish Air Ferries*, Bookmag, Inverness, Scotland, 1990

Conran, Phil: *Desoutter11, EI-AAD*, unpubl.

Corlett, John: *Aviation in Ulster*, Blackstaff Press, 1981

Corrigan, Douglas: *That's My Story*, Hale, London, 1939

Department of Civil Aviation, Melbourne: *Desoutter aircraft VH-UEE – ex EI-AAD 26*, August 1969, unpubl

Fallon, Jane: *Throttle full open – life of Lady Bailey*, Lilliput Press, 1999

Gallagher, Desmond: *Shooting Suns and Things*, Kingford Press, 1986

Hayes, Karl: *R.A.F. and U.S. Naval Air Service in Ireland, 1913-1923*, Irish Air Letter, 1988

Hayes, Paddy: *Break Out!*, The O'Brien Press Ltd, 2004

Hornfeck, Peter: *70 years of the Irish Civil Aircraft Register*, BN Historians, 1999

Irish Air Corps: *The Irish Air Corps celebrates 100 years of Flight*, M & J Graphics, 2003

Irish Air Letter : Their Irish Civil Aircraft Register records.

Irish Air Letter : Extracts from various articles

Koehl, Fitzmaurice & Von Huenefeld : *Three Musketeers of the Air*, Putnams, 1928

Lawford, Hayden K: *In Galway Skies*, 2003

Lee, Ronan: *Spirit of Erin*, Feb 2002, unpubl

MacCarron, Donal: *Wings over Ireland – the story of the Irish Air Corps*, Midland Counties publication, 1996

MacCarron, Donal: *A View from Above*, O'Brien Press, 2000

McCrossan, Oliver: *The Curragh Motor Races 1947-1954*, Dreoilin Specialist Publications Ltd, 2003

Military Archives, Cathal Brugha Barracks, Rathmines, Dublin 6

National Archives, Bishop Street, Dublin 8

National Library, Kildare Street, Dublin 2

O'Rourke, Madeline: *Air Spectaculars-Irish Air Displays*, Glendale, 1989

Pouchin-Mould, Daphne D.C.: *Iona Engineering Works and Iona National Airways*, unpubl

Royal Irish Automobile Club Guinness Segrave Library and Archive, 34 Dawson Street, Dublin 2.

R.T.E.: *100 years – Ireland in the 20th Century*, TownHouse and CountryHouse Ltd, Ranelagh, Dublin 6, 2001

Share, Bernard: *The Flight of the Iolar – The Aer Lingus Experience*, Gill and MacMillan, 1986

Skinner and Cranitch: *Ireland and World Aviation*, Director Publ, 1988

Traynor, Michael: *Through the clouds over Limerick and beyond*, 1997

Weldon, Niall G; *Pioneers in Flight – Aer Lingus and the Story of Aviation in Ireland*, Liffey Press, 2002

INDEX

A

Abbeyshrule 139, 143, 227, 230, 250, 252, 260, 262, 264, 276, 298, 300, 310

Aer Arann 129, 130, 131, 154, 161, 226

Aer Lingus 33, 35, 42, 53, 67, 78, 79, 85, 90, 92, 93, 95, 96, 99, 100, 102, 116, 121, 133, 139, 148, 148, 152, 153, 155, 161, 163, 186, 190, 191, 197, 198, 199, 237, 238, 239, 240,

Aer Rianta1 34, 161, 163, 185, 200, 207

Aer Turas 101, 102, 153, 163

Aerial Advertising Limited 229

Air Ecosse 162

Aircraft Associates Limited 94, 99

Alcock and Brown 39, 42, 223

Armstrong, Oliver .40, 41, 42, 44, 53, 78, 153

Athenia 56

Avair Limited 131, 148, 154, 161

Aviator 78

B

Bailey, Lady Mary 71, 72, 73

Balbo, Generalv53

Baldonnel 15, 16, 17, 19, 20, 21, 22, 23, 30, 39, 40, 41, 42, 43, 44, 47, 48, 49, 50, 51, 54, 55, 65, 72, 76, 77, 78, 79, 125, 126, 131, 150, 153, 154, 156, 161, 220, 240,

Birr 134, 205, 225, 229, 244, 248

Boyce, Thompson 116, 120, 242

Brady, Mick 35, 75

Bremen 16, 17, 43, 44, 75, 104, 220

British Air Ferries 183

Bruton, Chris 79, 139

Bundoran 37, 38, 58

Butler, Sr. Katherine 29, 67

Byrne, Alderman Alfie .48, 52, 46, 74

Byrne, John 112, 223

C

Cahill, Caroline 12, 11, 15, 24, 103, 103, 104, 123

Cahill, Constance 84, 123

Cahill, Henry 102,103,104,124

Cahill, Hugh 8, 12, 14, 15, 16, 17, 18, 19, 20, 21, 22, 23, 24, 26, 29, 30, 32, 33, 34, 35, 39, 40, 42, 43, 45, 47, 48, 51, 56, 57, 63, 64, 66, 74, 77, 79, 82, 83, 85, 90, 95, 103, 104, 124, 164, 191, 198, 208, 225,

Cahill, Pearse 19, 22, 24, 32, 35, 48, 49, 56, 57, 66, 81, 82, 83, 84, 85, 86, 87, 88, 89, 90, 93, 94, 95, 96, 97, 100, 101, 103, 104, 105, 106, 107, 108, 109, 116, 120, 121, 122, 124, 126, 129, 133, 140, 148, 151, 153, 156, 162, 164, 184, 188, 191, 198, 200, 206, 208, 220, 221, 223, 224, 225, 226, 227, 228, 229, 230, 232, 235, 240, 338, 342, 344,

Cahill, Peter .84, 123, 129, 133, 134, 149, 312

Carrickfin 129, 134, 144, 151, 155, 156, 200, 205, 244, 278, 290

Channel Air Bridge 183

Channel Express 158, 158, 197, 198, 199, 200, 218

Cloghran 161, 188, 201, 207, 220

Clyden Airways 163

Cobham, Sir Alan 47, 50, 51,55, 67, 72, 220

Cobham's Circus 52

Collooney 26, 37

Coogan, J.C 35, 38

Coonagh 70, 113, 137, 264

Cork Airport 134, 163, 235, 237, 238, 250, 326

Corrigan, Douglas 'Wrong Way' 79, 157

Cross Guns Bridge 14, 17, 33, 41, 42, 56, 87, 97, 102, 103, 110, 124, 208, 208

Currie JohnR. 21, 25, 26, 48, 63, 65, 67, 68, 78, 93

Cusack, Robert 93

D

de Havilland, Sir Geoffrey 32, 70, 71

Dease, E.J 68, 74

Desoutter 17, 18, 19, 20, 21, 22, 23, 24, 32, 37, 131, 164,

DHL 137, 162, 163, 164, 182, 184, 187, 188, 189, 190, 197, 198, 201

Di Mascio, Ray 229, 296

Dublin Aero Club 76, 78

Dublin Air Ferries 26, 60, 74, 75, 77, 78, 79, 80

Dublin Airport Flying Club 191, 232, 236, 262

Duffy, Paul 156, 184, 227

E

Earhart, Amelia 38, 40, 72

EI Air Exports 197, 198

EI-AAA 15, 220

EI-AAC 74,78

EI-AAD 20, 27

EI-AAF 32, 35, 37, 38, 58, 59

EI-AAG 32, 38, 41, 58,59

EI-AAH 47